By Grit & Grace

Series Foreword

Along with the editors of *By Grit & Grace*, Fulcrum Publishing is proud to announce the launching of a new series, *Notable Westerners*, of which *By Grit & Grace* is the first volume. This new series will explore the real stories behind the personalities and events that continue to shape our national character.

The American West—land of myth, the epitome of an independent American spirit. When we think of the women and men who shaped the West, we tend to think in terms of caricatures, of larger-than-life heroines and heroes. Notable women and men have always loomed large on the open and wide landscapes of the American West. From the earliest Native American leaders to more recent westerners, these influential people have attracted the attention of travelers, historians, and writers. Often, such visitors focus on how these heroines and heroes of the region were important in creating and reshaping images of the West.

By Grit & Grace and all forthcoming books in the *Notable Westerners* series will explore the personalities and influences of such outstanding western characters. Editors Glenda Riley and Richard W. Etulain draw on their long experience in western history and their wide associations with western historians to bring together pithy, penetrating sketches of westerners of varied racial, ethnic, gender, and social backgrounds. To these volumes, contributors bring expertise in their field, knowledge of significant individuals, and lucid writing styles.

The result is a variety of essays providing insight into the movers and shakers of a unique region of the United States. The American West not only helped shape the American national character, but provides a continuing source of fascination for Americans and non-Americans alike. Scheduled to appear in the fall of each year, beginning this year with *By Grit & Grace* and continuing in 1999, each volume will present vignettes of the women and men who helped build the Old West, as well as the twentieth-century West. Forthcoming books in the series will explore other notable women and men (including lawmen and gunfighters, generals and chiefs, pioneers and homesteaders, and actors and actresses) whose lives were equally significant in influencing the history and culture of the American West and thus the United States.

By Grit & Grace

Eleven Women Who Shaped the American West

Edited by

GLENDA RILEY AND
RICHARD W. ETULAIN

Fulcrum Publishing

Book design by Deborah Rich
Cover design by Bill Spahr

Library of Congress Cataloging-in-Publication Data
By grit and grace : eleven women who shaped the American West / edited
by Glenda Riley and Richard W. Etulain.
p. cm.
Includes bibliographical references and index.
Contents: La Tules / Janet Lecompte — Jessie Benton Frémont /
Mary Lee Spence — Beautiful deceiver / Janet Fireman — Calamity
Jane / Richard W. Etulain — Annie Oakley / Glenda Riley — Mary Ellen
Pleasant / Quintard Taylor — Iron Eye's daughters / Valerie S. Mathes —
Elinore Pruitt Stewart / Susanne K. George — Abigail Scott Duniway /
Ruth Moynihan — Mother Katharine Drexel / Anne M. Butler.
I S B N 1-55591-259-1 (paperback)
1. Women pioneers—West (U.S.)—Biography. 2. Frontier and
pioneer life—West (U.S.) 3. West (U.S.)—Biography. I. Riley,
Glenda, 1938– . II. Etulain, Richard W.
F596.B99 1997
920.078—dc21   97-25057
[B]   CIP
Printed in Canada
0 9 8 7 6 5 4

Fulcrum Publishing
16100 Table Mountain Parkway, Suite 300
Golden, Colorado 80403
(800) 992-2908 ❧ (303) 277-1623
www.fulcrum-books.com

❧ Contents ❧

✤ Acknowledgments ✤

The editors would like to thank several people and organizations for their help and support in preparing this book. First of all, we are much indebted to the authors for taking the time from their full schedules to prepare essays for this collection. Their professionalism and insightful analyses are particularly appreciated.

Glenda Riley would also like to express gratitude to Ball State University, especially the Alexander M. Bracken Fund; to the Department of History at Ball State; and to Bess Edwards and the Annie Oakley Foundation in Greenville, Ohio.

Richard W. Etulain would like to thank the Center of the American West and the Research Allocations Fund at the University of New Mexico for supporting his research. He is also indebted to Professor James McLaird of Dakota Wesleyan University for reading and commenting on his essay on Calamity Jane.

Both editors are grateful to Charles Rankin, editor of *Montana: The Magazine of Western History,* for allowing them to draw on material first appearing in that journal or in other publications of the Montana Historical Society. In addition, the editors wish to express their appreciation to Bob Baron, Sam Scinta, and Sara Hanson of Fulcrum Publishing for their encouragement and aid.

GLENDA RILEY
Ball State University

RICHARD W. ETULAIN
University of New Mexico

❧ Introduction ❧
GLENDA RILEY

During the past decade or so, the West of the imagination has changed dramatically. Previously, film westerns relied upon Gary Cooper and John Wayne, while television gave us *Gunsmoke* and *Bonanza*. But where were the women in those days? They were either absent or cast in stock roles. Miss Kitty, the "madam with a heart of gold," is a prime example of a stereotypical western woman. Only occasionally did a woman with determination and fortitude appear, as in the films *Cat Ballou* or *Heartland*.

These "pretend" western women were almost always Anglo. Pale-skinned and light-haired, they were usually passive and quiet, civilizing the West and its male inhabitants whenever they could. Or they might work as prostitutes or schoolteachers (remember Etta Place in *Butch Cassidy and the Sundance Kid*). Others played equally predictable characters, perhaps a temperance crusader attacking the town's saloon with a hatchet.

Today, however, film and television offer such tales as *The Ballad of Little Jo*, in which a woman disguises herself as a man to survive the rough, masculine West; or *Dr. Quinn: Medicine Woman*, in which a woman doctor not only heals but reforms the people of a crude western town. The question is, did women like Jo and Dr. Quinn really exist in the West? Or have scriptwriters made them up to satisfy audiences filled with women who harbor twentieth-century feminist sentiments?

Happily, the answer is that strong, clever women did live in the real West. Jo Moynihan was an actual person, and she was not alone. For example, "Mountain Charley" (Mrs. E. J. Guerin) was a widow who masqueraded as a man to find work after her husband died. Although Dr. Quinn was not a historical figure, thousands of women did work as nurses and doctors throughout the West. Some learned by apprenticeship, but others studied at such schools as the Woman's Medical College in Chicago. Farther west, Dr. Kong Tai Heong was the first Chinese woman doctor to practice in Hawaii. After training at the Canton Medical School, she migrated to Honolulu in 1896.

Thousands of other forceful and accomplished western women lived in the West. Of course most of these women did not have to leave the domestic realm, act and dress like men, or enter the professions and politics to influence the West. In an era when a housewife was a woman achieving in her own right, such women served as domestic artisans who made food, clothing, and other goods; birthed and raised numerous children; acted as moral guides to family members and friends; produced "butter-and-egg" money that often sustained a farm or other family enterprise through its bad times; and fulfilled numerous other roles.

Although of varied racial and ethnic backgrounds, such women used technology during the early years that was basic or downright primitive. Yet they achieved a wide variety of tasks: whitewashing cabin and adobe walls, making medicines and treating the ill, producing candles and soap, processing food, cooking in open fireplaces or on wood-burning stoves, making cloth and clothing, and washing clothes "on the board." In the evening, by the light of fireplaces or candles, they might make shoes, braid straw hats, knit socks, or fashion hide gloves, some of which they sold to bring in "cash" money.

When the market economy developed in any given area of the West, the new system revolutionized women's lives. Ironically, instead of lessening women's work load, technology often increased it. For instance, rather than devoting time to collecting tallow and making candles, women trimmed wicks and cleaned kerosene lamps. They used treadle-powered sewing machines to produce clothing with increasingly complicated styles. They washed clothes in machines, but, lacking technology such as indoor plumbing and electricity, women had to turn the agitators by hand and carry clean water to the machines and dirty water from them. Women who had domestic help fared somewhat better, but they still had to spend hours every day supervising domestics, budgets, and other aspects of running a large household.

There existed then, many ways to pioneer the American West. Some people helped develop the West with plows, others with badges and rifles, and others with Bibles and pulpits. For many domestic women, the churn, kitchen, and chicken house often marked their boundaries.

Remarkably, thousands of women reached beyond the confines—and immense workloads—of the domestic scene. Often women acted and dressed like men or entered the professions and politics to influence the West. They especially sought paid employment outside their homes. Gazetteers, city directories, and newspaper advertisements indicate that urban and rural western women increasingly sought outside employment and entered the professions such as doctors, nurses, ministers, and morticians. Among other jobs, western women worked at those one might expect, such as domestic servants, boardinghouse keepers, milliners, seamstresses, and prostitutes. Women also held positions one might not expect, including attorneys, blackjack and monte dealers, telegraph operators, field hands, and miners.

In addition, women participated in a panoply of reform and community activities. By the beginning of the twentieth century, women's clubs existed all over the West. Their interests ranged from conservation of the environment to great books, libraries, temperance, health, sanitation, and religion. Club women and philanthropists helped develop the West, whether by holding charity fairs to raise money for a church building or by establishing a park in a raw frontier town.

Unfortunately, the media and the mythmakers have either overlooked women of color in this scenario or presented them as even greater clichés than Anglo women. In the film *Stagecoach,* for example, the keeper of the stage-stop laments the disappearance of his Indian wife and his horse—not because he lost his wife, a "squaw," who could be easily replaced, but because it would be difficult to find another good horse. Similarly, the media often characterized women of Hispanic-heritage as sensual "hot tamales," African American women as kindly "mammies," and Asian women as scheming "dragon ladies." Despite such slighting or stereotyping, women of color were not only omnipresent in the West, but significant to its growth.

Like Anglo women, women of color—American Indian, Hispanic-heritage, African American, and Asian—participated in the maturation of the American West. But unlike Anglo women, they frequently shouldered the additional burdens of racial prejudice and discriminatory policies. No words can describe the anguish window signs, such as "No Mexicans Hired Here" and "No Chinese Wanted," caused women desperate to help support their families and children.

Despite these obstacles, many women of color found ways to cope and to achieve. Although others may have overlooked their contributions, women of color knew their own worth. As a case in point, Ah-Yuen, an Asian woman cook and homesteader in Evanston, Wyoming, regularly rode in the Pioneer Days parade well into the 1920s.

To illustrate the variety of women's experiences in the pioneer West, this collection presents a variety of early western women, illustrating class status, ethnicity, race, marital status, age, or religious beliefs, all of whom had a hand in shaping the American West. The result is a rich portrait of western women, one that reveals the breadth of their heritages and achievements.

The collection opens with some of the most mythologized western women in history, the image-makers. These are the figures who, in one way or another, contributed to the legend of the Wild West. Because of their own accomplishments or those of people they inspired, these women became well-known throughout the nation, and even throughout the world.

In the first selection, Janet Lecompte describes Gertrudis Barceló, or La Tules, who was a reputed monte dealer and saloon keeper in Santa Fe, New Mexico, at the time Americans arrived and claimed Santa Fe for their own in 1846. To Anglo sensibilities, La Tules seemed unfettered, and perhaps even evil. Lecompte effectively refutes this view while providing an illuminating portrait of a notable western woman.

During the same era—the mid-nineteenth century—Jessie Benton Frémont maintained a home and fulfilled the many functions that made the spectacular military and political career of her husband, John C. Frémont, possible. It was, in fact, John Frémont who helped wrest the southwestern states from Mexico. Mary Lee Spence argues that Jessie Benton Frémont was a woman of quick wit and extensive intelligence who, had she lived in the twentieth century, might have risen to political prominence herself.

Another image maker of the mid-nineteenth century was Lola Montez. Janet R. Fireman indicates that Montez, a reputed beauty and a dancer of minor talent, performed in frontier California and made Grass Valley her home between 1853 and 1855. Despite her short stay in the West, Montez became something of a legend in far-western history.

Next Richard W. Etulain considers Calamity Jane, or Martha Canary. Even though the late-nineteenth-century West's most notorious bad-girl lived a full, exciting life, she did not do half the things mythmakers attributed to her. Calamity Jane did not, for example, marry Wild Bill Hickok nor have a child with him. Neither was she a successful Wild West performer, as contemporary novelist Larry McMurtry would have us believe.

Instead, Annie Oakley did dominate the Wild West arena. In this regard, Glenda Riley contends that although Annie Oakley was raised in Ohio and spent little time in the West, she became the model western woman. Between 1885, when she signed on with Buffalo Bill's Wild West, and her death in 1926, Oakley shot and rode her way to national, and even international, attention.

The second group of essays concentrates upon women who were also brave and hardy—yet less famous. Although their names are little known to most people, these women contributed greatly to a developing western society. Following very different paths, they devoted their efforts and energies to the refinement and betterment of the American West.

One notable figure was African American Mary Ellen Pleasant, who arrived in San Francisco during the mid-nineteenth century. Quintard Taylor analyzes this entrepreneur who used her profits to improve the existence of other African Americans in the West. Taylor also speculates about the impact of Pleasant's reform efforts and her eventual forsaking of them.

Later in the nineteenth century, the LaFlesche sisters left their mark on western history—Susette as a reformer on behalf of her people, the Omaha Indians, and Susan as a medical doctor. Valerie Mathes asserts that Susette and Susan not only navigated the treacherous shoals of assimilation during the late nineteenth century, but also walked with dignity into prominence during the early twentieth century.

An early-twentieth-century woman who advocated the West as a land of economic opportunity for women was Elinore Pruitt Stewart. A single woman homesteader (who soon married) in Wyoming, Stewart became a well-known author. Susanne K. George demonstrates that Stewart's life and accomplishments illustrate how some women took advantage of the Bootstrap Myth by seizing the opportunities offered by the American West and thus realizing their dreams.

Abigail Scott Duniway of Oregon had different aspirations for western women. During the early twentieth century, Duniway campaigned, wrote, and lobbied on behalf of woman's suffrage. In her essay, Ruth Barnes Moynihan explains how Duniway devised clever tactics to support the Nineteenth Amendment, which established woman's suffrage and was finally adopted in 1920, and how Duniway used power as effectively as any male politician.

Finally, Anne M. Butler shows how Mother Katharine Drexel used her energy and her wealth to establish the Sisters of the Blessed Sacrament for Indians and Colored People. Through a long career that spanned the late nineteenth and early twentieth centuries, Drexel came to the aid of many American Indians and African Americans in the West. By the 1910s and 1920s, much of Drexel's energy went into refining mission efforts among American Indians and organizing new missions among African Americans.

Clearly then, each in their own way, these women helped pioneer and develop their native or adopted land, the West. They illustrated admirable grit and often elusive grace to achieve their goals, personal and public. They were "gutsy" women long before the term was coined.

These women number but eleven among the millions who lived in the early American West. Yet stories of other women are legion. Some have been retrieved from the historical dustbin, many have not. As a result, historians and other researchers have much work ahead of them in rediscovering the western women history has overlooked.

One might ask: Is contemporary media pandering to feminist-minded audiences? Or did strong, achieving women actually live and work in the American West? Did such women as Little Jo and Dr. Quinn exist? Yes, many times over, as the essays in this collection clearly demonstrate.

❧ 1 ❧
La Tules:
The Ultimate New Mexican Woman

JANET LECOMPTE

❧ IN THE 1830s AND 1840s SHE WAS THE LEADING monte-bank dealer of the Mexican territory of New Mexico. Her name was doña Gertrudis Barceló, and she was known as "La Tules," Tules being the diminutive of Gertrudis, and the article declaring that she was the one and only Tules of importance. Matt Field, editor of the *New Orleans Picayune,* was visiting New Mexico and wrote to his newspaper that "the highest court her favor, and the lowest look at her with wonder."

Field met her in 1839 as he was strolling through the streets of Santa Fe with Louis Robidoux, an *alcalde* (mayor-judge) from St. Louis. As a gaudy mule-drawn carriage dashed past them, a middle-aged woman bowed from the carriage and a young, dark-eyed beauty smiled. The alcalde explained that the lady was the celebrated "Señora Toulous," and the girl was her niece, "an adventurous belle lately arrived from the city of Chihuahua." The bow and the smile from the carriage were interpreted by the alcalde (who rarely received such a courtesy from the great lady) as an invitation to visit her at home.

Home for Tules was 37 Calle de la Muralla, the next-to-last house on a street now known as Hillside, which began at the old Santa Fe city wall and stretched eastward to a marshy meadow. Tules's house was a rendezvous for fashionable men.

There Field met Governor Manuel Armijo, several of his officers, and Tules's beautiful niece surrounded by young suitors. The Americans spoke

La Tules.   *Like the other sketches herein, this one of Tules was sketched by Brewerton himself. It is the only known living portrait of her, although Brewerton allows her no charms whatsoever. (From G. Douglass Brewerton, "Incidents of Travel in New Mexico,"* Harpers New Monthly Magazine, *April 1854)*

little Spanish, the Mexicans little English, and blundering attempts at conversation kept the company in convulsions of laughter. For the Americans, the visit was a "novel and singular delight," enlivened by wine and the "side-splitting merriment of the good-natured governor."

Field described Tules's *sala* as a room fifty feet long and twenty feet wide, carpeted at one end and furnished with spare elegance. Mattresses that became beds at night were folded into sofas against the walls during the day and covered with costly Mexican blankets. At one end of the room was a large window latticed with wood, and on the walls were framed mirrors, as in most New Mexican houses. The visitors found Tules's wall decorations refined in comparison with the profusion of "coarsely engraved and colored pictures, rude images of saints, religious charms, broken looking glasses" in humbler dwellings.

Tules's sala revealed to Matt Field not only her studied simplicity but also her sense of humor. On one wall was an ornate clock of American manufacture with hands fixed at 12 and 6. The señora drolly explained that she only wound the clock on holidays, not wishing it to grow old too fast.

Time had not dealt so kindly with Tules herself. She was thirty-nine years old when Field first met her, and although he did not comment on her age, he remarked that her face was far from beautiful. Her only pleasant feature was "an eye of shrewd intelligence lit up … with that expression of mischievous brightness which can make any countenance agreeable." But also, her figure was trim, her manners free and graceful, and the ease she displayed while dancing a waltz "would have made her an object of attraction in a *soirée dansante* at Washington."

She was greatly admired, wrote Matt Field. Her rare presence at a dance rendered it a fashionable affair, and common folk looked on her with as much respect as they paid the governor and priests. Even Santa Fe trader Josiah Gregg, who despised Tules, had to admit that there was "no lady of more fashionable reputation" in Santa Fe.

Matt Field shows us Tules at home, a charming hostess, relaxed, laughing, enjoying her guests and responding to their enjoyment of her. We will get few glimpses of her personality, for we know her mainly through American accounts, and Americans described her as a hard-nosed businesswoman or as a woman of "loose morals."

Most Americans were appalled at the openness of gambling in New Mexico. There was plenty of gambling where they came from, but not by women, children, or priests, nor on main streets in full daylight, and certainly not on the Sabbath. Good women, of course, did not gamble at all in the United States nor did they (heaven forbid!) run a gambling hall.

In the United States a respectable married woman led a life of endless domesticity and good deeds and was called a "lady." The other kind was called a "female," a term that some Americans used for Tules. American men tolerated no competition from "the weaker sex"; they expected women to be submissive, conscious of their own inferiority, powerless by law and custom, and dependent on a man except in matters of morality and housekeeping.

When confronted with Tules, Americans reacted strongly. Plainly she did not think of herself as inferior, nor did she center her life on home and family, and she dealt in sin without showing a particle of guilt. Americans' diaries and accounts usually portrayed her as ugly, greedy, brazen, and immoral, and this judgment of her has persisted to the present.

The fact that Tules's work was gambling did not lessen her self-esteem, for she proudly volunteered to the 1841 census-taker that she was a *tahúr*, "gambler." Nor did her profession diminish her standing with New Mexicans. Women gambled everywhere in Mexico, even the elite of Mexico City (although more

The Padre Wins.   *Brewerton's readers would have found his drawing of a gambling priest scandalous or at least unbelievable. (From G. Douglass Brewerton, "Incidents of Travel in New Mexico,"* Harpers New Monthly Magazine, *April 1854)*

discreetly than the common women). Madame Calderón de la Barca, the Scottish wife of a Spanish diplomat in Mexico, wrote in 1842 that gambling was Mexico's "national sport," and that since monte banks generally won, gamblers were among the richest and consequently the most respected persons in the country.

So it was in Santa Fe. Men, women, and children gambled on tables set up under the porticos of buildings around the plaza, in wineshops, in homes, at any time of day or night, and on Sundays after church. Governors, judges and other civil officers, who had sworn to uphold the law against gambling, gambled; as did priests because gambling was not considered a sin and the church had no strictures against it.

In Republican New Mexico, a capable woman like Tules had a wider choice of lifestyle and career than a woman in the United States of that era. Legally, Tules could pursue any employment not connected with the clergy, military, or government bureaucracy; but few careers, other than with the church, the army, and the government, were open even to men in frontier New Mexico, and most were engaged in the production of food and shelter.

Elsewhere, Tules could have been a leader in any enterprise, for her character combined the courage, ambition, and commitment of a successful businessman with a woman's charm and tact, but New Mexico offered her no better choice for her talents than that of professional monte dealer, and in that occupation she was steadfast and finally successful.

Her accomplishment was turned against her by visiting Americans. In his *Commerce of the Prairies* (the most influential book about Santa Fe and the Santa Fe trade), Josiah Gregg expressed his disgust at many things he saw in New Mexico. Paul Horgan, Gregg's biographer, shows that Gregg's ill-health and ill-nature made him a humorless, irascible misanthrope.

Nothing infuriated Gregg more than the rise of Tules in her disreputable profession, unless it was the ill-gained power of her friend, Governor Manuel Armijo. To further express his censure, Gregg attributed squalid and immoral beginnings to both doña Tules and don Manuel—she as a whore, he as a low-caste sheep thief. In fact, Tules and Armijo had titles of *doña* and *don* respectively, and both were literate, a combination that indicated aristocratic origins.

In his sarcastic style Gregg tells Tules's story, condemning both her and her people, "to show the light in which gambling is held by all classes of society [and] to illustrate the purifying effects of wealth upon character." "Twelve or fifteen years ago," wrote Gregg after he returned from his last trip to New Mexico in 1840, Tules "lived (or rather roamed)" in Taos, a woman of "very loose habits." Finding it difficult to make a living in Taos, she moved to Santa Fe and became a gambler at the favorite game of monte bank. After years of poor luck, she finally won enough to open a bank of her own and earned a fortune and social prominence. Now, wrote Gregg, she is "openly received in the first circles of society."

Many American writers still copy Gregg, describing Tules as a "a woman of shady character," "a common prostitute," "a whore and a gambler," but no known sources, except those based on Gregg, locate her in Taos or suggest that her habits were "loose." Later accounts accuse her of adultery with Governor Armijo, but Gregg's was not one of them.

The Barceló family arrived in New Mexico around 1820 either from the province of Sonora or from the city of Chihuahua where Tules returned occasionally to conduct her games. Tules was born María Gertrudis Barceló in 1800, daughter of doña Dolores Herrero and don Juan Ignacio Barceló. Her brother, Trinidad Barceló, was nine years older than Tules; her two sisters, María de la Luz and Dolores, were two years older and twelve years younger, respectively.

The Barceló children, like their parents, had the trappings of class superiority. They were dignified with the title of *don* or *doña,* a Spanish title of nobility signifying warrior ancestors or wealth and distinction, but diminished in Republican New Mexico to a respectful term of address. A more solid indicator of elevated status was literacy. At least two of the Barceló children were educated: Tules could sign her name with a rubric after it, although her signature was unsteady from lack of use; Trinidad's signature was firm, and he became New Mexico's superintendent of schools.

The Barcelós were outsiders, being the first to bear that name in New Mexico. What sent them to this primitive frontier has yet to be discovered. Before their marriages to local folk, they lacked connections to a family network that provided most New Mexicans with security, power, and identity. The New Mexican extended family soaked up orphans and bastards, nieces and nephews, grandparents and stepchildren, but nothing in the records suggests that Tules had supportive kin outside her immediate family.

A need for a family network explains the Barceló family's apparent eagerness to be married to New Mexicans. Tules's sister María de la Luz married Rafael Sánchez in the village of Valencia south of Albuquerque on November 3, 1822. Six months later, on June 20, 1823, María Gertrudes (Tules) married Manuel Antonio Sisneros in the nearby village church at Tomé; two months after that, their widowed mother, doña Dolores Herrero, married don Pedro Pino, a name of distinction in New Mexico.

When Tules married Manuel Antonio Sisneros she was twenty-three, a ripe old age for a first marriage in New Mexico. She was also four years older than her groom and four or five months pregnant. Like any Mexican wife, Tules kept her maiden name along with rights of property and access to the courts. That she married shows that she wished to bear her children in wedlock, although countless Mexican babies from all classes received their mother's names and their fathers being recorded as "unknown." Americans blamed this "scandalous concubinage" on high marriage fees claimed by the priests and on women's lack of chastity.

Tules's childbearing brought her little joy. Four months after the wedding she gave birth to a son, Pedro, who died a month later. In January 1825, she bore Miguel Antonio, who died at the age of four months. If she bore other children, they are not of record, but she raised three girls, Carmel Sisneros, Rafaela Pino, and Rafaela's daughter Rallitos Washington. These four women comprised the nucleus of their extended family.

Rafaela Pino, born about 1822, was the "beautiful niece" recently from Chihuahua who was admired by Matt Field in 1839. Actually she was the natural or adopted daughter of doña Dolores Herrera and don Pedro Pino, but raised from birth by Tules. The girl was also known as Rafaela Sisneros (the surname of Tules's husband) until she married and took her husband's name of Gutiérrez in the American fashion.

Tules may have been a monte dealer long before she came to New Mexico, in order to support herself and her family. They were not well-off; her brother, Trinidad, complained of poverty in a letter of 1828 to the governor. But if money were not her sole motivation, Tules may have gambled because she was addicted to it, and she may have become a professional because her ambition was to be the richest, most famous, most admired gambler in New Mexico.

Perhaps as early as 1824 she was conducting games at the newly discovered Real de Dolores de Oro, the first placer mine in Republican New Mexico. The mine was located among piñon-dotted hills in a dry gulch of the Ortiz Mountains twenty-seven miles south of Santa Fe. Poor families, including women and children, gathered there after a rain with their baskets, goat horns, and shallow wooden bowls to wash the sands and collect tiny flakes of gold and an occasional nugget.

A day's work yielded the miners perhaps twenty-five or fifty cents worth of gold, which ended up partly in the pockets of Tules, and partly in wagons of Santa Fe traders returning to Missouri. Although Mexican law prohibited the export of bullion, Americans brought $180,000 worth of gold and silver from New Mexico to Missouri in 1824. The treasure was mostly silver bars and gold coins, but also gold dust in tiny leather bags concealed in the wagons.

By 1825 Real de Dolores had expanded to a gold camp where Tules set up her games to trap riches at their source. By law, gambling was forbidden. Under Spanish rule, gamblers were subject to loss of citizenship, and proprietors of gambling houses could be exiled. When Mexico became a nation in 1821, professional gamblers and owners of gambling houses were still subject to loss of civil rights, but the popularity of gambling made the law unenforceable.

Local statutes were more forgiving; at Real de Dolores gamblers were fined three pesos and the owner of the game six pesos. In 1825 Tules was fined a total of forty-three pesos for conducting illegal gambling games at various times throughout the year. By 1826 the little mining camp had become a busy little town; its officers issued licenses to gamblers, and the fees provided funds for the municipality. In 1826 Tules was fined twenty-five pesos on charges of gambling without a license. After 1826 Tules paid no fines in Real de Dolores; apparently she had departed without leaving a forwarding address.

Between 1826 and 1835 La Tules's life is unrecorded. During these years she may have "roamed" in Taos or served as an attendant at a gambling house, although Josiah Gregg's assertion is unsupported by other evidence. Or she may have conducted games in Chihuahua as she did later. By 1835 Tules had moved with her husband and family to Santa Fe and was dealing monte, but apparently not yet in her own gambling hall.

In 1835 Tules made use of the alcalde court to settle debts arising from her business. One gambler sued her for what the court decided was merely his bad luck in cards; she sued a soldier who owed her a gambling debt of a mule or twenty pesos; and she brought Santiago Clerce (James Kirker) to court to collect the four hundred pesos he owed her. Colonial Spain had required that a woman in a civil action obtain her husband's permission to appear in court, but Mexico did not require it. Tules appeared in court many times with or without her husband or his permission.

Tules also used the court to protect her honor from accusations of local gossips. In March 1835, a neighbor spread rumors that Tules was committing adultery with Lucius Thruston, a tall, well-mannered trader from Kentucky with whom she and her husband shared their house. Before the alcalde, Tules deftly maneuvered her accuser into denying that she had said such a thing. Both women signed the act of conciliation, Tules with her full name and rubric, the other woman with an *X*. Three months later Tules appeared before the alcalde again, extracting an apology from another woman for an unspecified slander, and again Tules signed her full name and rubric.

Her court appearances show that by 1835 Tules was already well established in Santa Fe, with sufficient renown to attract envy, sufficient stature and wit to vanquish her slanderers, and a doña before her name to mark her status. And she was literate, "a very extraordinary talent" wrote Gregg. This most self-reliant of women claimed the further right to entertain whomever she pleased and to conduct her business at any time and in any place that suited her. For exercising her freedoms, she paid with the malicious gossip that followed her all her life and even into the next century.

Before Tules had her gambling hall, she and other gamblers (mostly part-time amateurs) set up their games in private homes, in back rooms at fandangos, or on jerry-built tables under the portals outside shops around the plaza during fiestas. If somebody "denounced" the game, soldiers or city officials would break it up and fine the players and onlookers.

Tules needed a more stable location for her business than tables at fiestas and rented rooms. She also had to have a clear understanding with the local authorities; otherwise, her business could be terminated at the whim of an unsympathetic alcalde waving a statute at her. It was almost surely 1839 before she and her monte tables moved permanently into her famous gambling hall, for in that year Governor Manuel Armijo ignored the national law and in effect legalized gambling in Santa Fe.

In Republican New Mexico the penalties for gambling vacillated between fees and fines after Mexico came into being in 1821. When gambling was legal the alcalde and his deputies collected fees from all gamblers; when illegal, they collected fines, but only from those they could catch. Governor Manuel Armijo's ordinance provided for the licensing and taxing of gambling, thus decriminalizing gamblers, protecting licensed games, and ensuring revenues for the city.

Armijo's fees were collected monthly; owners of gambling houses were charged six pesos, players three pesos, and lookers-on one peso. The alcalde of Santa Fe sent out the patrol every night to collect fees from licensed gambling houses and their patrons at any hour. Encouraged by Armijo's ordinance, Tules opened her hall (probably with more courage than confidence, considering the transient tenure of Mexican politicians).

Tules's hall was located on what is now called Burro Alley between Washington and San Francisco streets in downtown Santa Fe. In the fall of 1839 Matt Field visited the hall but failed to note what later visitors (and modern writers) emphasized—the elegant furnishings of the hall, which probably did not exist until later.

Field watched Tules supervising a monte table where an assistant or a player (the alcalde on this occasion) dealt the cards, and attendants kept the player's glasses filled. The table was covered with piles of silver Mexican dollars and gold coins, constituting the "bank." Behind one of the tables Tules sat facing the players and dealt monte, a game of pure chance. In its simplest form, the dealer drew four cards from the bottom of the 40-card Spanish deck and laid them face-up on the table. The players then placed their bets on their chosen cards. The dealer turned over the cards in the deck one by one until a card matching the rank of a layout card was uncovered. Those who bet on that card were rewarded, and the others lost their money to the owner of the establishment. At the end of the evening Tules left by a side door, followed by attendants carrying bags of money.

Tules's business judgment, characterized by Matt Field as "deep policy and shrewdness," included a careful attention to details. For instance, when she bought a house in 1844 adjacent to her residence on Calle de la Muralla, she was meticulous in requiring that all former owners or their heirs appear with her in alcalde court to close the transaction. In her gambling hall details of good equipment and handsome furnishings added to the success of the business.

Tules's success also depended upon her impeccable courtesy and ease of manner. Matt Field commented on the "carefully modeled smile" that graced her homely countenance at the monte table. Others also described this smile:

Gambling Saloon in Santa Fe.   *Brewerton's drawing is probably of Tules's hall, for it fits the description in his letters. (From G. Douglass Brewerton, "Incidents of Travel in New Mexico,"* Harpers New Monthly Magazine, *April 1854)*

one customer wrote that doña Tules dealt monte with "a firm hand and a winning smile"; another who wrote disparagingly of her, noted her "melancholy smile" when she was losing.

Doña Tules was a lady, and her deportment was as elegant as her gambling hall. Matt Field watched her as she gambled until dawn with a rough-mannered American who implied that he was being cheated. She received the insult as graciously as though it were a compliment and continued the game with imperturbable good humor until the American had lost all his money.

Tules was the only woman in Santa Fe, probably in all of New Mexico, to start a business, continue it, improve and develop it, and succeed with it. Tules's prosperity did not shut down all the other dealers in town; she rented them space in her hall and perhaps took a cut of their profits. It must have been an honest operation as well, otherwise local court records would have informed us of fraud in stronger and more precise terms than the vague hints in American accounts of "ill-gotten wealth" and "machinations of the dealer."

Lieutenant Brewerton's was the fullest account of the hall when it lost its elegance to the damages wrought by U.S. soldiers in 1848. Brewerton described it as a low, flat-roofed, whitewashed adobe house in the shape of an L, which could be entered through a low doorway on Washington Street. The door led to a vestibule smelling of cheap brandy, a few billiard tables, and a bar where cut-glass decanters held fiery *aguardiente* from El Paso del Norte and Monongohela whiskey from a famous Pennsylvania distillery. Beyond the bar was the casino, a long low-ceilinged room dimly lit by chandeliers, candelabras, and narrow windows. On one table was a roulette wheel; three tables were dedicated to monte, with raised wooden rims to keep coins from rolling off, or, as Lieutenant Brewerton suggested, to hide the "machinations of the dealer."

Brewerton did not find the hall handsome, and by American standards it may not have been. But it was the most opulently furnished building in town, far more luxurious than the crude mud-and-timber *Palacio* where the governor lived and worked. Modern writers have further embellished the hall with "magnificent" chandeliers carrying "a thousand candles," and rare Brussels carpets on plank floors. But in 1848 Brewerton described the hall as "dimly-lit" and the floors as "earthen," stained with the brown spittle of tobacco-chewing Americans.

According to Matt Field, Tules was "the supreme queen of refinement and fashion in the republican city of Santa Fe." She earned this title by introducing to the women of Santa Fe the tight-waisted, floor-length gown *(túnica)* worn in the major cities of Europe and the United States. The gown was not entirely unknown in New Mexico, for among Josiah Gregg's trade goods in 1834 were "gowns of English chintz," but this elegant fashion did not win general favor until Tules modeled it.

Despite its popularity, the gown was entirely alien to the New Mexican way of life. The daily costume of New Mexican women was a loose cotton chemise (too low-cut and revealing for American taste) with an ankle-length, gathered skirt that was lifted to wash or wade in the river. Instead of the European bonnet, New Mexican women wrapped around their heads and shoulders a long, wide scarf called the *rebozo,* which served as a hat, a coat, a sling for carrying a baby or produce from the market.

In this comfortable clothing most New Mexican women made tortillas, swept mud floors, tended gardens, picked apples, washed clothing in the river, plastered walls, carried water-jars on their heads, rode horseback astride, chased chickens and little children, and danced all night. Women wading in the river and exposing their "limbs" or nursing babies in public were shocking to Susan Magoffin, a trader's eighteen-year-old bride who wrote in 1846, "I am constrained to keep my veil drawn closely over my face all the time to protect my blushes."

At first sight a visitor in 1841 named George Wilkins Kendall deplored the native costume, which he found "Eve-like and scanty," but he soon changed his mind and described it as "really graceful, easy—ay, becoming." By the mid-1830s a few affluent New Mexican women had adopted the one-piece gown, described by Kendall as a bodice stiffened by stays and a floor-length skirt of "monstrous width or fullness," underneath which was a corset laced tight, distorting the body into "flat or angular, or conical, or jutting shapes."

Mexican *fandangos* (dance parties), given every night in one or another part of the city, had no space for the new fashion; salas were too narrow and dances too athletic and rapid for skirts that were full, wide, and long. Nevertheless, by 1841 the gown had become popular with most of the women in Santa Fe and as far south as Chihuahua, where many Santa Fe traders extended their commerce.

The introduction of the gown coincided with various economic conditions that speeded its adoption. After the depression of 1837 in Missouri, and threats and invasions of Texans from 1840 to 1843, trade was slow, goods were cheap, and the women of Santa Fe could now afford to buy new, expensive fabrics. In 1843 Santa Fe traders imported more goods than ever before, doubling and tripling the size and value of their earlier wagon trains.

Encouraged by the demand for cheap goods, many New Mexicans joined the Americans in both the Missouri and the Chihuahua trade and in towns south of Chihuahua. Tules herself sent $10,000 to St. Louis in 1843 to buy goods, but only for the Santa Fe trade. When New Mexicans entered the Santa Fe trade, the trade itself became a force in socializing American and New Mexican men (many women had already done their part by marrying Americans). Mexicans and Americans became partners in wagon trains and consignments of goods; American traders continued to infiltrate New Mexican business and politics, and in 1846 they were a factor in the United States conquest of New Mexico—a "conquest of merchants" it has been called.

By 1841 a census showed that most of the women of Santa Fe had turned into *costureras,* or seamstresses, creating túnicas out of trader's goods, and business-women out of housewives. The gown sent a popular message: "I am a woman of leisure; I need not work." Women seen on the streets of Santa Fe began to wear the same high heels, corsets, hoops, bustles, and boned collars worn by American women. After the conquest, two official reports noted that all but the poorest of New Mexican women dressed like Americans except for the bonnet, which was generally rejected in favor of the practical rebozo.

Tules herself was no slave to the fashion she had introduced. She dressed as she pleased, as simply as any country girl or as grandly as a queen. At the monte table she wore the common New Mexican costume of a loose-fitting chemise and short full skirt without ornament of any kind. At balls she wore a silk gown ablaze with rich jewelry, her fingers covered with rings, her neck weighted with heavy chains of gold, one supporting a solid gold crucifix.

In 1841 a census of Santa Fe showed that Tules's household included herself, aged 41, gambler; her husband, don Manuel Sisneros, aged 37, farmer; Rafaela, daughter, aged 22, unmarried; and three servants. In 1842 Tules went to Chihuahua to set up her gambling games and paid no gambling fees or fines in New Mexico that year. Amado Chaves tells a family story that when Tules went to Chihuahua in 1842, she left her husband in Santa Fe to take care of the business and the family. The story is questionable, for we know that Rafaela and her five-year-old daughter, Rallitos Washington, accompanied Tules to Chihuahua.

Amado Chaves's stories are usually about half true. Born in 1851, Chaves was superintendent of schools in the early decades of the twentieth century and claimed kinship with doña Tules through Rallitos's marriage to his uncle Lorenzo Labadie. Rallitos was a beautiful child with blue eyes and blond hair, the product of Rafaela's affair with an American named Washington, whom Chaves mistakenly identifies as Colonel J. M. Washington, commanding troops in Santa Fe in 1848, eleven years after Rallitos's birth. (The seducer was probably Luis Washington, the only other man of that name on record, who married one María Salas in Santa Fe in 1836 and then disappeared.)

When Rafaela took another lover, as Amado Chaves was told by a cousin, Tules determined that this man should not escape his duty. As he sneaked into Rafaela's room through the window, he was met by Tules with a gun and a priest with a missal, and the marriage was instantly performed.

Tules's husband, Manuel Antonio Sisneros, made his last documented appearance in the 1841 census. Tules does not mention him in her will, nor does she describe herself as his widow. Amado Chaves wrote that Manuel Antonio left Tules and moved to Manzano where he died excommunicated and in disgrace, but this is not true, as Chaves himself says later. It was Amado's uncle, José Cisneros, who met this fate, not Manuel Antonio Sisneros, whose end is not known.

During 1842, as Tules set up her games in the city of Chihuahua, she wrote to her friend Governor Manuel Armijo that she was in good health and had celebrated Easter with fireworks and bulls; that her games were well-attended; that she had been invited to the inaugural ball honoring the new governor of Chihuahua, but had chosen not to go. She closed the letter with expressions of affection to Armijo and his wife from herself and Armijo's godchild, who Armijo called "the little girl Rallitos."

Armijo answered Tules's letter on February 1843, acknowledging its content, and saying in closing, "Give my remembrances to my god-children and to all your family, and I regret that I do not have the pleasure of giving you a fond embrace. Your affectionate [Manuel Armijo]." This is the first we hear that Armijo was godfather (a very close relationship) to Tules's adopted daughters. The letter is also the sole personal documentation of their friendship yet known, but by no means all that has been surmised.

In the early summer of 1846 an American artist named Alfred S. Waugh, who had chatted with the governor as he painted his portrait, wrote of Tules that "with this lady his Excellency is very intimate; indeed, I believe, he is a partner in her business." Waugh's suggestion that Armijo and Tules were partners in the gambling business or in the Santa Fe trade is possible, but proof is lacking. Waugh's description of their relationship as "intimate" suggests that Tules might have been Armijo's mistress, as Amado Chaves and other later writers state as fact. Waugh also writes that "to this Señora [Tules], the Governor communicates all the affairs of the state … ." Subsequent writers have adopted Waugh's suggestion that Tules was both mistress and mentor to Armijo.

Partners or not, lovers or not, Armijo and Tules spent much time together. The governor frequently walked from his office in the Governor's Palace to Tules's house or place of business—so frequently, in fact, that two different would-be assassins planned their attacks on the governor as he was on his way to visit her, perhaps for a jolly party, such as Matt Field described, or perhaps for a private assignation.

After the Mexican-American War began in May 1846, Armijo fled south before an American army of occupation, returning in disgrace to New Mexico in 1848. Colonel (soon to be General) Stephen Watts Kearny marched to Santa Fe and occupied the city on August 18, 1846. The American soldiers got a sullen welcome, but General Kearny was determined to win the trust of the people of Santa Fe.

On August 30, 1846, Kearny gave a ball at the Governor's Palace which was well attended by all the principal people of the town, "Madame Tula" included, wrote Lieutenant Emory in his diary. At another of General Kearny's balls, Susan Magoffin described the fashions as seriously out-of-date, and Tules as a "stately dame" with the "shrewd sense and fascinating manner necessary to allure the wayward, inexperienced youth to the hall of final ruin."

At a later ball, Susan noticed that the women dressed in Mexican style, danced and smoked *cigaritos*, "from the old woman with false hair and teeth (doña Tula), to the little child." Susan's ugly picture of Tules in 1846 contrasts with Matt Field's enthusiastic description of her in 1839. In fact, after arrival of the American soldiers, Tules's reputation as "supreme queen of refinement and fashion" faded, and the elegance of her gambling hall began to decay.

Tules did not hesitate to show her acceptance of the American invaders. On the very afternoon that General Kearny occupied the Santa Fe plaza,

Lucius Thruston, who had boarded with Tules in 1835, invited the general and his officers to have supper with the celebrated "Madame Tula." Lieutenant W. H. Emory, journalist of the Army of the West, and several others accepted Tules's invitation. They found her hall spacious and well-furnished, and its proprietor "a little passée" but still the "most vivacious and intelligent Mexican" they had seen. It is significant that only in his private journal does Lieutenant Emory record his visit with this notorious woman; not a word of it appears in his official report.

Later in the year Tules entertained another army journalist, Lieutenant J. W. Abert. Her house, wrote Abert, was covered with mirrors and was very stylish, and she served him El Paso wine and a cup of foamy hot chocolate. He noted in his diary that she "was the confidential adviser of Armijo, etc." the "etc." hanging like an insinuation at the end of the sentence. Lieutenant Abert mentioned his visit to Tules's house only in his private journal; his official report said nothing about it.

General Kearny departed for California with a small portion of his soldiers on September 25, 1846. The remaining soldiers, all young and undisciplined volunteers, were in Santa Fe for another year and a half with little to do but drink, gamble, and raise havoc. The soldiers' destructive behavior outraged many New Mexicans, but Tules saw the conquest as inevitable and was determined to make her personal peace with the invaders.

Accordingly, she offered American officers her cooperation and hospitality, and accepted theirs. She provided housing for officers in one of her houses; she welcomed the soldiers in her gambling hall; and she kept smiling. It is easy to imagine that her countrymen criticized her for aiding the enemy, just as the Americans criticized her for crossing the boundaries confining American womanhood. Nevertheless, she continued to aid the Americans, whether for the good of her people or the profit of her business.

In December 1846, she was credited with informing American officers of an incipient uprising of Santa Fe patriots who meant to assassinate the new American governor and his cabinet. New Mexico writer Erna Fergusson derides Tules as "wholeheartedly *gringa*" for her betrayal of the patriots, but sources differ as to whether the informant was Tules, a servant, or a mulatto wife of one of the conspirators.

Years later Private William H. Kennerly told another unverified story: When Colonel Doniphan desperately needed a thousand dollars for his troops, Tules loaned it to him, but only after Colonel David D. Mitchell flattered her by escorting her to a ball.

When Lieutenant George Brewerton visited Tules's hall in 1848, he was strongly fortified by his conviction that gambling is "that most debasing of

Grand Entreé into Santa Fé.   *Brewerton pictures a cavalier on a steed, a peon on a burro, and various women, priests, and citizens in front and on top of an adobe building in Santa Fe guarded by a soldier. (From G. Douglass Brewerton, "Incidents of Travel in New Mexico,"* Harpers New Monthly Magazine, *April 1854)*

vices … an entire devotion to which is the besetting sin of the whole Mexican people." The lieutenant had no trouble locating the owner of the hall, whose face "bore most unmistakably the impress of her fearful calling, being scarred and seamed, and rendered unwomanly by those painful lines which unbridled passions and midnight watching never fail to stamp upon the countenance of their votary." But Tules was still smiling, if weakly—Army doctor H. M. Dunlap wrote in 1847 that "when fortune favors her, her keen small black eyes seem about to start from their sockets, and a melancholy smile covers her wrinkled mouth when losing."

On February 2, 1848, the Mexican War ended. Four days later Colonel Sterling Price ordered that gambling houses to pay a license fee of $500 every three months and limit their clientele to officers and citizens over the age of twenty-one. Somehow Tules managed to survive Colonel Price's attempt to end gambling in Santa Fe, probably because her competitors dropped out and left her all the gamblers in town, including, of course, women, children, and priests. She was still running her gambling hall in 1849 when she imported a harpist from Chihuahua to entertain her customers. That is the last we hear of the hall, and almost the last we hear of Tules herself, for she was nearly fifty years old in 1849 and perhaps not in very good health.

In October 1850 Tules drew up her will with characteristic attention to detail. One copy was in Spanish, another in English, and it was witnessed not only by her doctor, a U.S. Army surgeon, but also by six leading men of Santa Fe. The will began with a statement of her extraordinary financial achievement as a Mexican woman: "First, I declare and state that I am entirely free from debt and that the property of every kind that I am now about to dispose of has been accumulated by my own labor and exertions."

Next, she bequeathed her jewelry, clothing, furniture, carriage, house, and land in Santa Fe to her beloved sister doña María de la Luz Barceló; and another house, where her other sister doña Dolores Barceló had been living, to "Rallitos Gutiérres alias Sisneros, a young girl whom I have brought up from infancy and who now resides with me." The will listed her other child as Carmel Barceló, age fourteen (the census of her household in 1850 also listed Rafael Sisneros, aged ten.)

Tules left half her mules to her brother Trinidad, the other half to her friend and neighbor Santiago Flores, and to his wife Refugia she bequeathed one-third of her money for the purpose of educating, clothing, and support- ing Rallitos Washington and Carmel Barceló (whom she had also raised from birth) until the girls were twenty-five years old or married. The other two-thirds of her money went to her sister doña María de la Luz and her brother don Trinidad. The will provided for just dues of church and government and concluded with her signature, "María Gertrudis Barceló," with her accus-tomed rubric.

After drawing up her will, Tules lived another year and a half. When it came time for her to die, according to Amado Chaves, she at first refused to confess her sins, believing God would judge her by her charitable deeds on earth. Her sister Dolores persuaded her to repent and take confession, and after that Tules sent her sister to identify those in need, and to distribute her largesse.

In another version of the redemption story told to Amado Chaves by his cousin, Tules continued to be Armijo's mistress until the priest of Tomé, Madariaga, persuaded all women living in sin to leave their men and join the church. Tules left Armijo and became very charitable to the poor. But Padre Madariaga died in 1839, which spoils Amado's other story that in 1846 Tules was Armijo's mistress and the power behind his throne.

Tules's funeral service, procession, and burial on January 17, 1852, were elaborate and attended by nearly all the people of Santa Fe and many from elsewhere. Predictably, American observers were outraged at the ostentation and expense. Lieutenant George Brewerton declared that Tules was buried with "all that pomp and ceremony with which ill gotten wealth delights to gild its obsequies"; W.W.H. Davis objected that the funeral cost over $3,000, which, in his mind, confirmed the abuses of the Church and the vanity of Tules. Countering these criticisms, Fray Angélico Cháves pointed out that the fees charged for such ceremonies were the sole support of church and priests.

Around the turn of the century, as coffins in the old Santa Fe cemetery were being moved to a new location, a lid fell off one of the coffins exposing a corpse to a passing schoolgirl who asserted, half a century later with no proof at all, that the corpse she saw was that of doña Tules, and that it had red hair. Accordingly, Ruth Laughlin's novel about doña Tules describes her as red-haired, and Erna Fergusson gives her a red wig.

According to Matt Field in 1839, New Mexicans considered doña Tules the outstanding woman of Santa Fe. To many Americans Tules was the most disreputable female in New Mexico, a woman with a man's ambition and capability who earned a fortune by spending her days and nights in a den of sin, her person shamelessly open to public scrutiny and the insults of crude men. Ignorant of Tules's history and culture, Americans judged her harshly by their own ideal of submissive, inferior, powerless, dependent women.

As the American stance against women's rights and gambling softened in the twentieth century, Tules's significance increased. Writers now drape her in different points of view, like a department-store manikin. This is nothing new, of course—Gregg used her to expose the nastiness of New Mexican society; Brewerton used her as an example of the ugliness of gambling; other American writers used her as an example of New Mexican depravity and as an excuse for the American conquest of New Mexico. Now historians use her as a frame for revisionist analyses of race, class, gender, and feminist theory.

No writer can really know Tules because the Americans who wrote about her hardly understood her at all. Only in Matt Field's description do we see her human qualities—her wit and charm; her warmth and courtesy; and her toughness, self-control, and stamina as a gambler. Tules's powerful presence was markedly different from that of the New Mexican girls and matrons vending their produce, dancing at fandangos, singing and chattering together at their tasks. But Tules was one of them all the same, deviating from their culture in no way except degree.

She did not violate the social norms of New Mexicans, but lived well within the prescribed limits of her gender and class. In her family relations, her care of Rafaela and Rallitos, and in the thoughtful provisions of her will, she was the good New Mexican matriarch; in her business, in her dealings with male gamblers and army officers, she was the modest and courteous shopkeeper, selling her games as other women sold their vegetables.

But of course she was more than matriarch or street vendor. She was the ultimate woman of Republican New Mexico, taking her independence to the limits possible to New Mexican women, stretching her opportunities as far as they would go. She lived her life exactly the way she chose, gambling always that the game she loved to play was worth the penalty Americans made her pay.

SOURCES AND FURTHER READING

This article expands my earlier study of La Tules entitled "La Tules and the Americans," *Arizona and the West* 20 (summer 1980):215–30, where footnotes supply precise references for much of the material herein, including those from the Mexican Archives of New Mexico. Accounts of travelers who wrote about Tules's world include, *Matt Field on the Santa Fe Trail,* collected by Clyde and Mae Reed Porter, edited by John E. Sunder (Norman: University of Oklahoma Press, 1960); Stella M. Drumm, ed., *Down the Santa Fé Trail and Into Mexico: The Diary of Susan Shelby Magoffin, 1846–1847* (New Haven: Yale University Press, 1926), 118–21; Josiah Gregg, *Commerce of the Prairies,* ed., Max. L. Moorhead (Norman: University of Oklahoma Press, 1954).

For Gregg's character, see Paul Horgan, *Josiah Gregg and His Vision of the Early West* (New York: Farrar Straus Giroux, 1979); George Wilkins Kendall, *Narrative of the Texan Santa Fe Expedition,* 2 vols. (New York: Harper and Brothers, 1844); John F. McDermott, ed., *Travels in Search of the Elephant: The Wanderings of Alfred S. Waugh, Artist in Louisiana, Missouri, and Santa Fe, in 1845–1846* (St. Louis: Missouri Historical Society, 1951); W.W.H. Davis, *El Gringo; or, New Mexico and Her People* (New York: Harper & Brothers: New York, 1857).

The delightful letters of Mme. Calderón de la Barca, *Life in Mexico During a Residence of Two Years in that Country* (New York: E. P. Dutton and Co., 1931) describe upper-class women in Mexico City, from which can be drawn similarities and contrasts with those of Santa Fe women.

Tules is the heroine of two rather dated novels. Anna Robeson Burr's *The Golden Quicksand* (New York: D. Appleton-Century Company, 1936) depicts her as a svelte and sexy siren in black lace and pearl earrings; Ruth Laughlin's *The Wind Leaves No Shadow* (Caldwell, ID: Caxton Printers, 1973) makes her a sweet and spunky woman escaping one peril after another. The most accurate of many popular articles about Tules is the well-aged piece of Walter Briggs with Howard Bryan and Fray Angélico Chávez entitled "Venal or Virtuous? The Lady They Called La Tules," *New Mexico Magazine* 49 (March/April 1971):9–16.

Works on Republican New Mexico, from popular to scholarly, include Ruth Laughlin, *Caballeros* (Caldwell, ID: Caxton Printers, 1947); Erna Fergusson, *New Mexico: A Pageant of Three Peoples* (New York: Alfred A. Knopf, 1971); Bernard DeVoto, *The Year of Decision, 1846* (Boston: Little, Brown and Company, 1943), which places the American conquest in a national context; and Marc Simmons *New Mexico: An Interpretive History* (New York: W. W. Norton & Company, 1977). For more scholarly studies, see David J.

Weber, *The Mexican Frontier 1821–1846: The American Southwest Under Mexico* (Albuquerque: University of New Mexico Press, 1982), with its extensive bibliography. See also two histories, one political by Howard Roberts Lamar, *The Far Southwest, 1846–1912: A Territorial History* (New York: W. W. Norton & Company, 1970), and an old but ever-useful work of Hubert Howe Bancroft, *History of Arizona and New Mexico*, vol. 17, in *The Works of Hubert Howe Bancroft* (San Francisco: A. L. Bancroft, 1889).

For a favorable Catholic interpretation of Tules's life by a broad minded, contemporary priest, see Fray Angélico Chávez, "Doña Tules, Her Fame and Her Funeral," *El Palacio* 57 (August 1950); for a modern Chicana view of Tules, see Deena J. González, "La Tules of Image and Reality: Euro-American Attitudes and Legend Formation on a Spanish-Mexican Frontier," in Adela de la Torre and Beatríz M. Pesquera, eds., *Building with Our Hands: New Directions in Chicana Studies* (Berkeley: University of California Press, 1991). Court records showing the actions of women of Republican New Mexico based on custom and legal rights are used in Janet Lecompte, "The Independent Women of New Mexico, 1821–1846," *Western Historical Quarterly* 12 (January 1981):17–35.

For a deep study of the parent culture as it related to women, differentiating the legal and actual rights of women, see Silvia Marina Arrom, *The Women of Mexico City, 1790–1857* (Stanford, CA: Stanford University Press, 1985); Arrom concludes that Mexico City women were not necessarily representative of women in other parts of Mexico, as Tules's career illustrates. Asunción Lavrin's outstanding work on colonial Mexican women suggests the origins of the independent New Mexican woman of the Republican period. See, for instance, "In Search of the Colonial Woman in Mexico: The Seventeenth and Eighteenth Centuries," in *Latin American Woman: Historical Perspectives,* ed. Asunción Lavrin (Westport, CT: Greenwood Press, 1978).

The "gown" segment uses chapter ten of Josiah Gregg's *Commerce of the Prairies* for estimates of amount and value of goods and number of traders and wagons each year from 1822 to 1843. Most references to the growing use of the gown are in sources already cited; the preponderance of "costureras" is based on censuses analyzed by Beth Lyndon, "Occupations in Santa Fe, New Mexico: 1821–1870" (Honors' thesis, The Colorado College, 1986).

In reconstructing Tules's life, census records are important, especially those of Virginia Langham Olmstead, *New Mexico Spanish & Mexican Colonial Censuses, 1790, 1823, 1845* (1975), and *New Mexico 1850 Territorial Census,* 4 vols. (1976), and published by the New Mexico Genealogical Society, Albuquerque, as well as local schedules in the Mexican Archives of New Mexico, Records Center and Archives, Santa Fe.

The United States' conquest of New Mexico is viewed in documentary excerpts by George Winston Smith and Charles Judah in *Chronicles of the Gringos; The U.S. Army in the Mexican War 1846–1848; Accounts of Eyewitnesses & Combatants* (Albuquerque: University of New Mexico Press, 1968). Journals and letters of soldiers and travelers in Santa Fe, 1846 to 1848 are legion; those used herein are Lieutenant Abert's diary edited by John Galvin, *Western America in 1846–1847: The Original Travel Diary of Lieutenant J. W. Abert* ... (San Francisco: John Howell—Books, 1966) and "Extracts from the Journal of Lt. Emory" *Niles National Register 71* (November 7, 1846 [dated in error "Sept. 30, 1846"]):158.

Official government reports of Emory and Abert are in Lieutenant W. H. Emory, *Notes of a Military Reconnoissance, from Fort Leavenworth, in Missouri, to San Diego, in California, including parts of the Arkansas, Del Norte, and Gila Rivers* 30th Cong., 1st sess. (Sen. Exec. Doc. 7) Serial 505 (Washington, D.C. 1848); an abridged account is Ross Calvin, ed., *Lieutenant Emory Reports* (Albuquerque: University of New Mexico Press, 1951).

Accounts of other American soldiers include John T. Hughes, *Doniphan's Expedition containing an account of the Conquest of New Mexico* (Cincinnati, OH, 1847), reprinted in William E. Connelley, *Doniphan's Expedition and the Conquest of New Mexico and California* (Topeka, KS, 1907); George Rutledge Gibson, *Journal of a Soldier under Kearny and Doniphan, 1846–1847,* ed. Ralph P. Bieber, *The Southwest Historical Series,* vol. 3 (Glendale, CA: Arthur H. Clark Co., 1935); George Douglass Brewerton, *Overland with Kit Carson: A Narrative of the Old Spanish Trail in '48,* ed. Stallo Vinton (New York: A. L. Burt Company, 1930); and William Clark Kennerly, *Persimmon Hill: A Narrative of Old St. Louis and the Far West* (Norman: University of Oklahoma Press, 1948).

Other sources are "The Doctor in Santa Fe, Being a Part of the Journal of Dr. H. M. Dunlap, Santa Fe, 1847," manuscript in Missouri State Historical Society, Columbia; "Typed Statement of Amado Chaves," Misc. Papers, Records Center & Archives, Santa Fe, and W.H.H. Allison, "Santa Fe as It Appeared During the Winter of the Years 1837 and 1838," *Old Santa Fe 2* (October 1914). Accounts based on Amado Chaves's stories are Ralph Emerson Twitchell, *Leading Facts of New Mexico History* (Cedar Rapids, IA: Torch Press, 1912), 2:508n.; Twitchell, *Old Santa Fe: The Story of New Mexico's Ancient Capital* (Santa Fe: Rio Grande Press, 1963), 338–39, 467–68; and Marc Simmons, *The Little Lion of the Southwest* (Chicago: Swallow Press, 1973), 79.

2

Jessie Benton Frémont: A Daughter of the East, a Bride of the West

MARY LEE SPENCE

❧ IN THE POPULAR MIND OF THE TWENTIETH CENTURY, Martha Canary (Calamity Jane) probably has more name recognition than Jessie Benton Frémont, but of all the women portrayed in this book, Jessie is the most notable of the women and the woman who had the most powerful political connections. Until she made her permanent home in Los Angeles in late 1887 at the age of sixty-three, her residences in the West were few. But from the very earliest years of her life, her person and her interests were identified with the West. Her father was the powerful Missouri senator, Thomas Hart Benton, who espoused western interests in and out of Congress for more than three decades. Her husband, the dashing western explorer John Charles Frémont, whom she married at the age of seventeen, riveted her attention even more sharply on the West.

Even though Jessie was not averse to subtly reminding readers that she was a senator's daughter or the wife of a colonel (later general), she was no shrinking violet, content to exercise influence through the male members of her family. Politics and power fascinated her, and more than most women of her time, she assumed a role for herself. Sometimes, she was torn about the direct use of power by women and drew back, but the temptation to embellish the historical record and to put the Benton/Frémont interpretation on history was irresistible. Her writings attribute to her father and husband

Jessie Benton Frémont in 1861 at home on Black Point, overlooking San Francisco Bay. (Courtesy of The Bancroft Library, Berkeley, California)

premier roles in shaping and carrying forward the growth of the West, and it had been her "great good fortune" to blend the two lives.

Jessie's fascinating life, spanning the last seventy-five years of the nineteenth century, reflects the whole tapestry of the trans-Mississippi West: its exploration and varied geography, the conquest of Mexican territory, the sea and overland migrations, economic development, and the building of cities. But Jessie was more than a sectional figure; she was very much a national figure, caught up in national politics and the Civil War.

Jessie remembered three childhood homes. One was Cherry Grove, the home of her maternal grandfather, James McDowell, near the Blue Ridge Mountain town of Lexington, Virginia, where she had been born on May 31, 1824. She was the second oldest of four sisters and two much younger brothers. It had also been the birthplace of her mother, Elizabeth McDowell, who, after a long courtship, married Thomas Hart Benton, already a U.S. senator.

The second was the St. Louis home of her father and grandmother, Ann Gooch Benton (the wife of the deceased land speculator Jesse Benton). The Bentons went there every other year, not only for family reasons, but also for Benton to mend political fences and campaign for reelection. Here Jessie was exposed to a strange new world. The Catholic religion and the

French language still seemed to dominate; army officers in worn uniforms went by on horseback; fur empresarios, Santa Fe traders, and real Indians mingled along the bustling waterfront. St. Louis had become a major commercial metropolis, the gateway to the West, and Jessie's ears absorbed much exciting talk of expansionism and the need to open new routes to tap frontier resources.

The third home was the Benton's official residence in Washington, first in boardinghouses and then in the permanent residence on C Street. She could recall how her father took her with him to the White House to visit President Andrew Jackson, with whom he had made peace and a political alliance, or how he sometimes deposited her in the Library of Congress under the watchful eye of the librarian. While he was in the Senate, she would page through *The Birds of America* and the collections of illustrated travels. When she and her older sister Eliza (called Liz) reached school age, Benton employed a series of tutors, but Jessie seized every opportunity to escape to her father's library, where she cajoled Benton into correcting her exercises and supervising her reading. And when they went on their travels to Virginia and St. Louis, a little English valise held the books and maps for their father's teaching. Sometimes they were much above the young Bentons' comprehension, but they grew into them. "Especially," she wrote, "we never got away from Plutarch and the *Iliad.* The gods and goddesses descended on us everywhere."

As Jessie reached her teens, she became her father's secretary and confidante, and in the process was educated by a master craftsman in Washington politics and personalities. At the dinner table, too, she met politicians, diplomats, scientists, scholars, and rough westerners. At fourteen she and Eliza were sent as boarders to Miss English's Female Seminary in Georgetown, but Jessie thoroughly despised the "Society School." On a visit home, she seized the scissors, cut her wavy auburn hair, and announced that she would not return. Benton was thoroughly displeased, but she never went back to school. She had already met John Charles Frémont at a school concert at the seminary, but would not see him again for many months.

Frémont had been born in Savannah, Georgia, on January 21, 1813, the first child of an itinerant Frenchmen, Charles Fremon, who had enticed Anne Beverley Whiting Pryor to run away from her elderly husband, Major John Pryor of Richmond, Virginia. The parents lived as a couple but were never able to obtain a legal divorce, so John would bear the stigma of illegitimacy all of his life. Fremon died in 1818, leaving Anne with several small children. By 1823 the little family had become residents of Charleston, and John eventually enrolled in the scientific department of the College of Charleston but did not graduate. His charm and intelligence, however, had caught the eye of Joel Poinsett, an influential South Carolina politician, who helped him obtain various posts in surveying and eventually a commission in the U.S. Corps of Topographical Engineers. After field experience in the Minnesota country with the distinguished French scientist Joseph N. Nicollet, John came to Washington to help prepare the great map that would display the results of their explorations. Benton sometimes dropped by to observe the work and began inviting Nicollet and Frémont to informal evenings at his home, where the conversation often centered on the need to explore the lands west of the Missouri River.

The Bentons' attempts to quash the budding romance between their daughter and John failed. The two eloped on October 19, 1841, the day Benton left on a trip to Kentucky and St. Louis. After the secret marriage, Jessie returned to the Benton home, but the news had already leaked out. As soon as he heard it, the senator hurried back to Washington. One relative reported that the irate Benton would not let Jessie remain in his house. The marriage was published, and John took his wife to his lodgings. In time, Benton became reconciled, and the couple moved into the Benton home. As chair of the Senate Committee on Military Affairs, the senator used his influence to support the career of his son-in-law and to fulfill his own dreams about the West.

In 1842 Frémont was given command of an exploring expedition to the South Pass and the Wind River Mountains of Wyoming. He returned to Washington in time for his daughter Lily's birth and shortly afterwards spread over Jessie the wind-whipped flag which he had raised on one of the higher summits in the Wind River range, apparently to console her for not having produced a boy.

In 1843–1844 he led an expedition into Oregon and California, visiting Great Salt Lake on the way out, dramatically breaching the Sierra in midwinter, and traveling down almost the entire length of California before cutting east. During his absences, Jessie took her old place at the end of her father's library table as scribe and confidante and waited anxiously for news of her husband. She wrote a mother of one of the men on the expedition that she might have to resort to "some desperate remedy such as plain sewing to relieve" her nervous state.

When John did return from both expeditions, she helped him write lively, readable reports, filled with human touches, even frontier gossip. Curious Americans received a wealth of information, both miscellaneous and utilitarian, about the West; and emigrants were able to travel by the maps that his cartographer helped him draw. The reports and maps were ordered published by Congress, and subsequently a number of commercial editions appeared at home and abroad. John became a national hero; Jessie a celebrity. He was breveted captain, and then while he was away on his third expedition (1845–1847), which took him into California again, he was commissioned to be a lieutenant colonel in the Mounted Rifles. Jessie's spirits soared and she jubilantly wrote to him that he was ranked with Daniel Defoe. "They say that as Robinson Crusoe is the most natural and interesting fiction of travel, so Frémont's report is the most romantically truthful."

In California, Frémont aided and abetted the Bear Flaggers in their revolt against Mexico. The Stars and Stripes soon replaced the Bear Flag at Sutter's Fort, and Frémont organized members of his exploring party and settler volunteers into the California Battalion to cooperate with the navy in wresting California from Mexico. After the task was accomplished, news began to filter into Washington of the disharmony among the military officers. When General Stephen Watts Kearny arrived in California with his troops, he began sparring with Commodore Robert Stockton for supremacy of command. Frémont, whom Stockton had appointed governor of the conquered territory, was the man caught in the middle.

When Christopher Carson, Frémont's guide for the first three expeditions, came to Washington with dispatches from California, Jessie, deeply disturbed, went twice with him to call on President James Polk. She was unable to elicit from the president an approbation of her husband's conduct. Ultimately, Frémont acknowledged the authority of Kearny, who marched him east, arrested him at Fort Leavenworth, and charged him with mutiny. Later the judge advocate added two additional charges: disobeying the lawful command of a superior officer, and conduct to the prejudice of good order and military discipline.

When Frémont arrived at what is now Kansas City, Jessie was there to meet her anguished husband and to give love and support. They no sooner reached Washington than he was called to South Carolina by the critical illness and soon to follow death of his mother. When newspapers reported that potential prosecution witnesses in the coming court-martial had received orders for distant places, Jessie, ever vigilant in her husband's defense, sent the reports to the president, appealed to his power to do justice, and boldly argued that pro-Kearny officers should not be allowed to escape questioning in this way. Fearing that Polk might think she was overstepping her womanly role, she added: "Do not suppose, Sir, that I lightly interfere in a matter properly belonging to men, but in the absence of Mr. Frémont I attend to his affairs at his request."

The court-martial was held at the Washington Arsenal. Jessie was involved in defense strategy and as secretary and copyist for Benton and another one of his sons-in-law, William Carey Jones, who prepared the arguments. Since as civilians, the two men could not speak in a military courtroom, John conducted his own defense. Kearny's testimony cast Frémont in the role of bargaining for the governorship of California; the defense strategy was to show that Kearny bore false witness. The long and bitter trial was painful for Jessie. Frémont was found guilty on all charges and specifications and ordered dismissed from the service. Seven of the thirteen members of the court, however, recommended him to the clemency of the president. Polk was not satisfied that mutiny had been proven; he sustained the second and third charges, but remitted the penalty, and ordered Frémont to report for army duty. The proud explorer refused to admit in any way the justice of the decision against him and submitted his resignation from the service. Benton was convinced that Frémont had paid the penalty of not having entered the army through the gates of West Point. "He had done worse: he had become distinguished." As for Jessie, she wrestled with the demon of despair.

With Jessie's assistance again, Frémont completed a *Geographical Memoir upon Upper California,* while he waited anxiously for Congress to appropriate funds for a new expedition to the West. When the measure failed to pass, he and Benton sought private financing for a winter expedition that would explore the feasibility of building a railroad from St. Louis to the Pacific. John and Jessie, whose second child had been born in July 1848, made plans to settle in California, where he was the claimant to Las Mariposas, a vast property near Yosemite, which as yet had no set boundaries or confirmed title.

Jessie, with Lily and six-week-old Benton, accompanied John to the frontier. Three days out of St. Louis, the baby died on the Missouri River steamer, but the grieving family continued on to Boone Creek. John left for the West on October 20, and Jessie returned East to make preparations to travel to California by way of the Isthmus of Panama.

She was one of four females among the nearly three hundred and fifty passengers aboard the side-wheeler *Crescent City* when it churned out of New York harbor on March 15, 1849, bound for Chagres River in Panama. The ultimate destination for most of them was the California gold diggings. The three other females were Jessie's six-year-old daughter, Lily; their newly hired servant who was soon put under guard in another cabin for stealing their clothing; and an Irish woman traveling with her husband. Nine days later they reached Chagres, and had it not been for fear of being shamed in the eyes of her father, Jessie would have returned immediately to New York on the steamer as the captain begged her to do.

The small tender that came out to meet them carried them only a few miles up the Chagres River, where most of the passengers changed to dugout canoes for the three-day, forty-mile journey to Gorgona. One of the developers of the Panama route, William Aspinwall, had arranged for Jessie and her protector, brother-in-law Richard Taylor Jacob, to be given places in the "whale-boat" of the Pacific Mail Steamship Company. Jessie invited the Irish woman to join them and over the former's protest, the thieving servant also claimed a place. The Frémont party rested each night on cots with clean sheets in one or another of the riverside camps built for the American engineering team surveying the route for a projected railroad, whereas most of the other travelers risked their health by sleeping on the ground or in the huts of Indians.

The Frémont party was nearing Gorgona when Jacob suffered a sunstroke and had to return to the United States. Jessie was urged to return, too. Her trip was impossible, officers of the engineering corps told her, but the gritty twenty-five-year-old woman was determined to push on and meet her husband in San Francisco as planned. After Panama City, she would also be without the protection of Captain Tucker, a trusted employee of Aspinwall, who was escorting the Frémont entourage across the isthmus.

Before leaving Gorgona, Jessie and others were invited to a breakfast at the town alcalde's house, which was a structure on poles with a thatched roof and wattled sides, resembling "a magnified vegetable crate." The soft-spoken warning of another guest prevented her from showing horror when the chief dishes were served—"a baked monkey, which looked like a little child that had been burned to death" and an iguana, or large lizard, of which she had seen many along the river.

The twenty-one mile trip from Gorgona to Panama City was not without its perils: steep mountains with narrow trails and rapid streams to cross. Travel was by muleback now. Jessie's mount was a fine one, but most of the others were small, badly fed, wretched little creatures full of viciousness. Both riders and baggage suffered considerably. Captain Tucker was exultant that Jessie seemed unafraid, and "as there were no complaints, or tears, or visible breakdown," she wrote later, "he gave me credit for high courage, while the fact was that the whole thing was so like a nightmare that one took it as a bad dream—in helpless silence."

The first few days in the walled city of Panama City had their pleasant aspects. She and Lily were invited to stay in the home of Señora Arcé y Zimena, whose nephew Jessie had known when he was Panamanian ambassador in Washington. She read, wrote letters, dined with ladies of the upper class, walked on the ramparts in the cool of the day, and from their balcony overlooking the main plaza, she and Lily could see the old cathedral with the roof and spire inlaid with mother-of-pearl, the wizened jeweler plying his trade in the open air, the customs house, and the calaboose, where barefoot guards whiled away their time fighting cocks. All too often the Episcopal clergyman, with white robes and bared head, followed a solitary rough coffin, attended by a few men dressed in red flannel shirts, to the temporary burial ground beyond the land gate. Panama City was increasingly crowded with forty-niners and tropical diseases were taking their toll. On all lips were the question: When would the ships arrive to take them to California?

As Jessie and Lily waited impatiently, rumors began to reach Panama that Frémont's overland expedition had met disaster in the rugged mountains of southern Colorado. Then came the letter from Taos, dated January 27 and February 6, 1849, from her husband (forwarded by her father) confirming the rumors and giving details of his battle against the winter weather and the loss of 10 men, 120 mules, and all equipment. He assured her that he had been injured in neither mind nor body and would resupply, move west over a more southern route, and meet her in San Francisco.

The strain and the tropics left Jessie ill; her lungs were infected and she coughed blood. Gradually, she recovered and again brushed aside all pleas to return east. By May 18, she and Lily were bound for San Francisco aboard the Pacific Mail Steamship Company steamer, *Panama,* coming from around the Horn. When her hacking cough revived in the hot, airless cabin, a room was made for her on the quarterdeck with the big flag doubled and thrown over the boom. Although she learned in San Diego that her husband was in California, she was disappointed that he was not there to meet her when the ship steamed through the narrow strait that had already been named the Golden Gate. John arrived ten days later and the little family went to Monterey, a hundred miles to the south.

Had it not been for her image of "the proud lonely man making a new start in life," she might have quailed at boarding the *Crescent City,* and the sudden realization that she was severing ties to friends and family, especially to her father, and of venturing into strange faraway places. The whole court-martial had been a shattering and disillusioning experience for her. Who could she trust? And gone, too, was some of the assurance that the world would go her way. She may have lost some of her innocence, but her trials had also made her stronger, albeit more cynical and less forgiving. The experiences with forty-niners on ship and the isthmus broke down her aloofness, and in the words of her recent biographer, Pamela Herr, the journey became "a passage into a male realm, an exhilarating place she had occasionally known with her father and with John when they worked together on the reports."

John did not take his family to Las Mariposas. It was too far out of the way—too wild and rough with danger from Indians and bears, and with miners flooding into the area. He made several trips to the area, and gold began flowing into the family coffers from the mining taking place there and also from a steam sawmill he had established at Pueblo San Jose. During their brief stay of seven months in California, the Frémonts lived for a time in a wing of the adobe villa of Señora José Castro in Monterey or simply wandered, often stopping to visit old California families at their ranchos, or residing sometimes in a prefabricated house from China in San Francisco's Happy Valley, or even in a hot room in San Jose. Frémont was quietly campaigning for political office, and Jessie was jubilant when he was elected U.S. senator by the newly organized state legislature.

Back across the Isthmus of Panama went Jessie and Lily with John. They all suffered fevers before arriving in New York in March 1850; indeed Jessie, gripped by malaria, had languished for a month in Panama City at the home of her old friend Señora Arcé before being carried in a stretcher across the mountains. After they recovered from their illnesses, they savored their reentry into Washington society and the many parties and dinners. The return with gold and a senate seat had wiped out the disgrace of the court-martial and Jessie felt vindicated. Even the growing sectional tension over slavery could not dampen her spirits. Her joy quickly evaporated, however, when California was finally admitted to the Union as a free state and the congressmen were sworn in. John drew the short senate term and felt compelled to return to California to campaign for re-election.

Jessie, who was two months pregnant, and Lily again went with him— their third arduous crossing of the isthmus in less than two years. But after 142 ballots, the state legislature carried over the election of a senator to the next term, and John gave up on politics, instead turning his attention to developing his properties, especially the rich gold-bearing quartz veins on Las Mariposas. He was away from home on June 22, 1851, when the San Francisco fire (ironically set by the "thieving" servant who had crossed the isthmus in 1849) burned the pretty cottage where the Frémonts were living, forcing the evacuation of Jessie, Lily, and the two-month-old baby boy, John Charles.

Early in 1852, the Frémonts again traversed the Isthmus of Panama, stopped briefly in New York, and then sailed for England, where they stayed at London's elite Clarendon Hotel. John went to raise capital for Las Mariposas; Jessie anticipated acceptance into court society, and she was not disappointed. Dressed in pink satin, lace, and pearls, she was thrilled and delighted when she was presented to Queen Victoria. With her husband, she was swept up in a pleasant round of teas and dinners at important London houses and with figures like Joshua Bates, an American connected with the Barings, and Sir Roderick Murchison, president of the Royal Geographical Society, which had presented John the Founder's Medal for his services in promoting the cause of geographical science.

But the splendor was tainted by humiliation. Newspapers gave a disturbing picture of affairs on Las Mariposas with respect to irregularities in mining leases. There were also rumors that the property had been sold by Benton, acting under a power of attorney from Frémont, who, upon arrival in London, had repudiated the sale. The crowning blow came when the explorer stepped into a carriage to attend a dinner with Jessie and was arrested for nonpayment of drafts, which he had drawn upon the secretary of state when he was governor of California. The drafts had subsequently been passed into the hands of a London firm, which now brought charges. Frémont spent the night of April 7 in Sloman's Lock-up on Cursitor Street, Chancery Lane. Jessie frantically sought bail money, ironically from the very agent with whom Frémont was warring. When he told her he had not money for bail, either from his own funds or Mariposas' agency funds, Jessie lost her equilibrium and usual grace, roasting him with the words: "You are a great rascal—my father says so." In the end the American investment banker George Peabody came to the rescue, and soon afterward the Frémonts fled to Paris to protect John from further arrests.

They took up their residence in an elegant Italianate house on the Champs Elysées with a full retinue of servants and luxuries of every kind. Through the kindness of an elderly French nobleman, who was also a Las Mariposas investor, the Frémonts were put on the *liste intime* and received invitations for the fêtes and balls of Louis Napoleon, who proclaimed himself emperor in December 1852.

In February 1853, Jessie gave birth to a daughter, whom they named Anne Beverley, and in March came a letter from Benton indicating that Congress had authorized surveys of the principal routes to the Pacific Ocean to determine the most practical and economical route for a railroad. He urged John to return and ask for a place on the survey of the central region between the 38th and 39th parallels. Frémont crossed the channel to clean up his affairs in London and to borrow £13,000, securing it by a mortgage on all of his one-half interest in Las Mariposas. The remaining half was owned by others, principally the San Francisco banking firm of Palmer, Cook & Company, which had also loaned money to the explorer. Frémont sailed from Liverpool, leaving Jessie, the children, and two French servants to follow from Le Havre on the *Arago*.

The family took a house near Benton's, but heat and the illness of Anne caused Jessie to seek relief at the Silver Spring home of good and long-term friends, the Francis Preston Blairs, whose married daughter, Elizabeth Blair

(Lizzie) Lee, also lived there. Lizzie was with her when the baby died in Jessie's arms. The intimacy of that tragic night cemented the friendship of the two women.

When Frémont failed to receive the command of the government survey, he decided to make his own survey—his fifth and last—and perhaps win new laurels that would wipe out the defeats of the past. Benton may have contributed funds, but observers noted a coolness between him and the explorer. The senator no doubt remembered the failed fourth expedition and the cancellation of the sale of Las Mariposas, but other reasons may have contributed to his aloofness—possibly a growing mistrust of Frémont's judgment, a feeling Jessie thought her brother-in-law, William Carey Jones, had encouraged.

With John's departure for the frontier, Jessie again "began the waiting, and hoping, and fearing." When she received a telegram that he had turned back from the frontier to seek medical attention in St. Louis, she hurried to his side. Homeopathic medicine improved his inflammatory rheumatism, and when John left to rejoin his waiting men, Jessie accompanied him up the Missouri River as far as Independence. She was excessively sad and nervous all winter, partly due to the declining health of her mother, and then in April came a Mormon official to Washington with the news that Frémont and his men, half-starved and exhausted, had found refuge in the little Mormon village of Parowan. Jessie was "shocked" and "chilled" by the harshness with which her father gave her the news; he seemed more concerned about a bungled expedition than by John's sufferings. To the public, however, Benton gave the most optimistic of reports and when his son-in-law returned by sea in late May 1854, he lauded his accomplishments.

By late August, John was once more on his way to the Pacific Coast, this time alone, and by way of Panama. The *National Intelligencer* reported that he went to fix astronomically the position of the crossing he had discovered the previous spring, but in reality it was Las Mariposas and other business affairs that he went "to fix." Jessie stayed behind; her mother died in early September; her father's home burned on an icy day in February 1855; and shortly after John's return she gave birth on May 17, 1855, to her fifth and last child, a boy, who was christened Francis Preston after Francis Preston Blair.

The Frémonts and the Blairs were growing closer together both personally and politically. Under the Missouri Compromise of 1820 slavery had been excluded from the territories laying north of latitude 36°30′. Thirty-four years later the passage of the Kansas-Nebraska Act, repealing that sacred compact and permitting settlers to vote the question of slavery up or down in the territories, set the nation on a blind march toward the abyss of secession

The Frémonts representing "Young America" versus "Old Fogyism."

and civil war. Old parties split and realigned, new parties such as the Republican and American, formed; every issue was considered from the point of its effect upon slavery, and Kansas "bled" as the pro- and anti-slavery forces warred to bring the territory into their respective ideological camp.

As the presidential election drew near, parties searched for a presidential candidate who could win in 1856. Because of his reputation as "the Pathfinder" and "conqueror of California," but with almost no political baggage, Frémont was courted by both the Democratic and Republican parties. He made a special trip to Nantucket to discuss the issue with Jessie, who had gone there to recuperate from childbirth and to escape the coolness of her father. As neither could support the extension of slavery into Kansas and Nebraska, as the Democratic nominee would have to do in order to maintain the loyalty of the southern wing, John allied himself with the Republicans, who were still too new to have a wide following. Blair was solidly behind him, but the staunch old Democrat, Benton, also hostile to slavery, feared the election of a purely sectional candidate would exacerbate conflict and would not support his son-in-law's candidacy. Later, on election eve in St. Louis, he gave an opposition speech that Jessie termed "a sort of Brutus stab," and set her to wondering if she were of "the right stuff for a political woman."

In the fervent campaign that followed John's nomination, Jessie tried to maintain a discreet public image, but she was much in the eye of the public, and sometimes the ticket seemed to be more "Frémont and Jessie" than "Frémont and Dayton." One banner bore the inscription "Jessie for the White House," and Republicans sang songs like "Oh Jessie Is a Sweet Bright Lady" to the tune of "Comin' thro' the Rye." Never before had a woman been so featured in a political campaign, and never before had women been so visible at rallies or as workers. Many echoed the sentiment of abolitionist, Lydia Maria Child: "What a shame that *women* can't vote! We'd carry our 'Jessie' into the White House on our shoulders, *wouldn't* we?"

Behind the scenes in their fashionable New York City home at 56 West Ninth Street, Jessie worked tirelessly for John's election: receiving a multitude of visitors, supervising correspondence, countering slanders and charges that he was a Catholic, and collecting materials for several campaign biographies, even going in disguise with Lizzie's husband to Virginia to gather information about his family background. In the chapter that she virtually wrote for John Bigelow's biography of Frémont, she neatly papered over her husband's illegitimacy and emphasized a distant relationship with George Washington.

In a surprisingly close election, Democrat James Buchanan won. It must have been an especially bitter pill for Frémont to lose the four electoral votes of California where numerous "Bear Clubs" had been organized to support him. With all her heart, Jessie had coveted the presidency for John, and for herself, too. Her dreams were destroyed and she was bitterly disappointed, but except for some show of anger and pain in letters to dear Lizzie, she outwardly bore the defeat gallantly and cheerfully. Relations with her aging father, who unknown to her had cancer, mended somewhat and finally she could write Blair, "I find myself thinking it was the 'world well lost' since family harmony and peace for my Father's old age has come out of defeat."

After the election John went to California; Jessie took the children to France and rented a large country villa ten miles from Paris, but news of her father's serious illness brought her quickly back to the United States. She arrived the same day as John. Within a few months the whole family was on its way to California, again by the way of the isthmus, but this time they crossed in railroad cars.

They went immediately to Las Mariposas—Jessie's first visit to their seventy-square-mile property—and settled into a small whitewashed cottage near the little town of Bear Valley, which was the hub of Frémont's mining operations. It was here that she learned of her beloved father's death. The malaise that had descended upon her after the election continued, and she suffered from headaches and a "miserable weakness about the heart," but for the most part, she remained outwardly cheerful.

She again assumed her role as John's scribe and became thoroughly acquainted with his ambitious plans for developing the mining properties as well as with his constant legal and financial problems. And she gave the Blairs, and later the public, graphic accounts of a mining dispute that came close to violence, of a camping trip to nearby Mount Bullion, and of eastern visitors, including an old political ally, Horace Greeley of the New York *Tribune.*

But still she felt "as if the mountains of Bear Valley bounded" her world, and she longed for a more congenial life. Early in 1860, John purchased a home and thirteen acres for her on the tip of Black Point, a finger of land jutting into the Bay of San Francisco, which later became Fort Mason. She wrote Lizzie that it was "more beautiful than any Sea Dream that Tennyson or any poet ever fancied." She was glad to escape the isolation of Bear Valley and to enjoy the comforts of city life with its opera, private parties, lectures, and newspapers. She waged an unsuccessful crusade to save a former black servant from the gallows, and she met interesting people like Thomas Starr King, the new Unitarian minister; Bret Harte and Herman Melville, writers; Carleton Watkins, the photographer; and Edward D. Baker, the new Republican senator from Oregon.

John was in Europe trying to raise capital for Las Mariposas when the Civil War broke out. At the urging of the Blairs, President Lincoln named him a major general in command of the western department with headquarters at St. Louis. Jessie and the children met him in New York, and soon all of them were in St. Louis—a city in turmoil, with many Confederate sympathizers, as indeed was true of Missouri in general. There was no settling in a safe eastern city for Jessie; she was determined to play a part in the war. "The restraints of ordinary times do not apply now," she wrote.

Jessie plunged into work as her husband's unofficial aide and confidante and also, with the help of William G. Eliot, a Unitarian minister and founder of Washington University, organized the Western Sanitary Commission, a forerunner of the Red Cross. Much went wrong for Frémont, not all of his own doing. Arms and supplies were lacking; military defeats took place, complaints about his aloofness and his organization of an elite bodyguard led by foreign and flamboyant officers were heard; and war profiteering by his cronies occurred. He had difficulties, too, with the ambitious Francis Preston Blair, Jr., the son of his old political supporter, who damned Frémont in letters to his brother, Postmaster General Montgomery Blair, who in turn passed them on to the president.

Frémont sealed his own fate when, on August 31, 1861, after consulting only Jessie and a Quaker abolitionist, he placed Missouri under martial law and issued a proclamation freeing the slaves of Missouri rebels. Lincoln asked Frémont to modify the proclamation, which had been greeted enthusiastically by the abolitionists. At this point, Jessie carrying a letter from her husband, took the train to Washington to see the president. She remembered walking late at night with Edward P. Cowles to the White House, fatigued and in her dusty travel dress, to deliver the message. By her account, the president received her coolly, and when she tried to explain the situation in Missouri and the importance of winning the support of European countries by freeing the slaves, he remarked, "You are quite a female politician." Two years later, he remembered her as having "taxed me so violently with so many things, that I had to exercise all the awkward tact I have to avoid quarreling with her." Jessie was angry, probably strident, but if Frémont were conspiring against the president, she would have had too much political savvy to tell of disloyalty.

The next day, she had a bitter meeting with Francis P. Blair, Sr., who reminded her of what all the Blairs had done to bolster and advance the interests of the Frémonts, but she was too imperial for him. The long friendship between the two families faded, and Lizzie wrote sadly to her husband, "Were there ever people who were so false to themselves & to others?" Still she did not cease to love Jessie, but the two women did not meet again until 1883 when Lizzie, who had heard disturbing reports about Jessie's poverty, called on her old friend in New York City.

After Jessie's return to Missouri, John briefly jailed Frank Blair twice for insubordination, acts that Montgomery Blair attributed to "General Jessie." The president sent out various officials to investigate the situation in the western department and on November 2, 1861, removed Frémont from his command near Springfield, Missouri, as his forces readied to battle the Confederates the next day. John became the martyred leader of the radicals who demanded that the abolition of slavery be made an object of the war.

As for Jessie, she quickly wrote *The Story of the Guard,* which gave an account of the heroic victory of the Frémont bodyguard at Springfield and at the same time subtly defended her husband's command of a hundred days. She informed her publisher, Ticknor & Fields, that she planned to use the book's royalties to benefit the families of the men who died during the battle. She also helped John prepare a documented statement for the Committee on the Conduct of the War. "She has scarcely slept or rested," wrote an acquaintance. "To see her husband vindicated, is the restless burning of her soul, and she is mistress of every statistic, every item, that can weigh for or against him."

In mid-March of 1862 Lincoln named Frémont commander of the mountain division, and Jessie went with him to Wheeling, then in Virginia. When three months later, the president decided to reorganize the army in the East, thereby making Frémont subordinate to his old enemy, John Pope, he resigned his command. He remained on army pay for a time, but never

THE STORY OF THE GUARD:

A CHRONICLE OF THE WAR.

By JESSIE BENTON FRÉMONT.

" Their good swords rust,
And their steeds are dust,
But their souls are with the saints, we trust."

BOSTON:
TICKNOR AND FIELDS.
1863.

Title page from Jessie Benton Frémont's first book. The butterfly is the symbol for Las Mariposas Estate.

received another assignment. The radical wing of the Republicans nominated Frémont for the presidency in 1864, but when it appeared that Lincoln might not be reelected in a three-party contest, Lincoln's negotiators persuaded Frémont to withdraw. Although the Frémonts denied that there had been "a deal," Montgomery Blair was dismissed from Lincoln's cabinet, and later when John sought the territorial governorship of Arizona, he reminded the Republicans of the political debt owed to him.

During the Civil War, the Frémonts sold the debt-ridden Las Mariposas and in April 1865 purchased a hundred-acre estate overlooking the Hudson, near Tarrytown and named it Pocaho. Jessie concentrated on children, house, garden, and society; and John on his many railroad investments and speculations, which often took him away from home. For her there were trips to New York City (they had kept their brownstone), to Washington, D.C., to St. Louis in 1868 where she unveiled a large monument of her father, and to Europe in 1869 and 1872. The life of domesticity and luxury ended in 1873 with the bankruptcy of the Memphis, El Paso, and Pacific Railway Company and the trial of Frémont in absentia in a Paris court for swindling Frenchmen who had purchased bonds of the company.

Although Jessie was depressed and even made physically ill by the scandal and the dizzying drop from wealth to poverty, her old mettle came to the fore. She sought the help of the shrewd Pennsylvania lawyer Jeremiah Black in salvaging what she could of their dwindling fortune, asked the popular writer James Parton to present to the public her husband's side of the railroad story, and began herself to write for a living, an occupation that would continue for almost twenty years. She produced a series of reminiscences and biographical sketches for the New York *Ledger,* a well paying weekly, and then an account of her 1849 crossing of the Isthmus of Panama and gold-rush experiences for *Harper's.* At this time, she said of herself, "I am like a deeply built ship; I drive best under a strong wind."

Despite her efforts, the Frémonts were forced to sell Pocaho and move into what Jessie jokingly called "poverty flat" at 924 Madison Avenue. In 1877 their household treasures—paintings, furniture, and books—were sold at auction. Jessie and friends worked for a political appointment for John, and the opportunity came when Rutherford B. Hayes was inaugurated president. He was an old admirer of the "Pathfinder," his wife was a friend of Jessie's, and his private secretary, William King Rogers, would soon become a business associate of Fremont's in various enterprises in Arizona and Mexico. On the day that Hayes appointed Frémont governor of Arizona Territory, he presented Jessie with a magnolia blossom, and two years later Jessie sent the president a memorial platter with magnolias and violets, her flower, painted in the center. It was accompanied by a gracious note, reading in part, "It is [to] your appreciation of the General that we owe this return to peace."

Seventeen years had elapsed since Jessie had left California, but she enjoyed the train trip west in 1878 to the new post, and especially the Frémonts' glorious reception in San Francisco and the visit to their old home area of Black Point, although it had been confiscated by the federal government during the Civil War. She and John were accompanied by daughter Lily (now thirty-six), son Frank, an Irish maid, and their staghound. In San Francisco they added a Chinese cook to their entourage. Travel between Yuma, the scorching railhead of the Southern Pacific Railroad, and the capital city of Prescott, tucked high in the pines 230 miles to the northeast, was by three army ambulances, each drawn by six mules.

Jessie, at fifty-four, must have found much that was difficult in the new life on the Arizona frontier, but she refused to be "rolled in cotton wool" and treated like a fragile flower. She and Lily made window drapes for the rented governor's "mansion" and quickly entered into the life of the community. Each afternoon she went to the public school, the Prescott Free Academy, to give a history lesson and instruct a young army officer in the French language. She devoted long hours to writing (much of it for John), participated in the social activities of the town and nearby Fort Whipple, collected Mohave pottery for friends in the East, and persuaded the Catholic bishop to ask the motherhouse of the Sisters of St. Joseph of Carondelet to grant nuns in Arizona the privilege of wearing cooler clothing. The natural beauty of the mountains fascinated her, and she nicknamed Thumb Butte, behind the town, "the Sphinx," and described sunsets in rapt terms. Jessie was impressed with the simple strength and endurance of the women she met, and some of the Prescott residents, such as the writer, Anna Fitch, and the judge, Charles Silent, became enduring friends.

Almost a year to the day of her arrival, without ever having been out of town, Jessie left Prescott for good. Under fire for a six-month absence from the territory, John needed her "on the spot" in New York as his agent in the placing of mining properties and as his personal lobbyist in Washington while he was forced to remain in Prescott. She stayed with son Charley and his wife, with friends, or in a hotel, as she worked hard and remained optimistic that the Frémont fortune would be restored. She saw or wrote often to the president's private secretary and other government officials about mining matters, the necessity of ousting a "thwarting" territorial secretary, and for special favors. Thrice before his resignation of the governorship in October 1881, John joined her in New York for business promotion, but fortune eluded the Frémonts.

When John's official stipend ended, Jessie quietly turned to writing again as a source of income, producing more than fifty articles for *Wide Awake*. She called her harmless sketches "fireside history"—personal reminiscences about presidents and congressmen, diplomats, and socialites. In 1885, with the assistance of John and Lily, she embarked on a more ambitious writing project. The new book was to be John's memoirs, but in Jessie's mind it was "our book." It was designed to give the facts of history, at least from the Frémont point of view, but also to give credit to her husband and father for their roles in shaping and carrying forward the development of the West. Perhaps it was the probing of Josiah Royce, philosopher and historian, about Frémont's role in the conquest of California or the financial success of Ulysses S. Grant's *Memoirs* that spurred Jessie to pull out of storage the papers and illustrations she had been preserving for more than thirty years.

The advance from the publishers (Belford, Clarke & Company) permitted the Frémonts to take a house in Washington, D.C. Lily did research in the libraries at the Capitol, John dictated, and Jessie did all the writing. But what was to be "*the* American book of the 19th Century," was a disappointing failure. There were no new revelations, and the large volume did not carry John's story beyond the conquest of California.

The three Frémonts moved back to a cheap dwelling at Point Pleasant on the New Jersey coast in 1887. Their finances, spirits, and health worsened and Jessie received electrotherapeutic treatments. When their physician advised a warmer climate for John, Jessie sought financial assistance from a fellow Panama traveler of 1849, Collis P. Huntington, who had since made a fortune in railroading. He provided tickets to California and a generous sum for expenses. When they arrived in Los Angeles, their old Arizona friend, Charles Silent, was there to greet them and to help and advise them all during their period in California.

The California real estate ventures that John tried to promote were no more successful than his previous ventures. Jessie continued to write, and she also stepped up her efforts to have Congress compensate them for the confiscation of Black Point and to have John restored to the army as a major-general and placed on the retired list with pay. Friends were successful with respect to the latter, and two months before Frémont's death in 1890 in New York where he had gone on "business," he was awarded a pension of $6,000 annually. Congress, prodded by newspaper stories that Jessie had been left destitute, passed a bill giving her a widow's pension of $2,000. The ladies of California built her and Lily a four-bedroom, redwood home at the corner of Hoover and Twenty-eight Streets amid a grove of orange trees and tactfully indicated that the gift was not charity, but a memorial of their regard for her husband. A streetcar line on Hoover, for which they received lifetime passes from two former Prescott friends, connected them with the whole city of Los Angeles.

Although devastated by John's death, Jessie soon embarked on the task of completing the article he was writing with respect to his part in the conquest of California for *Century* magazine. Her passion now was the defense of her husband's name and image, a name and image that had become hers as well. Royce's charge that Frémont, in seeking glory, had disobeyed his official instructions in 1846 and actually thwarted the Washington government's plans for a peaceful acquisition of the Mexican Department of California was but one of many criticisms being leveled against the career of the old explorer and aroused the "complete fight" in Jessie. After the *Century* article was completed, she and Frank, who had obtained leave from his army post, wrote what was intended to be the second volume of the *Memoirs*. "Great Events during the Life of Major General C. Frémont … and of Jessie Benton Frémont" was never published nor were her own "memoirs" in two versions.

Jessie's bitterness at past injustices gradually faded as she lived out her life in the "even serene gentle" climate of California, surrounded by good friends and the loving care of her daughter. She was especially close to Caroline Severance, who lived only a few blocks away and who had become a widow in 1892. Severance, a leader in the national woman's rights movement in the East and in Los Angeles, founded the Friday Morning Club, a woman's organization. It focused on civic reform and involved both Frémont women.

Jessie was also enlivened by the friendship of Charles Fletcher Lummis, the colorful founder of the Southwest Museum and an admirer of Southwestern culture and the role Frémont had played in California history. He published several of Jessie's pieces, including the poem "Dolores" in his *Land of Sunshine* (later *Out West*), pronounced her "the most interesting woman I ever met," and later missed her "more than any other woman that has ever died." As she had with Bret Harte, Jessie did what she could to promote with possible patrons the career of John Gutzon Borglum, who lived primarily in Los Angeles between 1884 and 1896. He painted Frémont's portrait and did a small delicate head of Jessie.

Jessie was already suffering from rheumatism and a growing deafness when a fall in 1900 confined her to a "rolling chair." She died in 1902 and after funeral services at Christ Episcopal Church, her ashes were taken for burial beside Frémont in Rockland Cemetery overlooking the Hudson River.

The lives of Jessie and John Frémont were so intertwined that it is impossible to write about one without also writing about the other. Their relationship was a complex one. All through their marriage, beginning with the expeditions, John was often away and sometimes seemed to be only a guest in his own home. Early in the marriage he may have felt some rivalry with Benton for the attention and devotion of his wife, but after the death of the "Old Roman," Jessie felt she had "magnetized" Frémont into home life. If she had heard rumors that he had gotten a French maid pregnant in 1856, had a mistress in 1861, or flirted with the American sculptor, Vinnie Ream, in 1869, she never gave any indication. She was the ever loyal wife—ever defending him, ever covering for his mistakes and lapses in duty. After the election of 1856, she may have become less a part of his life. Lizzie Blair Lee thought him "faithless" and Jessie's loyalty to him "excessive," but their children and most friends saw only the greatest of devotion. In 1880 Lily wrote, "Father ... misses mother immensely"; Charley thought she might not survive the news of Frémont's death; and Frank, looking back years later, remembered "an intensive homelife."

As the lives of Jessie and John were intertwined with each other so were their lives intertwined with the West. John's true accomplishments were in the geographical exploration of the Trans-Mississippi West, but had it not been for Jessie he probably would not have achieved great national fame and world recognition. She was a bright woman, with a flair for words, a sharp eye for a good story, and a broad knowledge of history, literature, and human nature. With her help, but with no indication that she was a collaborator, the western expeditions came alive on paper. Readers became involved vicariously in the shooting of the canyons of the Sweetwater, the navigation of the Great

Salt Lake in an eighteen-foot Indian rubber boat, and the month-long battle with snow in crossing the Sierra Nevada in mid-winter. Would-be emigrants to the West read them for the information they contained; stay-at-homes for sheer enjoyment. At least one perceptive reader, Ralph Waldo Emerson, wondered if Frémont was too concerned with image—"with the eternal vanity of *how we must look*." Jessie helped create images of her husband that she later felt obliged to defend.

She did more than dramatize John's accomplishments and create images. She attempted to embellish the historical record, to create myths, to shape history. In her writings, officials in Washington would have cancelled Frémont's second western expedition, save for her action; "that but for Mr. Frémont's action California would have been English," or that "he was incapable of putting self before duty," or that he had "launched the key word *Emancipation*."

Although primarily associated with western exploration and the reports of those explorations, the Frémonts had other strong ties to the West and are identified as "westerners" in spite of living many years in the East. California gave John his first political office and fueled his and Jessie's ambition for the presidency. The mines of Las Mariposas made them millionaires, or so it was said, although in reality, loans often supported their lavish style. His federal office in Arizona gave them temporary monetary relief. Ultimately, California again became Jessie's home for her final fifteen years.

Jessie had the spirit of a pioneer and the ability to adapt to the western environment and to austerity, but there was no doubt that she loved luxury, the civilized comforts of the East, and the sophisticated world of intellectuals and of gaslight theaters. In spite of the high cost of freight over the mountains, the little cottage in isolated Bear Valley had been furnished in 1858, presumably by an agent, with velvet carpets, a fine piano, bronze clocks, and marble-topped furniture. The home at Pocaho, with an estimated value of $300,000, contained a $4,000 painting of the Golden Gate by her neighbor, Albert Bierstadt; a portion of the library of Alexander von Humboldt; and portraits of her and "the General" by Giuseppe Fagnani. Charley had his own boat and Frank a Steinway grand piano, while a staff of well-trained servants—maids, grooms, coachmen, gardeners, even a French chef—kept the estate running smoothly. Even though finances were becoming shaky, the family acquired a little island off the coast of Maine, where they planned to build a summer cottage.

Although fond of luxury, Jessie was not unaware of the less privileged. In addition to her opposition to slavery and her humanitarian work during the Civil War work, she often acted in a personal way to help others: sending

*Jessie Benton Frémont in her Los Angeles home. Above her desk is John Gutzon Borglum's
painting of John C. Frémont. The painting of Jessie was done by Thomas Buchanan in 1856.
(Courtesy of The Bancroft Library, Berkeley, California)*

money to families of servants, persuading publishers to read young authors'
manuscripts, cajoling officials to give appointments, writing on behalf of a
black woman hoping to purchase a house in Washington, D.C., and protesting
the dropping of a woman from the payroll of the Patent Office. It was her pen
that made Kit Carson a legend, and after his death she sought to protect his
memory from shameful misrepresentation by the poet Joaquin Miller. That she
was sensitive to the predictment of the Mexican Californians, whose culture
was threatened by the Yankee invasion, was evinced in her writings.

Given the pattern of her life and her frequent quotation of Portia's lines
from Shakespeare's *Julius Caesar:* "Being so fathered and so husbanded, should
I not be stronger than my sex?" one might have expected her to support
suffrage for women. But when Elizabeth Cady Stanton asked her in 1866 to
head a petition drive, she refused, explaining that "women in their present
position manage men much better." In channeling her towering ambition
and energy into her husband's career, she was both a nineteenth-century
woman and a realist. Often she had written that "feminine courtesy and
deference are the crutches the public expects a woman to use." She found

that when she made forays into the male realms of politics and war, she came away bruised. Had she lived a century later, her "masculine grasp of affairs" and her "feminine intuitions of policy" might well have carried her to impressive political heights of her own. An extraordinarily gifted Victorian woman, Jessie Benton Frémont had lived life with grit and grace.

SOURCES AND FURTHER READING

Jessie Benton Frémont's personality and several voices are captured in her writings, principally in her letters, a representative number of which were edited by Pamela Herr and Mary Lee Spence in *The Letters of Jessie Benton Frémont* (Urbana: University of Illinois Press, 1993). Her first book, *The Story of the Guard* (Boston: Ticknor and Fields, 1863), defended her husband's conduct as commander of the western department during the Civil War. Many of her published articles were subsequently collected in three volumes. *A Year of American Travel* (New York: Harper & Brothers, 1878), republished from *Harper's New Monthly Magazine* (1877), recounted her first crossing of the Isthmus of Panama. With an introduction by Patrice Manahan, The Book Club of California reprinted it in 1960. *Souvenirs of My Time* (Boston: D. Lothrop, 1887) is largely stories about Washington, D.C. and Europe. *Far West Sketches* (Boston: D. Lothrop, 1890) preserves the narratives of life in Arizona and on Las Mariposas, including encounters with grizzly bears, a mining war, and the beauties of the Yosemite region. Jessie's "Origin of the Frémont Expeditions," *Century* 41 (March 1891), written after her husband's death, was a reply to his critics with respect to lack of instructions for his actions in California.

Donald Jackson, "The Myth of the Frémont Howitzer," *Missouri Historical Society Bulletin,* 23 (April 1967), exposes the fiction in the Benton and Frémont allegations that the chief of the Topographical Bureau wished to break up the second expedition. The multi-volume set of the *Expeditions of John Charles Frémont,* (Urbana: University of Illinois Press, 1970–1984), edited by Donald Jackson and Mary Lee Spence, prints letters and maps connected with the explorer's work with Joseph N. Nicollet, his own five western expeditions, the two reports written in collaboration with his wife, the court-martial proceedings in 1847–1848, and an artist's account of the fifth expedition.

Catherine Coffin Phillips's pioneering biography of *Jessie Benton Frémont: A Woman Who Made History* (San Francisco: John Henry Nash, 1935) has been largely superseded by Pamela Herr's fine biography, *Jessie Benton Frémont* (New York: Franklin Watts, 1987; reprint, University of Oklahoma Press, 1988). Mary Lee Spence's *The Arizona Diary of Lily Frémont* (Tuscon: University of Arizona Press, 1997) gives a picture of Frémont family life and activities in Arizona as well as Jessie and John's attempts to market mines in the East.

The standard biography of Frémont remains *Frémont: Pathmarker of the West* by Allan Nevins (New York: Longmans, Green, 1955). Andrew Rolle, *John Charles Frémont: Character as Destiny* (Norman: University of Oklahoma Press, 1991), is an interesting psychological study of the explorer.

3

Beautiful Deceiver:
The Absolutely Divine Lola Montez

JANET R. FIREMAN

And, after all, what is a lie? 'Tis but the truth in masquerade.
—Lord Byron, *Don Juan*

A GREAT TRAVELER ALL HER LIFE, Lola Montez arrived in the West, in San Francisco, with a lot of baggage. She had trunks, valises, wardrobes, and assorted other luggage, all filled to the brim with controversies and ambiguities, all packed personally by Lola Montez, and all padded with notoriety that had been disseminated by an intercontinental press following her story for the past two decades.

In 1853, California was still very much a work-in-progress and, as such, was an ideal setting for the contradictions Montez embodied. Her principal attraction was that she was a beautiful and wicked woman. She had been stereotyped by the press, and her image simultaneously appealed to Californians' prurient interests and allayed self-reproach they felt for their own wickedness. After a string of theatrical performances in San Francisco, Sacramento, and the Sierra foothills mining towns, Montez rested for a time among the pines and close to a quartz mill in Grass Valley, where a countrified existence seemed to counterbalance her erstwhile profligate and wayward lifestyle. Although the tranquility she assumed there did not stick, her time spent in the West engendered a legend of her as a western woman.

By the time Lola Montez arrived in San Francisco, she was very well established as a celebrity of the highest rank: she was famous for being famous. In fact, she may have been the second-most famous woman in the world, after Queen Victoria, who surely would have been horrified by the comparison. The elements of Montez's fame were based in notoriety, which she had achieved in the meteoric speed of five years from her dancing debut on the London stage to her expulsion from Bavaria in 1848.

This lithographic portrait done in 1847 depicts Lola Montez wearing and holding symbols associated with her principal assumed identity as that of a Spanish Catholic. (Courtesy of San Francisco Performing Arts Library and Museum)

Five years later, when she alighted from the *Northerner* and arranged to appear at the American Theater, San Franciscans knew they were in for a treat the likes of which they had not seen before. The city was a place of new arrivals, but Lola Montez's reputation promised that her presence in San Francisco would be spectacular.

From the early days of the Gold Rush, as far back as August 1849, San Franciscans had read about the exploits of La Montez. She had been called many names. Some of these were out of admiration *(The Divine Lola, the great female republican)*; some out of derision *(La Pompadour, Cyprian intruder)*; some were purely descriptive *(the eccentric Lola)*; and some recorded the many proper names she employed through the years. She was Eliza James, Maria Dolores de Porris y Montez, the Countess of Landsfeld, Maria de los Dolores Landsfeld, Marie de Landsfeld Heald, and Mrs. Patrick Purdy Hull. She was born Eliza Gilbert though most sources say her birth name was Marie Dolores Eliza Rosanna Gilbert. This was but one of her most pervasive and successful inventions because it served as foundation for the name she and other people used most frequently: Lola Montez.

Californians knew she was *someone*, but they weren't certain who. Montez was said to have been born in Spain, Cuba, or Turkey. She was the daughter of a Spanish nobleman or a Spanish gypsy, or a rajah, or of the Sultan of Turkey, or perhaps of Lord Byron. In fact, Eliza Rosanna Gilbert was the daughter of Edward Gilbert, ensign in the Twenty-fifth Regiment of Foot, the King's Own Borderers, and the illegitimately born and ambitious Elizabeth Oliver, whom Gilbert married shortly after Eliza's birth in Limerick, Ireland.

From her teenage years, Eliza-Lola was a self-starter and undoubtedly the architect of her own fate, but she was also the architect of her own past. Much of the confusion about her—whether her parentage and place of birth or any other biographical fact—is due to Montez herself. She was an enormous liar. Over the years, she gave varying versions of her youth, but was steadfast almost to the end in claiming to be of Spanish heritage, or of mixed Spanish and Irish extraction. Born in 1820, she took ship for India with her parents when her father was transferred there in 1823. Shortly he died of cholera, and shortly her mother married Lt. Patrick Craigie. When Eliza-Lola was approaching her seventh birthday, she was sent to the home of Craigie's parents in Montrose, Scotland, for her education. After five years, the unruly girl was transferred to the care of Sir Jasper Nicholls, recently returned to London from India, where he was Craigie's commanding officer. Sir Jasper put Eliza-Lola in school at the Aldridge Academy in Bath, where she received an excellent education for a girl of her middle-class rank. The emphasis was on languages, and Eliza-Lola also was exposed to dancing, sewing, and drawing. In school—and everywhere else—she was restless, and a bit of a prankster. One of her false claims created later comes from this period in the real Eliza-Lola's life: that the cunning and calculating Becky Sharp in William Thackaray's *Vanity Fair* was modeled after her.

At the age of seventeen, Eliza-Lola took the reins. Her mother had traveled to England in the company of Lt. Thomas James of the Twenty-first Regiment of the Bengal Native Infantry. Although Lieutenant James was apparently infatuated with the attractive Mrs. Craigie, Eliza-Lola seems to have persuaded the thirty-year-old to elope with her when she learned of her mother's plan for her to marry a sixty-four-year-old widower in India. The Protestant wedding ceremony near Dublin marked day one of Eliza-Lola's estrangement from her mother.

The couple traveled to India when Lieutenant James was required to return to duty. Following a "she said/he said" dispute about infidelity, Eliza-Lola took the unpleasant step of moving in with her mother and stepfather in Calcutta, where her mother was unsympathetic to her daughter having left her husband, unpromising though he was. In the fall of 1840, Eliza-Lola sailed for England, possibly having contracted chronic malaria. During the five-month trip, a shameless shipboard romance with Lt. Charles Lennox was followed by shocking behavior of a co-habitation kind in London. The relationship with Lennox did not last, but Lieutenant James had had enough and won a judicial separation from his wife. Unknown to Eliza-Lola, this was not a divorce and did not permit remarriage.

At twenty, the reputation of Eliza Gilbert James was already stained by multiple scandals: elopement with an older man, a failed marriage, and adultery. The young woman was left with no means of support except for her wits. Another might have become a governess, or a lady's companion, but the soon-to-be Lola chose dance as a career. This wildly irrational choice—considering her lack of training and the difficulties to overcome for success on the stage—can only be seen as characteristic Montez boldness. Later she claimed to have studied with a Spanish dancing master in London; surely she went to Spain, perhaps motivated by the then-current fashion for things Spanish and by having seen the fabulously popular Fanny Elssler perform Latin dances.

If San Franciscans had read a lot about Lola Montez in one or more of at least ten dailies in the city, most of what they read was hearsay or for other reasons not to be believed. The reading public consumed fabulous accounts of her Munich palace where she bathed in lavender and dried herself with rose leaves; of her bigamous second marriage to a callow army officer eight years her junior; of Parisian gentlemen paying her ten thousand dollars for a single evening's entertainment; and of the retorts she proffered from the footlights to a man who had thumbed his nose at her during a performance in Washington, D.C. They had also read that she was glamorous and strikingly beautiful, which was absolutely true.

Lola Montez was one of the great beauties of her time, which is ground zero for her celebrity. Her "Spanish" beauty was also the bait for King Ludwig I of Bavaria, who shortly after laying eyes on her, insisted that her portrait be painted for the Schonheitsgalerie, his showpiece Gallery of Beauties. The contact made, one thing led to another, and her liaison with Ludwig became her greatest *succés de scandale*. That striking splendor was composed of an oval face with lush, very dark hair, a perfect white complexion, and the deepest blue eyes under Ava Gardner egotist-eyebrows. The components may sound conventional, but the effect was spectacular. Like Elizabeth Taylor in her late teen years and early twenties in the late 1940s and early 1950s, Montez's features were dominated by dazzling eyes and quickly changing, sensuous facial expressions. She was not lovely; she was loveliness incarnate. She was an enchantress.

Besides being renowned for her looks, Montez was famous for other traits that showed in relief in California's female-challenged society. She was known for her vanity, for the treasure chest of jewels she had acquired from admirers, and for her profligate ways with the vast amounts of money she acquired from uncertain sources. Further, she was said to be the most charming, the most generous, the most impulsive, the most conniving, the most perfidious, the most sinister, and the kindest of women. Perhaps because so much was known about her—and so much of that was contradictory—she was unreasonably, irresistibly tantalizing. As the most bohemian woman of her time, as an eccentric, and beyond all, as an enigma, it is not hard to understand why Lola Montez was so very famous by the time she set foot on California soil.

Aside from being famous for being famous, Montez was recognized as a dancer and as an actor. The fact is, Montez was not a very good dancer and her skill level was never considered high, though most of the time she was deemed captivating and drew large audiences. Montez's dance was eccentric, erotic, and novel. This—not skill—was her appeal, along with her beauty and notoriety.

A brand new person disembarked at Southampton in the spring of 1843. She was the recent widow of a Spanish officer who had been killed in the Carlist civil war, and her name was Maria Dolores de Porris y Montez. Almost immediately, she acquired the patronage of the Earl of Malmesbury, who within months arranged for her dancing debut at Her Majesty's Theatre, where her widowhood was cast aside and she was billed as the daughter of a Spanish patriot. Astonishingly, Montez's London debut on June 3, 1843, was an artistic—if not complete—success. Most of the audience liked her, and the newspaper critics found her gorgeous and very appealing, if not a very good dancer. But she was also denounced in the *Times* as a fraud by theater patrons who recognized her as Betty James, who had abandoned her husband and was an adulteress. Montez lashed out in a letter to the editor, insisting that the accusation was false and including a pack of lies about herself. But such a stir had been aroused that the theater suspended her engagement and the Spanish dancer departed for the Continent.

This scarcely initiated performer set out with an uncertain itinerary. She had met the unlikely numbered Prince Heinrich LXXII in London, who ruled the tiny principality of Reuss in southeastern Germany. Montez wrote to him, announcing her imminent arrival in Ebersdorf, Reuss's capital. In short order, she probably had an affair with the prince, definitely caused a stir, and was sent packing. But Montez secured a continental debut in Berlin, and there wangled her way into the presence of King Frederick William who was hosting Czar Nicholas I. She performed for both, and she finagled an invitation from the czar to perform in St. Petersburg. On her way to Russia, armed with letters of introduction, she danced in Warsaw, where she probably delivered her first footlight chat, made friends with several literary men and journalists, and got her name in print for a row with the police in which she drew a dagger from her garter. That she was always armed added another fillip to her reputation. Ejected from Poland by its Russian overlords, but not deterred from her goal to dance in St. Petersburg, she took with her an abiding fondness for Poles, many of whom she was to consort with in later years. In St. Petersburg, after engagements in Konigsburg and Riga, Montez danced only once, apparently because Nicholas disallowed further performances.

Having read that Franz Liszt—then at the height of his popularity—was on tour, La Montez contrived a meeting and engaged him in a torrid affair. Armed with letters of introduction from Liszt, Montez entered Paris and voilà! debuted at the Opera. There she was, performing at the theater of theaters in the European capital of culture, after no more than twenty-five performances to her credit. This achievement was emblematic of Montez's career, forged with luck, charm, and contrivance. Still, she was not a success at the Opera, where her dancing was reviewed as being too risqué. But Montez stayed in Paris, and feathered her cap with the friendship of a bohemian group of distinguished literati including Alexandre Dumas, *père*, with whom she had a brief sexual fling. In the fall of 1844, already trailing a thread of affection for journalists, Montez began one of only two great romances of her life, with Alexandre Henri Dujarier, editor of *La Presse*. Montez was happy as Dujarier's mistress and companion and looked to the prospect of marriage and a honeymoon in Spain. But tragedy struck when Dujarier was killed in a duel with a rival, the journalist Jean-Baptiste Rosemond de Beauvallon.

But the show had to go on, or more accurately, Montez needed money. She began to perform again after a year of co-habitational retirement and took to the road on tour to Spa, Bonn, Baden-Baden (from whence she was expelled), and back to Paris, where Montez had to appear at Beauvallon's murder trial. A sensation in elegant black lacy mourning clothes, Montez testified that she should have been the dualist against Beauvallon. Longing for new adventure in the summer of 1846, Montez took a new lover and traveled with him to Brussels, Ostend, and the German resorts. Once that love affair ended, she continued on the road, with engagements in Heidelberg, Hamburg, and Stuttgart, but was anticipating new conquests during the fall season.

Montez traveled to Munich, where the biggest prey—whom perhaps she stalked deliberately—was sitting on the gilded throne of Bavaria. Ludwig was the greatest amorous and financial trophy of her career. She was twenty-six and in her prime; he was sixty, was not handsome, stuttered, and was hard of hearing. The husband of an understanding woman whom he loved, Ludwig had carried on a number of liaisons with stage women. He was in fact devoted to the beauty of women, and to the beauty of Munich, which he had transformed into an architectural and artistic showplace. He wrote poetry and thought of himself as a poet.

When Montez arrived on the scene in October 1846, she was unable to arrange a performance in the Munich court theater, but she did arrange a meeting with the king. He was swept away. She danced a *cachucha* and a *fandango* and transmitted love rays from her gorgeous eyes to the king as she swooped and swayed. Montez's affair with Ludwig has been put through the wringer of interpretation but what became a graphic and active—though intermittent—sexual relationship, was not realized at first. Montez's arrival in Munich coincided with a moment when conservative, ultramontane forces had gained political ascendance under Karl von Abel, the minister of the interior and principal advisor to Ludwig. Montez marked Abel as her chief enemy early on and carried the thought with her for years to come.

Abel and his cohorts were dismantling the liberal provisions of a constitution that had been in place since 1819. Imbued with Parisian liberal ideas, Montez tried to convince Ludwig of the necessity for political freedom. She claimed to have turned the king around, who was Catholic, a confirmed autocrat, and tended toward the conservative, but who had been moving toward the religious center and was wary of the ultramontane push. Ludwig was also a Hispanophile and defenseless to Montez's "Spanish" charms. Abel ran a check and uncovered Montez's checkered past and false identity. He implemented plans to discredit Montez because of the influence she was wielding with the king and because of the scandalous liaison and the enormous amounts of money that Ludwig lavished upon her. The king gave her a house, which was enhanced by a six-figure redecoration, a carriage, jewels, and gobs of walking-around money.

Meanwhile, Montez showed increasing arrogance as the king's mistress, and in making her likes and dislikes known to Ludwig, swayed him on hirings and firings. Antics like carrying on a love affair with a Lieutenant Nussbaumer, and allowing her big dog to attack a horse pulling a brewer's cart, and then bopping the poor man over the head with her umbrella made her extremely unpopular. Within months, the public hated Montez.

Determined to get respect, Montez badgered Ludwig to elevate her to the nobility. Her lack of Bavarian citizenship presented a problem so great that the government was dismissed over their objections to granting it. In Bavaria, and in the London press, Montez was credited with getting rid of the right-wing Abel, whom the people disliked. Ludwig appointed a new ministry, Protestant and more liberal, and devised a way to provide Montez with citizenship, but he delayed a title for fear of the nobility's reaction. Meanwhile, the London and French newspapers were carrying the breaking news of rioting mobs and other trouble in Bavaria, and disclosed Montez's past. She responded with letters, including a re-invention of her mother having been born in Cuba of Irish extraction, but still alleged herself to have been born in Spain to a Spanish father.

At the same time there was growing public outrage against Montez, her intimacy with the king was also growing, and the lie was given to all her claims that the relationship was purely platonic. Ludwig was sexually obsessed by Montez, which surely clouded his judgment in the political arena. He was particularly fond of her feet—maybe part of his susceptibility to dancers—and to commemorate that passion, Montez made a gift to the king of an alabaster sculpture of one of her feet. Campaigning for his affections, Montez won a long-fought battle when Ludwig created her Countess of Landsfeld on his birthday, August 25, 1847. From that moment, Montez had achieved success beyond her earliest ambitions, and beyond those of many other women classified with her as an adventuress and courtesan.

But with her elevation to the nobility, Montez's behavior in Munich became only worse. She defied standards of moral conduct, she exercised her willfulness freely, and she was intolerably arrogant. The irony is that her ego-driven demeanor mocked and shocked the very society she strived to join. She took up with Fritz Peissner, one of the leaders of a liberal student group that had rallied around her, only one of a series of infidelities to Ludwig. Still, he adored her—and he paid the consequences. Montez's indiscretions and the king's continued protectiveness of her gradually led to his losing public support, though he had always been especially beloved by Bavarians. Closing the university, which was a hotbed of the political struggle between conservative ultramontane forces and those of a more republican, liberal streak, led to renewed riots, and to Lola Montez's exile to Switzerland.

Montez enjoyed sixteen months of glory in Munich—on which she was able to dine out for years to come. But for Ludwig, they were disastrous. Befuddled by his passion, he made plans to join Montez in Switzerland, even when he was hailed by Bavarians for having acceded to constitutional concessions that made his position on the throne as strong as ever. Foolishly, he abdicated in favor of his son, thinking that no one could possibly care what he did with his personal life if he were no longer king. But they never did live together happily ever after; Montez betrayed Ludwig, and she continued to manipulate him for years.

In geopolitics, 1848 was a watershed year. In the United States, the Treaty of Guadalupe Hidalgo simultaneously enlarged the United States and diminished Mexico, transferring California and a lot more of the West to U.S. sovereignty. Among the momentous political revolutions on the Continent in 1848, Lola Montez played a small part, which she both simplified and exaggerated after her exile. Because of the 1848 uprisings, the way people thought about politics, economics, and society changed. Talk of political liberalism and expanded capitalism was in the air, and when the press ascribed a leadership role to Montez in Bavaria, and when she herself invoked concepts of popular sovereignty and civil equality in the next phase of her career, the public gobbled it up, part and parcel. Besides portraying herself as

*Even this miniature copy of the portrait
commissioned by Ludwig in 1847 gives one a
clue as to why the king fell so hard for Lola
Montez. (Courtesy of California History
Room, California State Library,
Sacramento, California)*

a republican leader of the youth faction from the university, and alleging that she served as an adviser to the king on policy matters, Montez claimed to have convinced Ludwig to abdicate in favor of his son as a gesture toward the establishment of a constitutional monarchy.

In truth, this was so much nonsense. Montez was undoubtedly interested in progressive ideas, but she was no political activist. In fact, during the days leading up to the revolution, her most fervent political cause was convincing Ludwig to make her a countess. The ambiguity of elevation to the nobility with an attendant yearly stipend while espousing liberal ideals did not seem to occur to La Montez, although it did to Ludwig, who was diligent and intelligent. His thinking during what were terribly difficult times for a monarch who had micromanaged Bavaria for twenty-three years, and who considered himself among the most enlightened and sensitive of autocrats, was not influenced by Lola Montez, except on personal grounds. The role Montez played in Bavaria in 1848 was to complicate matters for Ludwig. Poor Ludwig: he loved Montez, whom he called his little "Lolitta." Like many heads of state, he wanted to have his cake and eat it too.

Lola Montez was no feminist, though the compliment has been bestowed on her. As a child, she had learned the value of self-assertion; from the beginning of her stage career, she had asserted herself, and she was proud of what she viewed as independence. She showed that she was a master of wielding a whip; and also of lashing out with her tongue. The offenses that instigated these whip-lashings were never physical assaults; they were what she perceived as insults. It was as if with whip in hand, Montez was asserting her rights, guarding her reputation, and responding to questions of her self-reliance.

But even if Montez was involved with her own political action committee of Munich's university students just before women gathered in Seneca Falls for the first women's rights convention in 1848, Montez made clear that her sentiments were not with Lucy Stone and other feminists. She was after her own betterment in the old mold, not those of all women, not in the form of anything that can properly be called feminism.

If Lola Montez played any significant role as a politician, it was as an astute personal political thinker, an opportunist. Demonstrations of this aptitude were her ability to cajole, convince, and generally manipulate an audience in her footlight chats, and in her eloquent, self-serving letters to many editors. She also wrote to Ludwig from Switzerland, where she mounted up debts and caused enough mischief to be asked to leave what she considered to be a dull place anyway.

In London living a lush life on Ludwig's nickel in late 1848, Montez entered society. Within a year, she met and married twenty-one-year-old George Trafford Heald, coronet in the fashionable Second Light Guards. Not much about Heald except his good income and regularization of her national status would recommend him to Montez as her consort. Heald was born in London, educated at Eton and Cambridge, and a member of the gentry. They celebrated two wedding ceremonies: first Catholic, and then Church of England, but despite seeming to have covered all bases, the weddings were the cause of considerable trouble. Montez, who had called herself a widow in the marriage registers, was arrested for bigamy, since Lieutenant James was still very much alive in India. The Healds traveled on the Continent in two separate trips, both of which coincided with legal proceedings and Montez's effort to stay out of jail. During their visits to France, Italy, and Spain, the Healds squabbled a lot, and by the spring of 1850 they separated for good.

La Montez was alone again in Paris during the spring of 1850, living in comparably modest rooms, having acquired only a small settlement from Heald, and because her cash cow in Bavaria was drying up. Trying to spin gold herself, Montez began to write a fantastic autobiography that was serialized in the newspapers. Meanwhile, Ludwig had finally grown out of his love for little Lolitta; the many lies she had told him and her venality left him devastated, but wiser. Montez returned all his letters, letters that contained astonishingly intimate details of his sexual obsession with her. Their correspondence ended in 1851, and he sent her the last of many bank drafts. Finally, the six-year episode with Ludwig was finished, but Montez spoke of him as her friend and always referred to him as a great and kind man.

After an absence from the stage of almost five years, Montez prepared again to dance. The circumstances were a repetition of those that put her on the London stage in the first place: severed spousal ties and virtually no means of support. In Paris, amidst an active social life—during which she may have become infected with syphilis—she studied dancing and incorporated new choreography into her limited repertoire, and as ever, met a number of influential gentlemen. One of these was James Gordon Bennett, editor and publisher of the *New York Herald*, who was amazed at her chain-smoking, and whose publicity machine was soon to assist Montez in America. But first, armed with her Bavarian notoriety, she negotiated a contract for a world tour. After spectacular success in Paris and nine other French cities, and throughout Belgium, she canceled the contract and signed with an American manager. In November 1851, she boarded the *Humboldt* for New York, overshadowed on board and at dockside in New York by the Hungarian revolutionary hero, Lajos Kossuth. Still, she was in the land of opportunity and individualism and, as she said, a place to make money.

La Montez opened on Broadway on Christmas Day. The show was a brilliant success, and supposedly took in more money than any ever had. When newspaper pieces appeared criticizing her personal and public lives, she wrote to the papers' editors, confident in her abilities to influence public opinion. In a letter later reprinted in San Francisco, she refuted lies she said were spread by her detractors, and shrewdly, she affirmed her joy at having arrived in America and being among the free and the brave. Yes! Lola Montez was a politician; she knew her audience.

In New York, her photograph was taken at Meade Brothers, and it survives as the earliest photo of Montez. It does not show a spectacular beauty to match the fame, probably because of the long exposure time required and perhaps because her loveliness was beginning to fade. Still, she embarked on a triumphant tour, with a first stop in Philadelphia, where she had a second photo made—this time with the Arapaho chief, Light in the Clouds. Then Montez traveled on to Washington, D.C., Richmond, Norfolk, Baltimore, and Boston, where a third photo was made. This unflattering shot has been reproduced frequently, and not without reason: it is probably the first photo of a woman with a cigarette in hand. The tour train rumbled on to Lowell, Portland, Salem, Hartford, New Haven, Albany, Rochester, Buffalo, and back to New York. Montez enjoyed success and caused a hubbub everywhere.

While Montez was on tour, the playwright C.P.T. Ware had composed a play she commissioned. La Montez pulled off a coup that must have been the envy of many actors. Even though she was not very good in the role—or in any others—she performed as herself in an autobiographical docudrama called *Lola Montez in Bavaria*, which premiered in New York. Surely this is the crescendo of reinventing oneself. Five parts of the play corresponded to

Above a double signature, Montez wrote, "I consider this lithograph the best likeness I have yet had taken of myself. The picture is taken from a daguerreotype by Messrs. Meade Brothers of New York." 1851 (Courtesy of the Harvard Theatre Collection)

five of the stages in Montez's self-created career: danseuse, politician, countess, revolutionist, and fugitive. She did it her way, showing her version of the many roles she had played, molding the public's mind to her way of thinking. They ate it up, and *Lola Montez in Bavaria* became her stock in trade.

But Montez's pièce de résistance was the Spider Dance. Originally a southern Italian folk dance called "La Tarantella," it had been part of her repertoire since her 1843 debut. Even in the United States when she performed primarily as an actor, playbills announced that Montez would do the Spider Dance as an afterpiece. It was her climax and her box office; in short, her signature piece even more than *Lola Montez in Bavaria*. Although it might have been announced on an opening night program, the Spider Dance was usually not presented until some days later as a strategy to build the house, and to encourage return visits.

Sometimes the Spider Dance was billed as "La Oleana," other times as "El Olé," "El Olle," "La Tarantula," or "El Zapateado," but it was apparently the same basic shtick, with improvisations, or with modifications in length, degree of frenzy, and stage effects. The basic story line was simple: A young woman in festive attire—Montez was always beautifully costumed—was invaded by a host of spiders, who overran her clothing and crept through her skirts. Trying to shake off the beasties, she danced. And she danced, and danced, with increasing fury and violence, stomping on the spiders as they fell. Occasionally, Montez might lift her skirts, displaying her highly esteemed ankles and a bit of calf. Other times, Montez herself assumed the role of spider, bounding about the stage in simulated horrific spider movements. Hard as it is to believe, the Spider Dance was thought to be racy, thrilling, and outright salacious by some.

In New York, the reviewers said Montez was a better actor than dancer, and she continued her tour of the United States southward, with a return to Philadelphia, and then again to Washington, D.C., and Baltimore, making a thousand dollars a week. She rested the summer of 1852 in the Catskills and prepared several new plays, which she took to Boston and Philadelphia in the fall. A winter tour took her to Charleston, through Georgia and Alabama, and then to New Orleans by January 1853. And there, in a city that prides itself on being wide-open to gaiety of all sorts, Montez enjoyed the longest stage run of her career: four weeks of packed houses. She continued on, up the Mississippi by steamboat to Cincinnati, where her Bavarian past played especially well to the large German audiences. Heading back south, Montez played in St. Louis before returning to New Orleans.

Throughout the U.S. tours, Montez was a star attraction, with elevated ticket prices and nearly full houses for every debut. Devotion to work had its rewards: the reviews were favorable, and she made a great deal of money. Furthermore, perhaps because of an expanded repertoire in which she acted more than she danced, for the first time in her career, more than just a few women went to see Montez. During her first stay in New Orleans, Montez heard a false report of Heald's death, but even so, continued to consider Marie de Landsfeld Heald as much her legal name as Lola Montez. And why not? They were both equally illegal. Two years after coming to America, her misrepresentations and her eccentricities were numerous and frequent enough to be attention-grabbing. There were several minor run-ins with the police, and squabbles with staff and theater personnel continued. Publicity through notoriety had become a defining fact of life for Montez. Despite the years, her charm and beauty abided, and by 1853 Lola Montez was a real and true living legend.

And as a living legend, La Montez headed west for a theatrical tour of California. She embarked from New Orleans on the *Philadelphia* on April 22, 1853, for the coast of Panama. Making the best of crossing the isthmus by making friends with influential gentlemen, she boarded the *Northerner* in Panama. On that voyage, she met Patrick Purdy Hull, a former Cleveland lawyer who had first gone to California with an appointment to work on the 1850 census and who had stayed on as a journalist. Within weeks, she married him.

California provided a good audience for Montez. Even as she arrived in May 1853, after the first few frantic years of the Gold Rush, California suffered from a leisure-life deficit. In both San Francisco and Sacramento, and especially in the mining towns where Montez performed, men—for the demographics alone assured that her audiences would be mostly male—had only a limited menu of leisure activities. Diversions in the mines and in the towns are well known: drinking and gambling to excess; singing, dancing, and fiddling or banjo-playing; engaging in commodity sex; and writing letters and in journals. Or they could pray.

Although it was not prohibited, for most Christians, dance was entirely separate from the practice of religion. Worship, or even broad observance, excluded dance; it was profane. And though Montez used Catholicism as an indicator of identity for the Spanish background she had invented, there was nothing Catholic—or religious in any way—associated with her acting or her dancing. Exotic and profane, Montez was an outstanding object of attention for leisure. Indeed, audiences spent a good deal of money to see her performances. Ticket prices were elevated for her appearances, as they were for other star attractions in California and in the East, but in California the cost of seeing Montez was especially dear. In San Francisco, the best seats cost five dollars, which was five times more than in New York, and ten times the price of admission in other eastern cities. Furthermore, by the time Montez arrived in the mines, the daily yields of placer miners had diminished enormously, and many were employed as quartz mining wage-earners while extraction became increasingly industrialized.

One of the earmarks of Montez's performances and public behavior was lack of restraint. Daring, exuberance, and devil-may-care abandon marked her Spider Dance especially, and all this must have appealed wildly to the miners' hungers for a change of pace, release, and salacious fulfillment. Indeed, audiences in Europe, Canada, and the United States, virtually slurped up Montez's display. To the majority of mid-nineteenth-century men, who at least publicly sought to portray self-restraint, Lola's walk on the wild side offered its own mother lode of vicarious pleasures.

In their pursuit of leisure activities, miners frequently brought the rivalries and tensions of their labor to the fun. Because the work of so many was directed towards the same end, gold extraction, the separation between earning a livelihood and leisure pursuit was drawn by the thinnest of lines. Montez's California performances were punctuated by vocal audience interjections and scuffles, and more than once, audiences took their reactions to the street. La Montez encouraged feedback in what became her expected and practically regular footlight chats. She transformed hisses and boos into interactive entertainment; stopping her performance, approaching on the stage apron, and remonstrating the disrespectful in the house. The result was usually increased adulation.

From the beginning of her career and fame, which coincided with public criticism, Montez professed to have enemies—people with entrenched power and others—who fulminated against her. The most commonly named of these were the Jesuits. Montez's enemies list was one of the most imaginative and clever devices of her self-invention. Furthermore, she said horrible things:

that Jesuits had tried to poison her with arsenic, that they had shot at her twice, and that they had attempted to kidnap her from Munich and carry her off to an Austrian prison. By referring to the Society of Jesus, she deflected attention to a pre-identified dark force. When criticized in California, she suggested that it could not be Americans finding fault with her, since she had been so well received at every U.S. venue at which she had appeared. She played upon the ethnocentrism, racism, and jingoism she knew her audiences to harbor.

That Lola Montez was Spanish—or posed as Spanish—does not seem to have been a factor in public disapproval, even though from colonial times Americans had inherited the Black Legend from England. The idea that by nature Spaniards—and all Hispanics by extension—were evil, greedy, bigoted, distrustful, and ignorant was attached by Anglo Americans to Mexicans in California, but often they referred to Mexican women as "Spanish" to indicate their higher regard for women. Amidst this negative American attitude toward Hispanics, in the mid-nineteenth century—in Montez's time—there was a reversal of Hispanophobia. Things Spanish became popular, and American writers like Washington Irving and William H. Prescott boosted an appreciation of *lo español* among the reading public. Spanish romanticism and issues involved in political upheavals in Spain appealed to American sensibilities. By the last two decades of the century, interest in Spanish culture became mainstream, and in fact became fashionable. This Hispanophile feeling centered in California, which was reinventing its past, largely through sentimentalism. Idealizing Spanish California gave impetus to Montez's legacy and stimulated a host of biographies. The fact is, in her own time and after she left California, Lola Montez benefited from an uneven but growing interest in and appreciation for Spanish things that had previously been absent from Anglo culture on both sides of the Atlantic.

In San Francisco before Montez played herself in *Lola Montez in Bavaria*, a knock-off farce of the same title was performed. In the theater of the time, and particularly in a place like San Francisco that was ravenously hungry for entertainment, tragedies were often followed by farces. Beginning in London in 1848, Lola Montez was the subject of some of these absurd box-office draws, such as *Lola Montes; or, Pas de Fascination*. By 1853, the published version of one of these burlesques had reached San Francisco, and it played immediately after *Hamlet* on one occasion and just after *Romeo and Juliet* on another, both just a month after Montez herself performed the original. In these farces, and another of the same genre that also had London origins, *Lola Montes; or, A Countess for an Hour*, La Montez was the object of cruel derision. An original one-act send-up, called *Lola Montez; or, Catching a*

Governor, was written and performed by one of the leading figures of the San Francisco theater community during Montez's initial three-week California engagement. The next week a second piece penned in California that mimicked and mocked *Lola Montez in Bavaria* was staged. This one was called *Who's Got the Countess? Or, The Rival Houses.* And at a rival theater, a song was written and sung to spoof Montez and Lewis Baker, the manager of the American Theater, where she was appearing:

> *Oh, have you heard the news of late*
> *Of what has happened in our State? —*
> *There has arrived a monarch mate,*
> > *Imported from Bavaria!*
> *If you would like to see the sight,*
> *And aint afraid the crittur'll bite,*
> *Just pay five dollars any night,*
> *And Baker'll get the show up right!*
> *She'll glance at you with those sparkling yes,*
> *And other means she will devise*
> *To make you puff her to the skies,*
> *While she the spiders will surprise!*
> *And all the Bakers in the town*
> *Will find the Countess does it Brown,*
> *When with the dust they must come own—*
> > *To the Countess of Bavaria!*

Lola Montez didn't seem to mind; she could take a joke, and she probably welcomed the free publicity.

Six weeks after her arrival in San Francisco, and with her performances completed, Lola Montez performed another little piece of drama. In a morning ceremony at Mission Dolores, she entered into wedlock with San Francisco newspaperman Patrick Purdy Hull. This was Montez's third marriage, her second of a bigamous sort, held in a Catholic chapel founded by Spaniards. What could be better to tie the knot for a Spanish and Catholic poseuse!

The honeymoon trip included Montez's debut in Sacramento. On opening night, with John Sutter in the audience, some people laughed when she danced. She stopped, stepped forward to the footlights, curtsied daintily, and spoke sweetly that if people did not like what she was doing then alright, she wouldn't do it. And she walked off the stage. According to other reports, her speech was not pretty, but rather was a tirade of the first order in which she accused the men in the audience of not being worthy of being men and that they should therefore exchange their trousers for her skirts. Projectiles from the audience, Montez's exit, and a musical interlude provided by the Hungarian violinist Miska Hauser preceded resumption of the dance. Still, the audience refused to appreciate her skills, and after another exit and entrance, finally the evening ended. Or it seemed to end, because Montez and her new husband were shivareed at their hotel, and authorities had to disburse the crowd.

The next evening at the theater, everything was different. Montez made a little speech of apology for the recent unpleasantness, in which she explained that she had danced the Spider Dance all over Europe, but that nowhere had audiences been more appreciative and nowhere had people been kinder to her than in America—and therefore, why should she not dance the Spider Dance in California?

Montez was heartily applauded and began a smash performance. She chalked up the whole nasty Sacramento night to experience and adventure and said that it was worth more than a thousand dollars. Even as the burlesques of the Spider Dance and of *Lola Montez in Bavaria* continued in San Francisco, she exhibited a die-hard spirit that paid well.

Two or three months later, the papers carried the story that the happy couple was no more; Mrs. Hull had ejected her husband. She toured the Sierra foothills, performing in Marysville, Grass Valley, Nevada City, and then returned to Grass Valley. And there her travels came to a halt and there began a bucolic interlude in Lola Montez's career. She bought a cottage, and invested in the Empire Mine.

Montez nested in Grass Valley—an unlikely spot for a red-hot cosmopolitan—and settled in with astounding élan. She took in a grizzly bear cub as one of her many pets at her Grass Valley cottage, where she indulged in *Sunset* magazine indoor-outdoor living. She had the bear chained to the fence surrounding her yard, which is depicted in a much-reproduced engraving published in 1854. Although it is a precious image—the petite and lovely Montez providing comfort and loving care for the symbolic call of the Sierra wilds and of California's independence; and although it was not common practice to keep a bear like a dog, it was not so remarkable as it has been portrayed. For one thing, Montez was an inveterate lover of "dumb things." Writers have often placed this trait as a counterpoint to La Montez's frequently flaring temper. She seems always to have had at least one dog, and in Grass Valley she looked after a number of dogs and cats, as well as songbirds, a turkey, a pig, a pony, and some goats and sheep.

But the bear—because it literally bit the petite Montez hand that fed it—became the most notorious member of the Montez menagerie. The bear was of course only doing what came naturally, and what was to be expected in a society in which bull-and-bear fights were an entertainment alternative to the performances of faux-Spanish dancers. Bull-and-bear fights were probably the most spectacular of the blood sports introduced by Mexican miners, all of which crossed nationality lines in their popularity. Although bullfighting and cockfighting were there for Montez to see, and although their Hispanic roots might have appealed to her own self-devised biography, the grandiosity—as well as the fuzziness and outrageousness—of a pet bear must have exerted special appeal.

From Grass Valley, the equestrian Montez, accompanied by friends and pack animals, took to the High Country on a trail ride over Donner Pass to Truckee Meadows. One member of the party became separated from the group, and after searching for him, they returned to Grass Valley. The root of the incident was innocent: one man who struck out on his own had taken the wrong trail, but like so many other instances, press reports had it that the incident was accountable to an argument that La Montez had picked, and the lone rider left the party out of disgust with her.

The kinder and gentler Montez was demonstrated not only in her love of animals, but in her special affection for children. In Grass Valley, the danseuse befriended Mary Ann Crabtree, and entertained the six-year-old Lotta Crabtree, who was already taking dancing lessons from a local teacher. An element of the legend (to which she did not contribute) has it that Montez taught Lotta to dance and wanted to take the child with her on tour. In fact, Mrs. Crabtree was an ambitious stage mother, and the child became a star, prefiguring a Mary Pickford/Shirley Temple combination, but with red, rather than brunette or blonde, curls. She tried, as Pickford and Temple tried later, to stay forever young, even though she burlesqued Montez as an adult in the 1860s.

The reason for Montez having no children of her own is unknown, but she did seem to take delight in the company of children. She organized parties with games and goodies for local kids, with no motive except to entertain the tikes. If purpose must be attached to every known doing of Montez, these sallies into party-making might be considered part of the "Martha Stewart version" of rustication, which Montez practiced. Within the bounds of her picket fence, Montez gardened ferociously, decorated her small house from floorboard to rafter, provided a salon where she hosted soirees, and offered delectables to scores of frequent guests.

In Grass Valley, a town of more than 3,000 people that was booming with the promise of big returns from quartz mining when she arrived, Montez did not seem as eccentric as she had elsewhere. She was well liked by her fellow townspeople and appreciated for her many acts of kindness and generosity to the poor and the infirm. Montez was remembered fondly and imaginatively when she departed.

By early 1855, Montez probably needed money, so she left Grass Valley. She may have intended to return, because neither did she sell her California real estate, nor did she take her belongings with her. In San Francisco she assembled a troupe and on June 6 took ship for Australia, which was to be the first leg of a round-the-world journey and tour.

In Montez's company was thirty-two-year-old Augustus Noel Follin, who had come to California in 1850, leaving a wife and children in New York. When Follin met Montez, he fell hard for her and, apparently under her influence, became an actor, using the stage name Frank Folland. He became her lover and was also her agent by the time they left San Francisco for Sydney via Honolulu, Tahiti, and Samoa. For the most part, Montez was happy with Follin; he was only the second true love of her life. But like Dujarier, who had died young and tragically, so was Follin to die before his time, and with great affect on Montez. The Australian tour was a box-office and critical success, but it was turbulent as all Montez's engagements were. She fired the whole troupe and was slapped with a lawsuit by them as she and Follin sailed out of Sydney harbor for points south. Montez performed in Melbourne, Geelong, Adelaide, Ballarat, and the Bendigo goldfield towns and then went back to Sydney, where she rested and tried to recuperate from recurring illness. The usual squabbles and tantrums and sensational publicity had assured a good run, but had been hard on the aging star. Although Montez was only thirty-five, she had been living rough for a long time. Chain smoking, the possibility of one or more chronic diseases, and having been beaten by a whip-wielding woman during the seven-month tour had taken their toll. Follin and Montez canceled the tour and departed for San Francisco in May 1855.

Homeward bound, things got worse. One day out of Honolulu, Follin was lost at sea, apparently due to accident. Montez was grief-stricken and entered a period of depression and increasing involvement in spiritualism, which she had first experienced in New England in 1851. Back in San Francisco, with a white talking cockatoo perched on her shoulder, she was becoming a different person. She read of George Heald's death in the papers, and she performed for a couple of weeks, but danced little. On other stages, burlesques of Montez were mounted again, but satires like *A Trip to Australia; or, Lola Montez on the Fanny Major* were not well received.

Within months, Montez sold her San Francisco house and four lots, consigned all her jewelry for sale at public auction, and directed the proceeds to be sent to Follin's stepmother for the education of his children. She specified that the kids were to study whatever suited them, but they were also to be instructed in a knowledge of God and of spiritualism. Montez cut short a Sacramento engagement, settled her affairs in a last trip to Grass Valley, made a farewell stage run in the city, and sailed out of the Golden Gate on November 20, 1856. Follin's death was obviously a turning point in her life.

In New York, Montez was still proud and impetuous, she still lied, and she still loved the limelight, but the edge had worn off her anger, arrogance, and egotism. In the five years remaining to her, she was still recognizable in body and spirit as the Lola Montez she had created, but the appearance and reality of both had withered. Close friendships were now the anchors of her existence in place of the self-interest that had propelled her in the past. Charles Chauncey Burr, a journalist who had been a lawyer and minister of the Universalist Church was one of these; and a childhood friend from Montrose, Maria Elizabeth Buchanan, and her husband Isaac, a prominent New York florist, were the others. Montez became a follower of Thomas Lake Harris, a Universalist who was interested in spiritualism and who founded the New Church of New York, but Montez's religiosity focused on redemption above all else.

Still, Montez needed to support herself. Almost as soon as she landed in New York, she looked up Susan Danforth Follin, the stepmother of her deceased lover. For a brief and weird interlude, Montez took on a partner for stage performances in Albany and Providence. They were billed as the Montez Sisters, Lola and Minnie, who was actually Miriam, Noel's beautiful and promiscuous twenty-year-old half-sister. Miriam's waywardness led to a parting of the ways within weeks, and Montez continued touring Pittsburgh, St. Louis, Louisville, and Chicago, where big crowds, rave reviews, and Montez's recurring illness were the principal features. Miriam left the stage, and in following years, had a number of lovers and husbands, gained a title of nobility, and became Mrs. Frank Leslie, achieving fame and honors in the publishing world.

Meanwhile, realizing that she was getting too old to play the roles in her repertoire, and that dancing was much too strenuous for her uneasy health, Montez effected a mid-life career change. She had always been a great talker and a riveting conversationalist. Packaging these skills with her life experiences, strongly held opinions, formidable stage presence, and fame, she launched an inordinately successful career as a lecturer. Elevating the art of conversation to a profession, Montez began in Hamilton, Ontario, in July 1857 with a talk called "Beautiful Women," containing true and false autobiographical stories and common sense beauty tips. Montez's maiden lecture tour continued to Buffalo, where she premiered with an anti-Catholic argument called "The Origin and Power of Rome," in which her own claimed Catholicism faded from the picture. With rave reviews piling up, she moved on to Montreal where she spoke on "Wits and Women of Paris" and then to Boston, New Haven, and Hartford. In Philadelphia, she introduced "Gallantry," in which she used Ludwig as a principal example. More lectures

followed in Baltimore, Washington, D.C., and Philadelphia, where she delivered "Heroines of History and Strong-Minded Women," in which she
made fun of the women's rights movement and championed traditional roles
for women, excluding only those few individuals who might be truly exceptional. The critics thought she was redeeming herself through her lectures. Her
manner, elocution, and expressiveness were applauded more than her message.
And were it not ever so? But now, instead of fiery dancing or impassioned delivery of her lines, Montez spoke with beautiful elocution in a modulated voice
absent of the exotic accent she had affected in the past. As a lecturer, she
dressed simply but elegantly, frequently choosing to wear a black dress set off
by a white collar, as Coco Chanel would prescribe later as always correct.

By December 1857, despite having been included with Horace Greeley
and Edward Everett as the leading public speakers on the lecture circuit,
Montez announced the end of her lecture career because she was going to
marry. She traveled to Le Havre with plans to meet Prince Ludwig Johann
Sulkowski, an Austrian exiled in 1848 whom she had met in Berlin. However, the groom was a no-show. Montez returned to the United States, discovering that she had been the dupe of a cruel hoax: Sulkowski had a wife
and children living on his prosperous upstate New York farm.

Disillusioned with love forever, living in modest rooms, Montez mounted
the lecture platform again, speaking to packed houses in fashionable Man-
hattan and Brooklyn. When questions arose about her past, she prepared
two autobiographical lectures to set the record straight, but they were pep-
pered with lies of self-invention about her Spanish origins, her European
adventures, and her political influence over Ludwig.

In May and June, Montez repeated her lectures and made a farewell to the
stage before moving uptown to Yorkville, where she began yet another career, this time as an author. In just one year, she published three books. The
first was the text of her lectures, which appeared in two American editions
and three pirated editions in London. This was followed by *The Arts of Beauty*,
which sold 60,000 copies in multiple editions, as well as British and Cana-
dian editions of 45,000 each. Her final book was the inferior *Anecdotes of
Love*, a compilation of snippets from many sources about historical love affairs of the rich and famous.

Financially secure from the proceeds of lectures and books; comfortable
in her Yorkville house with a little animal menagerie and garden; modern-
ized with an avant-garde short haircut; safe in the warm friendship of Maria
and Isaac Buchanan; and surrounded—as ever—by a cloud of cigarette smoke,
Montez hosted soirees and enjoyed life. Perhaps trust in this new sanctuary,
as well as a continuing search for the spotlight, impelled her to sail to Galway

for yet another lecture tour. In Ireland for the first time since she had eloped twenty years before, she was welcomed as an honored native daughter. After visiting relatives in Cork and lecturing there, she spoke in Dublin on "America and Its People," explaining the differences between social and political equality, predicting a war of the races, and emphasizing the opportunity afforded in the West for hard-working immigrants. Other lectures on the tour were "Comic Aspects of Fashion," and "English and American Character Compared," in which Montez prophesied that though still rough and turbulent, the American West would become the foundation of a new and original American character.

From Ireland, the most demanding tour in a lifetime of tours continued in Manchester, Glasgow, Edinburgh, Sheffield, Nottingham, Leicester, York, and other cities, terminating in London in April 1859. Although tickets for her lectures were much less costly than for stage performances, she took in a great deal of money.

Montez bought a house near Hyde Park and briefly planned to retire in London, but financial trouble and grave illness put an end to that idea. Her life had become like a novel or a movie that appears to be drawing to a close just when a new plot twist emerges. While recuperating at the country home of friends, Montez's new development materialized in the form of a spiritual diary, in which she showed that not only was she aware of her old self, but that she was trying to change: she was trying to learn to be humble and to be pious.

With health restored, she returned to New York, which was the final sea voyage for perhaps the most well-traveled woman of her time. Montez was accused of having expressed anti-American opionions during her British lectures. Proud to be an American, which she had achieved through her brief

Unsmiling and a little sour-looking during the long exposure, Montez deliberately drew attention to her fierce smoking habit by holding a cigarette when her daguerreotype was made in Boston in 1852. (Courtesy of Seaver Center for Western History Research, Natural History Museum of Los Angeles County)

marriage to Pat Hull, she defended herself, and soon was on the lecture platform again speaking to an SRO audience about "John Bull at Home." Yet another extensive tour followed to Philadelphia, Baltimore, Washington, D.C. (where the vice president, senators, and ambassadors attended), through Pennsylvania, Ohio, Indiana, St. Louis, Springfield, Chicago, Detroit, Toronto, Buffalo, Albany, and back to New York. Once again, she had brought in lots of money, but had suffered from illness a good deal of the time. Besides peace and stability, the New Yorker Lola Montez had finally achieved respect from many people, and had earned a rest.

But the bright lights of the dramatic life she had lived were not to flicker out without still more drama. On June 30, 1860, she suffered a stroke that left her speechless and paralyzed on her left side. She convalesced with the Buchanans and made a will. By fall she had recovered sufficiently to move to her own rooms in a boarding house. Montez regained speech and could walk haltingly when she received an unwelcome visit from her mother. Eliza Craigie, by this time a widow, had traveled from England in hopes of cashing in on her daughter's fortune. The visit was short and cold, but resolved Montez to make a legal transfer of anything she might still own in Bavaria to Isaac Buchanan. The document was signed, "Lola Montez, Countess of Landsfeld."

In the fall her health improved, and she counseled recovering prostitutes at the New York Magdalen Society's shelter and altered her will to benefit that institution as well as Maria Buchanan. By December, when Montez was nearly recovered, she caught pneumonia, which was her last illness. Her minister of the moment, the Reverend Francis Hawks of Calvary Episcopal Church, visited her many times, and later remembered Montez's inspiring eloquence in speaking about redemption—words uttered from a ravaged face but from a truly penitent soul. A month before her forty-second birthday, on January 17, 1861, the woman called Lola Montez—and many other things—died with her hand touching the Bible as a friend read to her from it. Close friends attended Montez's Episcopal burial service at Green-Wood Cemetery in Brooklyn, where the marble headstone, now worn and scarcely legible, reads "Mrs. Eliza Gilbert."

Lola Montez achieved a lasting, if odd and fuzzy fame: her name is broadly recognized, but rarely do people know much about her. If Americans are not very clear on her now, neither were they clear about La Montez in the past, largely due to her self-serving obfuscation of the truth—and downright lying. Further, although Montez's existence was chronicled minutely by the press while she was still breathing, and though her notoriety still provided copy long after her death, newspapers and magazines were subject to entrapment in the web of untruths she wove, to romanticization, and perhaps

Pursuing a socialite's life in London in 1848, Montez rode in Hyde Park, where she met her second husband. In this engraved portrait, she is outfitted as an equestrian, complete with whip. (Courtesy of Seaver Center for Western History Research, Natural History Museum of Los Angeles County)

to the temptation of tangling the tale further. Nor has Montez always been well served by her biographers until very recently. Too often, they accepted at face value what they read. Writers of novels, plays, poems, and movies have recognized a prime subject—and all have taken full measures of poetic license with Montez.

Montez exerts a pull from the grave that might have piqued her own later-life interest in spiritualism. Even in death, she takes people in, she charms them, she beguiles and deceives. Lola Montez was a reckless rebel against convention whose remarkable combination of charms and contradictions created a singular and imaginative life. Those traits also laid down the legacy of legend. She carried her worldliness to the American West, and although the time she spent there was not very significant to her career, nor was it close to being the most interesting segment of a multi-phased lifework, she left a deep imprint.

Montez's influence on the West was greater than its effect on her. Her original California plan was to just do it: perform and make money. That accomplished, she could have returned to New York right away. But because the region appealed to her or because she was weary, she paused in Grass Valley. Although most California authors and other Montez groupies insist that she planned to stay forever in the West, there is little evidence. By nature, Montez was restless, gregarious, and cosmopolitan. After enjoying the beautiful Sierra for a while—as she had enoyed the Alps, the continental spas and resorts, and even the Catskills—she moved on to pursue further fame and fortune in her natural urban environment. Montez's milieu was the metropolis; the West of the 1850s was far distant from the urbane and sophisticated cutting-edge that beckoned Montez.

Especially in California—but in other parts of the West as well—Montez has been awarded a disproportionately significant place in the pantheon of pioneers. Westerners are strangely proud that the beautiful and wicked Lola Montez—who may have been an opera diva, a ballet dancer, or perhaps a Latin movie star—stopped in the region to glamorize even further an already golden land.

SOURCES AND FURTHER READING

Preparation for "Beautiful Deceiver: The Absolutely Divine Lola Montez" began with a review of the available literature. As other Montez researchers have found, this is a gargantuan task. Although many other sources were consulted, this essay contains only a representative sampling of the best and most informative works, as well as some that are valuable in understanding both defenders and detractors of Montez. A good deal of what has been written about Montez speaks directly to the perpetuation and dissemination of Montez legend and lore, rather than to historical enlightenment.

Because the press followed Montez's career so closely—or so loosely but persistently—the periodical literature alone constitutes thousands of pages, and many news stories about La Montez were reprinted numerous times in this country and abroad. Additionally, because Montez toured so extensively and because her fame never diminished, there are hundreds upon hundreds of reviews of her dance, theatrical, and lecture performances. Besides newspapers, *Frank Leslie's Weekly, Harper's, The London Illustrated News, Fraser's,* and other magazines featured Lola Montez frequently.

Fortunately for the researcher particularly concerned with Montez's sojourn in the West, Doris Foley's *The Divine Ecentric: Lola Montez and the Newspapers* (Los Angeles: Westernlore Press, 1969) assembles a welcome if breathless summary of Montez as portrayed in California newspapers from 1853 through 1861. If the press accounts Foley relates were not always entirely accurate and objective, neither was Lola Montez in her self-serving autobiography, written in the third person, which is an appendix to *The Divine Eccentric.*

James F. Varley's splendid new biography, *Lola Montez: The California Adventures of Europe's Notorious Courtesan* (Spokane, WA: The Arthur H. Clark Company, 1996), has also made extensive use of California and other U.S. newspapers, but with greater discernment and analysis than Foley. Varley's book is a great read, full of colorful vocabulary, and is particularly insightful concerning what made Montez tick. Further, Varley has included new material on the possibility of Montez suffering from syphilis. Even though he recognizes her faults, and takes pains to separate truth from fiction, Varley seems bewitched by Montez. He asserts that Montez was the only woman who came to "early" California and who left a significant mark, and classes her with Joaquin Murrieta as the most frequently and erroneously characterized figures in California history.

In George C. MacMinn's *The Theater of the Golden Era in California* (Caldwell, ID: The Caxton Printers, 1941), the author treats Montez in a long chapter called "The Peak of Notoriety." Here there are plentiful details about Montez and her colleagues on the

California stage with helpful information on theater descriptions, management, and marketing practices. Oscar Lewis picked up every endearing and revealing snippet on Montez's country life in Grass Valley and her California performances, and bound them together with handsome illustrations in the fine press edition, *Lola Montez: The Mid-Victorian Bad Girl in California* (San Francisco: The Colt Press, 1938).

General book-length biographies of Montez, which number at least twenty, deal with the western years in shorter form than the rest of her life. The first biography published in English was written by Edmund B. D'Auvergne, as he put it, "in the key of love." *Lola Montez: An Adventuress of the Forties* (London: T. Werner Laurie, 1909) took as its starting point George Clement Boase, "Gilbert, Marie Dolores Eliza Rosanna," an article in the *Dictionary of National Biography* (London: South, Elder, & Co., 1890). Boase's *Dictionary of National Biography* entry is said to be the first "complete" study of Montez in English, but alas, it is no longer reliable, though it contains useful sources and image references. Using Boase's biographical details, which were muddled by Montez's prevarications and their perpetuation by anecdote and press reporting, D'Auvergne fashioned a life story hinged on Montez as courtesan par excellence. Not to the credit of complete veracity, many biographers since have taken their pitch note from D'Auvergne, "key of love."

Among the best biographies until recently is Horace Wyndham's *The Magnificent Montez; From Courtesan to Convert* (New York: Hilman-Curl, 1936), in which the "honeycomb of fable and fascination" surrounding Montez is identified, and through the critical use of European archival and published sources, a valiant effort is made to uncover the truth. In *Queen of Hearts: The Passionate Pilgrimage of Lola Montez* (New York: John Day, 1936), Isaac Goldberg observes that Montez lived as if she were the heroine in a novel. He wrestles inconclusively with the difficulty of finding the truth about her life. In the end, he decides that since all truth was relative to Montez herself, perhaps uncovering the masquerade does not matter. Helen Holdredge, in *The Woman in Black: The Life of Lola Montez* (New York: Putnam, 1955), relied too heavily on Montez's autobiography, and appears to have become quite carried away with the spiritualism that her subject only dabbled in without lasting and sincere conviction.

Many other treatments of Montez have been published in compound biographical volumes on courtesans, theatrical figures, and wicked women, such as Albert Payson Terhune, *Superwomen* (New York: Mofat, Yard and Company, 1916), and Ethel Colburn Mayne, *Enchanters of Men* (London: Methuen & Co., 1909). Outstanding among these is an odd but well-written sketch of Montez by William Bolitho in *Twelve Against the Gods: The Story of Adventure* (Garden City, NY: Doubleday, 1933). Here Montez is placed alongside of Mohammed, Casanova, Columbus, Napoleon, and Woodrow Wilson (!), among others—and the message is about greatness.

Lola Montez: A Life (New Haven and London: Yale University Press, 1996) by Bruce Seymour, a lawyer and independent scholar, is absolutely the best single volume on Montez and will surely prove to be the definitive biography. Seymour coedited recently located voluminous correspondence between Ludwig and Montez and relied on it and many other archival sources in Bavarian repositories never previously employed. Not only has Seymour disclosed positively shocking details about the sexual relationship between the king and his little Lolitta, and illuminated Montez's character through Ludwig's perspicacious understanding—and broken heart—but he has calculated the amount of money—about three million dollars in current market value—that Ludwig lavished on Montez during two years, and her yearly allowance thereafter, which was about four hundred thousand dollars. Additionally, Seymour has convincingly corrected Eliza Gilbert's birth date and circumstances and, overall, has documented and interpreted a difficult subject in a sensitive and revealing manner.

Almost every book on Lola Montez includes a few or more illustrations of her: paintings, engravings, lithographs, or photographs, and expectedly, there is a good deal of repetition. Diane L. Day, "Lola Montez and Her American Image," in *History of Photography* 5 (October 1981) has assembled a super collection of images made of La Montez once she arrived in America. The camera shows a woman aging before her time, and without the benefit of air-brushing and retouching, Montez appears considerably less glamorous than the viewer might expect. The cinematic camera has also portrayed Lola Montez, but a film has yet to be made that captures the whole Montez—whether in legend or reality. However, Max Ophuls's *Lola Montes* (France and Germany: Gamma-Film, 1955) is considered a classic. Flashbacks tell the story of the famous dancer as she recalls her love affairs. A grand life was ruined by scandal and poverty, and she ended up in the circus. This was a landmark film for its use of "poly-visual fragmentation" (or montage), not its historical accuracy.

Lola Montes: Or, A Reply to the "Private History and Memoirs" of that Celebrated Lady, Recently Published, By the Marquis Papon, Formerly Secretary to the King of Bavaria, and for a Period the Professed Friend and Assistant of the Countess of Lansfeldt (New York, 1851) is an interesting tome that sheds light on the degree of interest in Montez following her Bavarian exile. It refutes Papon, a confidence man who took in Montez, and then turned to Ludwig for support, and does it with the profound passion of polemics at the time. In another contemporary work about another Lola Montez, Heman Dyer, *The Story of a Penitent: Lola Montez* (New York: Protestant Episcopal Society for the Promotion of Evangelical Knowledge, 1867), treats Montez's final career change. This work of faith discloses Montez's later-life defenders' belief in her courage and goodness.

The essential reading about Montez includes some of her own work: *Lectures of Lola Montez including her Autobiography* (New York: Rudd & Carlton, 1858) and *The Arts of Beauty or Secrets of a Lady's Toilet with Hints to Gentlemen on the Art of Fascinating* (New York: Dick & Fitzgerald, 1858). *The Arts of Beauty* contains sound advice on eating right and exercising and is combined with tongue-in-cheek advice to men on how to behave better toward women. Montez's cosmetic and skin care rituals are remarkably consistent with current practices, and the beauty tips should be taken seriously from one who knew whereof she spoke.

In addition to the Ludwig and Montez correspondence that Bruce Seymour utilized, other manuscript sources are in the Bayerisches Hauptstaatsarchiv and the Bayerisches Staatsarchiv, and other repositories in Munich. Seymour has deposited his research materials at the Bancroft Library in Berkeley, where several Montez documents are in the manuscripts collection. The Harvard Theatre Collection in Cambridge and the Museum of the City of New York also contain Montez holdings.

4

Calamity Jane:
Independent Woman of the Wild West

Richard W. Etulain

When Martha Canary came riding with Wild Bill Hickok into booming Deadwood, South Dakota, in midsummer 1876, she was already known in the northern West as Calamity Jane. Just barely out of her teens, Calamity was gaining a reputation through sensational newspaper accounts as a young woman without moorings, rumored to drink and cohabit with abandon. In the decade and a half after that memorable summer in Deadwood, Calamity was frequently dubbed a "hellcat in red britches," a Lady Wildcat, and a female terror of the plains and became a favorite subject for journalistic hyperbole. But behind this adventuresome, gun-toting hellion was another person: Martha Canary, a young woman adrift in a pioneer man's world, without home, family, or occupation. When Martha was transformed into Calamity Jane, her less dramatic side disappeared under a landslide of purple prose. The pioneer young woman of the frontier lost out to the Wild Woman of the West. Behind the mythological figure of popular attire stands another woman who needs her story told.

Unfortunately, in the more than ninety years since Calamity's death, no one has uncovered much of her past. Since Calamity was probably illiterate, there are no signed records—not even a signature. But there is an overabundance of lively stories: Calamity came to town, went on a wild toot, and is currently in the cooler. The paucity of solid facts and the plethora of stylized stories force Calamity's biographer to sort through thousands of bits and fragments to stitch together a story, much of it at odds with most of her previous life stories.

Calamity Jane in a formal pose. Photograph taken in the 1880s in Rawlins, Wyoming, where Calamity lived from time to time. (Courtesy of the American Heritage Center, University of Wyoming)

The ancestors of Martha Canary can be traced to the late eighteenth and early nineteenth centuries. They appear first in Virginia, where her grandfather James Canary was born in 1788. By 1820 James was farming in Ohio, where all his children, Martha Jane's uncles and aunts, were born. After the death of James's wife, he moved in the mid-1850s to Princeton in Mercer County, Missouri. On April 25, 1856, he purchased 320 acres of land for $1,775 in what became known as the Ravanna Township. With James came four of his grown children and their families. They were farmers, much like thousands of other pioneers looking for fresh opportunities in newly opened territories. The Princeton area, barely a generation or so out of Indian control, consisted of rolling hills, with the Ravanna section, mainly of prairie land, remaining unsettled longer than the surrounding more fertile areas. The first settlers to Princeton came in the early 1840s, with the well-known Collings families arriving shortly before 1850. By 1860, the Mercer County population had expanded to 9,300 with nearly 1,000 residing in the Ravanna Township, now but two years in legal existence.

Scanty census records, a few other obscure notices, and vague recollections gathered more than a half-century later tell us most of what we know of Martha's first years in Missouri. In 1860, when the census-taker visited Martha's farmhouse in the Ravanna Township, about five miles east of the center of modern-day Princeton, he recorded the names of six residents. Martha's father, Robert, the youngest of James's children, was thirty-five and married to twenty-year-old Charlotte. The census listed their three children as M[artha], born in 1856, Cilas [Silas?], born in 1857, and Lana, a year old. Robert was born in Ohio, Charlotte in Illinois, but all three children in Missouri. A farmer owning 180 acres of land worth $1,500 and other personal property valued at $400, Robert could read and write, but neither his wife nor his two sisters living nearby could. Grandfather James may have lived with Martha's parents; at least his name appears immediately after Robert's family. He is listed as without property or personal wealth.

That record may be misleading, however. A few months after James purchased his 320 acres in April 1856, he sold 40 acres to his son-in-law Robert Southers, the husband of James's daughter Mary. Three years later, James sold an additional 100 acres to another son-in-law, James Kilgore, husband to James's daughter Lana (or Lanny). On the same day, October 8, 1859, he sold the remaining 180 acres of his original purchase to his son Robert for $500. (A second son, James Thornton, owned his own land.) In all, Martha Jane's grandfather had parceled out the 320 acres to his three children for $800 less than he had paid for it. Perhaps declining health warned him he must act; he died less than three years after he had sold his land to his children.

Although Robert and Charlotte lived six or seven years in Princeton before leaving in 1862 or 1863, they and their family indelibly impressed themselves on the minds of their neighbors. Interviewed in the 1920s, those neighbors recalled first of all the instability of Martha's parents. Robert was remembered for his lackadaisical attitude, his ineptitude as a farmer, and his inability to control his lively wife. But it was Charlotte who remained fresh in the neighbors' minds. When journalist Duncan Aikman visited Princeton to gather information for his book *Calamity Jane and the Lady Wildcats* (1927), he heard the story, possibly handed down from Thornton Canary's unsympathetic wife, that Robert met Charlotte in a bawdy house in Ohio and immediately married her, hoping perhaps to reform the red-haired vixen. Charlotte's brightly colored and eye-catching clothing, her cigar smoking, her public swearing, and her drinking made her a marked woman in a time when pioneer wives were to be innocent of all these. On numerous occasions she rode to town to drink and associate with questionable men, only to return tipsy on her mud-spattered and lathered horse. Another elderly informant recalled a never-to-be-forgotten incident when Charlotte galloped her horse into the yard of newly married teenage mother and threw a swatch of calico cloth at her feet, yelling out "Here … take that and make a dress for your damn bastard." Others recalled her laughing at and taunting Robert, her neglected children, and her uncouth public actions. Still another neighbor, admitting Charlotte's unorthodox and sometimes unruly behavior, nonetheless recalled her as a good-hearted woman willing to help the needy. No one, however, remembered Charlotte as a lady; her unconventional actions were cause for rumors and snide stories, during her time in Princeton and for more than sixty years later.

Although Martha was but six or seven when her family left Princeton, she too was recalled three generations later. She was remembered as a lively little girl who relished playing with children next door. But another recalled Martha as a child whose misbehavior and swearing isolated her from other children. Two or three of her schoolmates distinctly recollected that she attended a "subscription school" on a nearby farm, later known as the Keith School. If she learned to read and write in the year or two she attended that log cabin school, she seems to have forgotten those lessons as an adult. However, if Martha's family left in 1862, she may not have attended school before leaving Princeton.

After the death of Robert's father in June 1862, the Canarys sold their farm the following December. Some contemporaries recalled Robert telling them he hoped to find better land to the west. When Duncan Aikman talked to Princetonians in the 1920s, he vaguely sensed that Charlotte's proslavery sentiments (some called her a "secesh [secessionist] spitfire") made her unwelcome because many residents with Iowa or northern backgrounds opposed slavery.

Itchy feet, distaste for farming, and antislavery sentiments aside, the major reason for Robert and Charlotte's departure from Princeton lies buried in the Mercer County courthouse records. Within a few weeks of the death of James Canary, his Missouri heirs, especially the family of his son James Thornton, were pursuing Martha's parents in the courts, accusing them of withholding some of James's assets. Robert and Charlotte, the claimants asserted, were refusing to part with James's property, including farm implements, livestock, and personal effects, as well as failing to divide the cash James had on hand. Finally, they argued that Robert, after borrowing considerable sums from his father more than a year before the latter's death, failed to repay these loans. Since these borrowed funds were part of James's legacy, they too should be restored to James's inheritance and equally divided among his heirs.

Although Robert and Charlotte were hailed into court on these matters on several occasions in 1862, 1863, and 1864, they "appeared not." Finally, the judge declared for the plaintiffs, James's other heirs. But it was a hollow decision since the heirs apparently never shared the personal property and the withheld funds listed in the suits. Meanwhile, Robert and Charlotte quickly left Princeton for a less threatening place. Local tradition recalls that they moved directly north into Iowa, before heading west in 1863 or 1864.

Within two years, this journey, begun with such high hopes, turned downward to disappointment and ended in tragedy.

What route the Canarys took and how long the trip lasted remains a mystery. Perhaps they immediately joined a wagon train for Montana, as thousands of other Missourians were doing. Maybe they heard of the new gold strikes in the Alder Gulch boom in western Montana and headed in that direction, dreaming of a more satisfying life than they had experienced as an unsuccessful farm family. There is one shred of evidence about the trip, which is to be used with care. When Calamity's ghost-written autobiography appeared in the mid-1890s, *Life and Adventures of Calamity Jane,* probably prepared as a come-on for her appearances in a Wild West show, that eight-page pamphlet indicated, among an armload or two of other impossible happenings, that her family spent five arduous months traveling from Missouri to Virginia City, Montana. Although the details of the trip itself seem designed to exaggerate the drama and dangers of Calamity's girlhood, there is no reason to disbelieve the general outline of her story. She speaks of the times when the trails were so primitive and difficult that the travelers "had to lower wagons over ledges by hand with ropes" because the paths "were so rough and rugged that horses were of no use." During the trip, Martha says, she became a "remarkable good shot and a fearless rider for a girl of my age."

When the Canary family arrived in Montana, perhaps as early as 1863 but more likely in 1864, the mining camps were already caught up in a red-hot mining bonanza. More than 10,000 gold-hungry newcomers had crowded into the Alder Gulch region, with about half the population squeezing out an existence in Virginia City.

A single document, startling for what it reveals, records the downward spiral and sudden disintegration of Martha's family in Montana. On the last day of 1864, the *Montana Post* carried a brief story entitled "Provision for the Destitute Poor" that highlighted the difficulties of "three little girls, who state their names to be Canary." They had appeared at the home of James Fergus asking for aid. As one of the three commissioners of Madison County, Fergus was in charge of aiding the poor. There was a good deal for him to do. The winter of 1864–1865 had turned so vicious that little or no food could be brought into Virginia City, forcing, for example, the price of flour up to the extravagant price of $100 per 150 pounds. It is not surprising then that the Canary family, like so many others, was in need. But in this case the reporter boldly added, "the father, it seems, is a gambler in Nevada [City, Montana]. The mother is a woman of the lowest grade." Then the journalist closed, "A *calico slip* without any additional cloth, was all that defended (?) the poor children from the inclemency of the weather. ... We understand that the little ones returned to Nevada [City], where they have existed for some time." Possibly Robert and Charlotte had reverted to type, hoping to make a pile without grinding physical labor. Perhaps, the riches-to-rags dream so typical of idealistic gold-seekers had already forced them into occupations distant from what they had planned.

Whatever the determining circumstances, tragedy was the outcome. Calamity says in her autobiography that her mother died in early 1866 in Blackfoot City, Montana, then a booming mining town of 2,000 souls and nearly 100 miles north of Alder Gulch. A year later, after Robert and his surviving family retreated to Salt Lake City, he too died.

Even before she became a teenager, Martha was without parents or a home. Unstable and uncertain as it was, life with Robert and Charlotte had given her a semblance of home. Now even that was gone. What would she do? How could she find a home and provide food and clothing for herself and her younger siblings?

Years later Calamity's nephew, Tobe Borner, provided a few details about his aunt's next few years. When he pressed his mother, Lana, Calamity's younger sister, for the story of her early years, she told him that Calamity once blurted out defensively that she had turned to prostitution to provide for her sister and brother, Elijah (Lije). On another occasion, Tobe mentioned that the children were farmed out to Mormon families in Salt Lake City, but that Martha soon struck out on her own. One must remember that Martha was only eleven in 1867.

Calamity's autobiography briefly mentions what she did next. After her father's death, she says, she "went to Fort Bridger, Wyoming Territory, where we arrived May 1, 1868. Remained around Fort Bridger during 1868, then to Piedmont, Wyoming, with U.P. Railway." Fortunately for later biographers, a census-taker gathering information for a special territorial census taken in 1869 discovered Martha in Piedmont that summer. It was the second census and the only one in addition to that of 1860, in which Martha's name was recorded.

The physical and social setting of Piedmont provide a brief glimpse of Martha Canary in an isolated frontier setting at the beginning of her teen years. Piedmont resembled the string of overnight, "hell-on-wheels" towns that sprang up along the Union Pacific Railroad as it pushed quickly westward through Wyoming in 1868 and 1869. At first an out-of-the-way stage station, it soon became a water and wood refueling stop along the track before trains faced a steep incline. Then, in the late 1860s, a tent city leaped into existence, quickly replaced by homes of loggers, railroad men, other workers, and two or three good-sized Mormon families. When the census enumerator arrived in the summer of 1869, he discovered a jerry-built town of nearly twenty houses and ninety-two residents.

The social makeup of the town reveals much about one of Martha's early homes after the death of her parents. Seventy-seven of the residents were male, mostly single laborers, and of the sixteen women, nine were married, with six of the other females younger members of families. In fact, of the residents, thirty-one belonged to four families. Only "Martha Canary," as the census reads, was unmarried and without immediate family. Revealingly, her age was given as fifteen, not thirteen. She probably added the two years because no one would know her real age, and, more importantly, her lifestyle undoubtedly badly bruised society's expectations for a new teenager.

Much later in the 1940s and 1950s, two elderly gentlemen recalled Martha at Ft. Bridger and Piedmont. Both remembered that she lived in a boarding house run by Mrs. Ed Alton, a married thirty-one-year-old immigrant from England whose husband was a laborer in Piedmont. Mrs. Alton is listed immediately after Martha in the census report. One of the men told a Nebraska reporter that Martha had been his baby-sitter, but that her questionable behavior so alienated Mrs. Alton that "Mother blew up and fired" Martha. Since Ed Alton served at Ft. Bridger before he moved to Piedmont, he and his wife may have been instrumental in finding a home for the new teenager.

The months—or perhaps a year or so—at Piedmont reveal a pattern in Martha's early life. Alone, barely in her teens, and without education or training, she was like a modern-day homeless waif. She had to rely on the generosity of others. Although she evidently tended children and worked in Mrs. Alton's boardinghouse for a short spell, she was unable to adopt a family, and her unorthodox and unruly behavior soon alienated Mrs. Alton, as it would other women and men who tried to befriend Martha. She was already following her mother's model, but without a family or an occupation for support.

After the Piedmont interlude, Martha disappears from the scene. She is not listed in the 1870 census, and no newspaper reveals her controversial actions. There is the strong, persisting rumor, nevertheless, that after Piedmont, or even just before, Martha landed in South Pass City and Miner's Delight, two booming mining towns in western Wyoming. Some reports even state that she resided with Patrick Gallagher and his wife in South Pass City until her untoward actions forced them to send her away. For nearly six years Martha's whereabouts are unknown. But when she surfaced, her deeds were again the subject of controversy and comment.

If Martha Canary disappeared in 1870, she reappeared as Calamity Jane in 1875–1876. In five or six years, Martha lost her identity as a wayward young orphan dependent on sympathetic adults for all her needs, but she was reborn as

Calamity Jane: an independent, devil-may-care young woman of alarming and antisocial antics whose reputation was known throughout the bordering Rocky Mountain and Plains states. In 1875–1876, she drew attention and unfavorable comment as a stowaway on at least two expeditions; in 1876 she burst on the Deadwood scene with Wild Bill Hickok and his cronies; and the next year she became the heroine of a sensational and widely circulated dime novel. In short, a new kind of frontier woman had appeared, part fact and part invention, and captured the nation's attention. Concurrent with Calamity Jane's emergence was the demise of the young girl from Princeton, Missouri. Martha Canary never reappeared in the next quarter of a century. Henceforth she would be Calamity Jane, western wild woman.

In her autobiography, Calamity summarizes her life between 1870 and 1875 in a few sentences, but as usual some of these details are improbable, others unadulterated stretchers. She mentions being in Ft. Russell, Ft. Sanders, and Ft. Laramie, locations that seem possible given her previous residence in western Wyoming and her later stopovers in Cheyenne in 1875 and 1876. On the other hand, her claims to having served as George Custer's scout in Arizona in 1870 and 1871, at the age of fourteen and fifteen, is a bald falsehood since Custer was not in the Southwest during this period. One also doubts her brag of being with Generals Custer, Nelson Miles, and Alfred Terry; they were not involved in the "Muscle Shell or Nursey Pursey [sic] Indian outbreak" at this time. Contemporaries remembering back also

Calamity Jane attired in elegant buckskins, probably much like what she wore when she entered Deadwood in 1876. Photo said to be taken in the early 1880s in Evanston, Wyoming. (Courtesy of the American Heritage Center, University of Wyoming)

recalled seeing Calamity at Ft. Steele, usually in the company of a young soldier. One of those who recalled seeing her was John Hunton, then a young farmer-rancher in Wyoming. His journal, published a half century later, reported that Calamity, as well as several other young prostitutes, came to a "hog ranch" near Ft. Laramie to serve the soldiers there. Not surprisingly that, and any other similar activity, went unrecorded in Calamity's autobiography and in her newspaper interviews.

But in the spring of 1875 we do know that Calamity made her first trip to the Black Hills. Her excursion there was a part of a series of events stretching back to 1868. In that year the U.S. government made a treaty with the Sioux, allowing the Indians a large reservation in what became western South Dakota. Six years later in 1874 George Custer marched through the region scouting the terrain and gathering information. When his troops reported scattered traces of pay dirt, gold-hungry pioneers urged the government to throw open the Black Hills for prospectors. Pressured to make a quick decision, Washington officials organized the Jenney Expedition to examine the rumors of gold in the hills and possibly to lay the groundwork for a new treaty with the Sioux.

Under the leadership of Walter P. Jenney and accompanied by Lieutenant Colonel R. T. Dodge, the expedition left Ft. Laramie in May 1875, spent five months on the trail and in the Black Hills, and returned to Ft. Laramie in October. Several testified to Calamity's stowing away among Dodge's troops. Harry Young, a teamster at the time and later a bartender in Deadwood, asserted that Calamity tailed along with Dodge; Dr. Valentine T. McGillycuddy, the group's topographer, made the same assertion. "Mac," a reporter with the Chicago *Inter-Ocean* and traveling with the expedition, was even more specific: on July 3, 1875, he wrote that a young woman with the "high latitude nomenclature" of "Calamity" had "followed the expedition from the first till now." She had a reputation, he continued, "of being a better horse-back rider [and] mule and bull whacker (driver), and a more unctuous coiner of English, and not the Queen's pure, either, than any (other) man in the command." Probably during this trip, or shortly before it, Martha gained the name "Calamity Jane." Undoubtedly her unorthodox demeanor and actions rather than one specific act gained her the new nickname, as she and others claimed.

Within a week, Calamity was dismissed when her salute of the officer of the day drew snickers from nearby soldiers. Discovering that he had just returned the salute of Calamity Jane, the officer reported her to Dodge, who dropped Calamity from the expedition even though they were more than fifty miles out from Ft. Laramie. The next day, Calamity sneaked back among the men, only to be located and thrown out again. This "ceremony," notes one of Calamity's biographers, "was repeated daily during the whole trip."

After returning with the Jenney Expedition, Calamity took up with another command in February 1876. This time she joined with General George Crook's troops just before they moved north to take on the Sioux. One observer wrote in his diary, "Calamity Jane is here going up with the troops. I think there is trouble ahead." Calamity surreptitiously joined the command, not as a scout as she claimed, but perhaps as a teamster or bullwhacker, or even as a prostitute or campfollower. Within a few weeks Crook returned from that unsuccessful mission. Calamity may have made another quick round-trip to the north in early spring. A number of reports also indicate that Calamity accompanied Crook's second march northward in May. John Gregory Bourke, then an aide-de-camp to Crook, noted later that Calamity was rumored to be among the bullwhackers. Another trooper with Crook, Anson Mills, asserted that he had seen and talked to Calamity. Discovered as an imposter because, "she did not cuss her mules with ... enthusiasm," Calamity was detained and sent back with a group of wounded soldiers. She must have returned in early June, for, as we shall see, the officials of Laramie County were waiting for her.

On occasion, Calamity spun atrocious lies to cover the truth. Her autobiography related that in spring 1876, after carrying army dispatches on a "ninety mile ride. . . [and] being wet and cold," she "contracted a severe illness" and was hospitalized for two weeks. If true, instead of being with Custer or Crook in their dramatic conflicts with Indians in June 1876, she was out of action at Ft. Fetterman.

But the District Court records of Laramie County in Wyoming tell a much different story. On May 24, 1876, Maggie Smith (alias Calamity Jane) was indicted for stealing a bundle of clothing and other personal effects from two women three months earlier. A bench warrant, charging Calamity with "grand larceny" "against the peace and dignity of the Territory of Wyoming," was issued the next day. Arrested but pleading not guilty, Calamity was jailed in Cheyenne. After several days of proceedings, including testimonies from the alleged victims, the jury on June 8 declared "the Defendant. Not. Guilty."

Calamity immediately celebrated her release. She paraded down Cheyenne's streets in a gown loaned to her by the wife of one of the sheriff's staff, enjoying her freedom. Two days later, a jubilant Calamity, "greatly rejoiced over release from durance vile," gained access to a horse and buggy and headed for Ft. Russell. But, as the *Cheyenne Leader* recorded on June 20 in a story entitled "Jane's Jamboree," Calamity overindulged in "frequent and liberal potations completely befogging her not very clear mind." She pushed the horse on to Chug, fifty miles away, without stopping. Then, "continuing to imbibe bug juice at close intervals and in large quantities," Calamity trotted on to Ft. Laramie, ninety miles from Cheyenne. As Custer marched toward tragedy at the Little Big Horn, Calamity Jane drunkenly cavorted northward, celebrating her freedom. There is even the possibility that she moved on to join Crook's campaign at this point rather than before her jailing in Cheyenne.

The rhythm of Calamity's life, already in high gear by June 1876, whirled into overdrive during the next few months. She also moved onto central stage in the Wild West when she became a nationally known figure by fall 1876. Over the next two years she starred in a widely circulated dime novel and began to appear in books published by well-known eastern publishers.

Less than a month after Calamity's wild buggyride northward, she was on her way to Deadwood with Wild Bill Hickok. One man who claimed he accompanied the Hickok group, Joseph F. "White Eye Jack" Anderson, asserted that Calamity joined the group by accident. The officer of the day at Ft. Laramie asked the men to take Calamity with them. More than sixty years later as a man of nearly ninety, Anderson gave a participant's observation of the historic ride to Deadwood. Charlie and Steve Utter accepted Calamity as part of their group and promised to take care of her since "she was very drunk and was not dressed very well." "We all liked her," Anderson continued, "even though she was rough." He thought of Hickok as "not very friendly" with Calamity, but she "seemed to think a great deal of Wild Bill." Anderson remembered that Wild Bill and Calamity seemed not to know one another, that they were certainly not lovers, and that Calamity and "Steve Utter bunked together."

The troupe traveled up the trail to Deadwood and arrived in early or mid-July. One onlooker termed their arrival a "spectacular entry." Dressed in eye-catching new suits of buckskin, Calamity included, the entrants rode the full length of Main Street, greeting old acquaintances and gathering the attention of those wishing to become friends. Leander Richardson, a journalist visiting Deadwood in late July, described the new mining camp as a jerry-built madhouse of rough citizens. "Every alternate house was a gambling saloon," he wrote in *Scribner's Monthly*, "and each of them was carrying on a brisk business." And the townsmen were a mangy bunch. Richardson said of them, "Taken as a whole, I never in my life saw so many hardened and brutal-looking men together … ."

Three weeks later Wild Bill lay dead, shot in the back of the head by two-bit gambler Jack McCall. Calamity bragged in her autobiography that she captured McCall in a nearby butchershop, armed only with a cleaver, and making "him throw up his hands." Probably not. Richardson and other observers of the time do not mention her, although there is other evidence she may have been in Deadwood at the time of Wild Bill's death and funeral. Mythmakers, including Calamity, often tried—and still try—to make much of the Wild Bill–Calamity Jane relationship, even making them to be lovers and parents of a child. No strong evidence exists showing Calamity was with Hickok, other than on the trip to Deadwood and perhaps for a few short days before his murder. Among the most preposterous claims in this regard is Jean Hickok McCormick's unfounded assertion, a half century later, that she was the daughter of Calamity and Hickok and that Calamity had kept a diary about her love affair with Wild Bill.

Newspapers in and around Deadwood reported Calamity's doings during the next few months. At the end of 1876 she was rumored to be dancing in a Deadwood hurdy-gurdy. A few weeks later the *Cheyenne Daily Leader* told readers that Calamity was "reported to have married and settled down in Custer City," South Dakota. Other brief notices revealed that she traveled back and forth by stage to visit "the boys in blue" in what became South and North Dakota. Another newspaper mentioned that Calamity and her "darling Jim" at a Saturday night dance had "succombed to the green-eyed monster" before an officer quieted their antics.

Another side of Calamity also emerged in a variety of reports. She was often saluted as a friend of the down-and-out, as a person ready to help any human, and especially as a nursemaid of the sick. There was a strong, persisting tradition among Deadwood pioneers and later historians that Calamity played a public and fearless role in nursing deathly sick victims of smallpox in Deadwood in 1878. Although several naysayers have attempted to dismiss or downsize these stories of Calamity's valiant efforts, the eyewitness accounts of nearly a dozen recipients or participants in her ministrations make it difficult to discard these stories simply as attempts to balance good deeds with her otherwise questionable character and behavior.

But another kind of Calamity, one of national and enduring proportions, suddenly tumbled on scene in the second half of 1877. She became a noted Wild West heroine, and her new stardom flashed into existence in a few months. In early June 1877 a series of newspapers carried the story that Calamity resembled a Bret Harte character; that she came from Virginia City, Nevada; that she dressed like a man and lived an unrestrained life; and, finally, stated that despite a "rough and dissipated career," these hardships had not "altogether 'swept away the lines where beauty lingers.'" Much of this information, including the flowery descriptions and mistaken facts, seems plagiarized from H. N. Maguire's *The Black Hills and American Wonderland* (1877), a book by a Rapid City journalist, parts of which were serialized in a New York paper. And virtually the same words and facts are utilized to describe Calamity's character in her first dime novel, Edward L. Wheeler's *Deadwood Dick, the Prince of the Road; or, The Black Rider of the Black Hills* (October 15, 1877). A few months later, T. M. Newson's play *Drama of Life in the Black Hills* (1878) featured Calamity as a major character. Although depicting Calamity as a twenty-two-year-old woman, as "uneducated, uncared for," and as "an original in herself," he too drew on the bittersweet descriptions in Maguire's account. In a space of less than a year, through these widely circulated mediums, Calamity Jane was transformed from a controversial local character to a nationally known heroine.

Revealingly, the mythic Calamity surfaced at an emotional high point of the Wild West. During the five years from 1876 to 1881, from the killing of Custer and the assassination of Wild Bill Hickok to Billy the Kid's demise and the OK Corral shootout five years later, the entire country was awash in a frenzy about a fascinating frontier. The apotheosis of Calamity, in the pages of western newspapers, in a widely read history, in a florid dime novel, and in a pioneering western drama, made her a suitable companion to male figures finding their way into a Wild West pantheon.

The years from 1876 to 1878, therefore, were a turning point in Calamity's life. Now nationally recognized as a Wild West "character" and fictional heroine, she had also, although still in her early twenties, already exposed enough of the underside of frontier life for a lifetime of carousing and dissipation. If Wyoming and more recently South Dakota were theaters for her earlier exploits, she now moved on to explore opportunities in southeastern and southcentral Montana and central and southern Wyoming. Indeed, Calamity's wanderings in the 1880s and 1890s followed a lifetime pattern: from the early railroad towns to the newly established forts, to the boomtowns of Cheyenne and Deadwood, and then on to Billings, Miles City, and Livingston in Montana and Rawlins and Lander in Wyoming, she was particularly drawn to recently established areas. They were Calamity's "homes"—not for long and not very successfully, however. They were also the sites for her "marriages" and "husbands."

By the early 1880s Calamity was living in Coulson, Montana (the forerunner of Billings), and before long migrated to Miles City and Livingston. Newly established along the Northern Pacific Railroad, these raw towns were prime locations for new Calamity testings. In 1882 and 1883 she was rumored to be living on a ranch west of Miles City and then on another near Laurel; in both places she served as a cook, cut fence posts for ranchers, and may even have been involved in horse stealing operations. Around this time the famed frontier photographer L. A. Huffman photographed Calamity. She posed formally in a dark, stylish dress, trimmed with a frilly collar and cuffs, and also wore a white collar bow and a large hat. Calamity seemed a bit tense

"Only and Original Calamity Jane."
Photograph taken by L. A. Huffman,
probably in the Miles City, Montana,
area in the early to mid-1880s. (Courtesy
of the American Heritage Center,
University of Wyoming)

and uneasy, staring past the camera. A vibrant young woman in her mid-twenties, she was not unattractive and communicated a much more feminine image here than in the often-reprinted photographs where she was dressed in bulky, masculine buckskins. At about this time Montana newspapers reported that Calamity had given birth to a healthy baby boy, whom she was calling "Little Calamity." Later accounts make vague mention of Calamity's son. One wonders how she felt about motherhood given the circumstances of her own home.

Calamity claimed in her suspect autobiography that she left Montana in 1883 and "went to California," passing through Ogden, Utah, on her way to San Francisco. Next she abandoned the West Coast for Texas, where in 1885 she married Clinton Burke. She alleged that she bore him a child in 1887 and that they "remained in Texas leading a quiet home life until 1889." But contemporary newspapers of the northern, interior West tell a much different, more believable story. After brief jaunts to Idaho and northern Wyoming, Calamity invaded Lander and Rawlins. Little-known family ties drew her to Lander, where her younger sister Lena lived. Born three years after Calamity, Lena had married German immigrant John Borner (Boerner) while still in her teens and now had several children. Calamity tried to visit her sister as often as she could, having to avoid her brother-in-law who strongly opposed what he castigated as Calamity's wild, immoral life.

Another, later story suggests that Calamity felt warmly toward her siblings even though she rarely saw them. When a Montana prospector met

Calamity at the turn of the century and told her of his recent visit with her younger brother Elijah in southwestern Wyoming (Lije had just been released from a five-year prison term for obstructing a railroad and falsely claiming damages), the Montanan said Calamity "broke down and sobbed like a child." So overcome with emotion was Calamity in hearing of "her 'baby' brother, that being the pet name she had ... bestowed upon him," that she forced a present upon the bearer of the news. Calamity's nephew, Tobe Borner, on two or three occasions, also spoke of the close feelings between the Canary sisters.

In 1885–1886, fresh stories of Calamity and her controversial actions were grist for lurid headlines in southcentral Wyoming. Not the least sensational of the stories were those concerning two new "husbands." Rawlins newspapers in the latter half of 1885 and the early months of 1886 reported that Calamity was now Mrs. Martha (Mattie) King, whose drunken escapades landed her in jail. Six months later in fall 1886 Calamity and a new husband, William Steers, were often in the news; then, and for much of the next year, the couple acted out their stormy relationship in Wyoming newspapers. Perhaps as a result of that "marriage," Calamity was said on June 21, 1887, to be "in a rather delicate condition." In October she gave birth to a baby girl. Unfortunately, motherhood did little to rein in Calamity's immediate actions, although her tryst with Steers seems to have ended in 1888. Leaving Lander, and after short stops in Laramie, Cheyenne, and Casper, Calamity returned to Montana. Then, she disappeared. Although brief notices referred to her between 1890 and 1894, little of substance is known of her during these years. Some have wondered if she settled on a ranch or ran a boarding house in Montana with Clinton Burke and tried to make a home for her little girl. Ironically, if the Wild West Calamity refrained from drinking and antisocial actions, newspapers were at a loss of what to write about her.

Coming out of isolation, Calamity returned to Deadwood in October 1895, and reporters were immediately supplied with a new crop of lively stories. Accompanied by a girl about eight years old, Calamity told a newspaper that she had been living with her husband on a ranch near Ekalaka, Montana, but she tired of that life and hoped to find something to support her daughter and herself. Another rumor circulated that Burke had gotten into trouble and that Calamity was forced to leave her erstwhile haven. Not surprisingly, Calamity was soon on a toot, then another, and still another. Once again in town, she seemed unable to break the tightening hold John Barleycorn had on her life. Then a promising possibility presented itself.

Near the end of 1895, a representative of the Middleton-Kohl organization visited Deadwood and invited Calamity to take part in their programs for dime museums. By mid-January she was on her way east for the first time, with an eight-week contract for $50 per week to appear in several midwestern and eastern cities. On January 20, 1896, a sensational come-on advertisement for her first appearance in Minneapolis described her as "The Famous Woman Scout of the Wild West! Heroine of a Thousand Thrilling Adventures! The Terror of Evildoers in the Black Hills! The Comrade of Buffalo Bill and Wild Bill!" If that exaggerated billing wasn't enough to do in Calamity, her undisciplined life was. By late spring she was back in the Black Hills, having succumbed once again to alcohol. It was not her first try as a performer. A dozen years earlier, she had traveled to Chicago with the Hardwick show, but that troupe was forced to disband and sell its horses because of insufficient funding. Unfortunately, for all her liveliness and heroic reputation, Calamity was not an actress. She could not live up to larger-than-life representations of her in fiction or on stage; nor was she a sharpshooter like Annie Oakley of Buffalo Bill's Wild West. Standing before a crowd to talk of herself was not for Calamity either. Although others like Buffalo Bill could move easily from life to self-dramatization, Calamity could only be herself.

After the disaster with the Kohl-Middleton group, Calamity returned west, living off and on in Montana for the next few years, particularly in the area of Livingston. Clinton Burke disappeared and Calamity took up with Robert Dorsett as her new partner. That relationship quickly dissolved, and Calamity was reported as wandering the length of southern Montana hawking photographs of herself and her autobiography. When income from those

Calamity Jane as General Cook's scout. Photograph by C. E. Fenn, supposedly in Livingston, Montana, in the mid-1890s. (Courtesy of the American Heritage Center, University of Wyoming)

sales proved insufficient, she was forced into the Gallatin County poor house in February 1901. One newspaper reported the following July that Calamity appeared "wan and weary, twisted and bent, on the rapid decline." By mid-July she was residing, said one account, "on a dirty bunk in a negro house of ill repute, sick and half dead." Then a remarkable occurrence promised another opportunity for recovery.

Josephine Brake, an established eastern novelist with an interest in the West, hearing of Calamity's misfortunes and perhaps also motivated to use Calamity's Wild West reputation for her own purposes, came to Montana to find Calamity. Brake announced that she wanted to save Calamity, to take her east, and to give her the good home she lacked. But Brake also wanted Calamity to help publicize Brake's writings at the Pan-American Exposition in Buffalo. When Calamity arrived in New York and found, to her disgust, that she was being used, she abandoned Mrs. Brake and joined Col. Frederic T. Cummins's Indian Congress. That position likewise ended quickly, with rumors about a drunken spree and a runaway wagon helping to explain the dismissal.

It was Calamity's last attempt at performance; she did not become part of Buffalo Bill's Wild West, as some have asserted. In all these dramatic opportunities, Calamity demonstrated that she was unable to bridge the gap between experience and performance, a handspring that Buffalo Bill achieved with such grace and persuasion. But Buffalo Bill did aid the penniless Calamity by helping fund her eventual return west.

Calamity's final decline came quickly, like an out-of-control stagecoach careening down a steep incline. After Calamity returned from the debacle in New York without money or a job, she seemed to give up. Wandering back west, she exhibited occasional flashes of her earlier charisma, but by spring 1902, suffering from a lingering illness, she was committed to a county poor house in Montana. Understandably, given her lifetime of individualism, she refused to go; she "objected vigorously" despite the promise that the institution would give her "medical assistance" and take "care of" her. It was about this time that Calamity Jane told Montana cowboy Teddy Blue: "Why don't the sons of bitches leave me alone and let me go to hell my own route?" A new outbreak in November sent her to jail in Billings, and when released in December she made for Deadwood, declaring Billings "a tenderfoot town" where she was underappreciated.

Arriving in Belle Fourche in January 1903, Calamity seemed serious about reforming and about supporting the daughter who accompanied her. But Calamity's resolve soon dissipated, even though her friend Madam Dora DuFran hired her as a cook. Leaving, meandering back and forth between

Calamity Jane as a participant in Col. Frederic T. Cummins's Indian Congress, which participated in the Pan-American Exposition, Buffalo, New York, in 1901. Photograph by C. D. Arnold. (Courtesy of the American Heritage Center, University of Wyoming)

the Black Hills and northeastern Wyoming, Calamity wobbled her way back to Deadwood. Sick, depressed, and still indulging in steady alcoholic binges, Calamity was disintegrating, as photographs of this time clearly reveal. She was obviously unwell when she returned to Deadwood in July, and "seriously ill" when she left Deadwood by train for nearby Terry. Put under doctor's care, she nonetheless quickly slipped away, on August 1, 1903, from "inflammation of the bowels." After a funeral service that attracted thousands, she was buried next to Wild Bill Hickok in the Mt. Moriah Cemetery in Deadwood. The companionship she may have wished for in life seemed possible only in death.

So evolved the life of Martha Canary/Calamity Jane. Reared in an unstable and disruptive home, Martha was an orphan at eleven, dependent upon others who were unable to discipline her independent spirit. While still a teenager with unorthodox and even notorious habits, she had already been renamed Calamity Jane. With the dramatic ride into Deadwood in the summer of 1876 her life reached its apex. Two years later her name was popping up frequently in newspapers of the northern interior West, and her appearance in a widely circulated history, a dramatic dime novel, and a play initiated Calamity into the inner circle of heroes of the Wild West. From that apex, she began to self destruct in the 1880s and 1890s. Unable to remain rooted in one place, wobbling through a series of "marriages" and "husbands," and increasingly exhibiting abnormal behavior and mounting alcoholism, Calamity tumbled downward even as her magic name was recognized in widening circles. Two promising opportunities to act out her life and reputation in dramatic shows also collapsed because of her inebriate actions. The youthful, animal-like energy that sustained her through years of dissipation, instability, and drunkenness now betrayed her. At her death at age forty-seven, she was already a tired, sick, old woman.

But Calamity was more than a Wild West heroine, more than simply "one of the boys," more than a tragic figure. She was also an independent woman trying to find her way in an American West rapidly closing out its frontier years. On one notable occasion in the mid-1890s a reporter revealed another side of Calamity. His published interview tells us much about her. Reflecting familiar concerns, Calamity worried that her appearance and home were too untidy for a visitor. Visiting with the journalist in the company of her "husband" and daughter Jessie, Calamity told him that she had done many things in the past for which she was sorry. Now, she wanted to forget those controversial actions and to keep her family intact. In his story, the reporter surmised what few biographers have realized: most of all, Calamity desired to be a "wife" and mother, to be like other pioneer women. Regretably, that domestic side of her character remains hidden under hundreds of stories about her unorthodox actions as a Wild West hellcat.

If there were enough pages, the Calamity Jane of popular imagination would deserve equal comment. Early on, the dime novel Calamity of the late-nineteenth century easily dissolved into the romantic cinematic Calamity in such well-known films as *The Plainsman* (1936) and *Calamity Jane* (1953). Meanwhile, popular historians and pulp biographers portrayed Calamity as a lively, rambunctious, two-gun she-cat worthy of becoming "one of the Wild West boys" like Billy the Kid, Wyatt Earp, and Wild Bill Hickok. Often reading history backwards and caught up in the fact that Calamity is buried next to Hickok, popularizers, then and now, manufactured a nonexistent love affair between the two Wild West giants. But the dramatic sociocultural changes of the 1960s helped create a new Calamity. The revisionist spaghetti Western films and debunking novels like Pete Dexter's *Deadwood* (1986) and Larry McMurtry's *Buffalo Girls* (1990) dramatized a grey, ambivalent heroine. As the century drew to a close, the Calamity of late-nineteenth-century popular culture was more than a generation or two removed from the romantic tomboy of Doris Day's Calamity of the 1950s. If McMurtry's heroine and the female protagonist of the film version of his novel are taken as examples, Calamity had become an aging, disillusioned, postfrontier hermaphrodite waiting to die. In these most recent renditions, pre-1960s Calamities were as absent from the scene as was Martha Canary.

But Calamity Jane was more than a grey heroine bewailing a passing frontier. Her full story began with a spicy, stubborn girl, who became a vibrant if unmoral young Calamity Jane, and who then turned into a decaying middle-aged woman. If these evolving dimensions of her life are understood, Calamity represents much more than a stereotyped Wild West female; she becomes a gritty pioneer endeavoring to hold onto her reputation as a woman who defined and lived in a sphere of her own making. It is her tragedy that she was unable to achieve what she wished for.

Sources and Further Reading

Unlike most other Wild West heroines and heroes, Martha Canary (Calamity Jane) lacks a full-length, well-researched, and artistically produced biography. Billy the Kid, Buffalo Bill Cody, Annie Oakley, Wild Bill Hickok, and Wyatt Earp all have been treated in at least one full-length, thoroughly researched biography; some have been dealt with in more than one. But not Calamity Jane. Instead, those interested in studying Calamity's life must be warned away from, rather than led to, most biographies of her. But that situation may be changing. Several useful essays have appeared recently, and now scholars are at work on studies of her life and her significance in American popular culture.

The first of the extensive biographical studies was Duncan Aikman's *Calamity Jane and the Lady Wildcats* (New York: Henry Holt and Company, 1927). A journalist from El Paso, Texas, Aikman traveled throughout Calamity country in the mid-1920s to examine available records and to interview persons who had known Calamity as a girl and grown woman. Although infected with H. L. Mencken's debunking virus and guilty of too much journalistic license in his portrait, Aikman nonetheless gathered important remembrances and obscure information about Calamity still useful to biographers.

The next book on Calamity, Nolie Mumey's *Calamity Jane, 1852–1903* (Denver, CO: Range Press, 1950), did not appear until 1950. A medical doctor and local historian, Mumey collected dozens of pertinent newspaper articles about Calamity throughout Wyoming, Montana, and South Dakota but failed to examine critically these sources or to provide evaluation of Calamity's life. In addition, he unfortunately accepted Jean Hickok McCormick's assertion that she was Wild Bill Hickok and Calamity's daughter and also the published diary that Mrs. McCormick claimed was her mother's. Still, the book is useful for the newspaper items it reproduces.

Nearly a decade later Glenn Clairmonte published her novelized biography, *Calamity Was Her Name* (Denver, CO: Sage Books, 1959). Although it is not the worst biography ever written, as one Calamity scholar alleged, it is a flawed source because the author created imaginary conversations and relied on too many questionable sources. Nonetheless, the novel, disguised as a biography, is clearly written and remains, in many ways, a plausible interpretation of Calamity.

Published one year earlier, Robert Beed Sollid's thoroughly researched and probing *Calamity Jane: A Study in Historical Criticism* (Helena, MT: Western Press, 1958) is the best book to-date on Calamity. Particularly valuable is the author's analytical use of a wide variety of newspaper sources. Moreover, no one before or since has been as exhaustive as she was in turning up obscure evidence on Calamity's life. Reprinted in 1995 by the Montana Historical Society with an Introduction by James McLaird and an Afterword by Richard W. Etulain, Sollid's study remains the most useful source on Calamity Jane.

Nearly fifty years elapsed before the next biography of Calamity appeared, Stella Foote's *A History of Calamity Jane: Our Country's First Liberated Woman* (New York: Vantage Press, 1995). Regrettably, two large flaws undercut the value of her book. First, Foote also accepts the validity of the spurious diary and letters that Jean Hickok McCormick claimed to be Calamity's. Moreover, the author is unable to treat other sources critically and sometimes contradicts herself. She has published, however, a large number of important newspaper stories and gathers many of the most important photographs of Calamity.

Of the hundreds of pamphlets, book chapters, essays, and informal pieces published on Calamity, a handful deserve brief mention. Clarence Paine, a midwestern librarian and historian who planned a biography of Calamity, published three strong essays, two in the Chicago Westerners' *Brand Books* (Chicago: Westerners, 1946, 1947) and the third in Roderick Peattie, ed., *The Black Hills* (New York, Vanguard Press, 1952). Andrew Blewitt's essay in *The English Westerners' Brand Book* 5 (January 1963):1–9, is a very useful abbreviated overview. Elizabeth Stevenson's chapter on Calamity Jane in her *Figures in a Western Landscape* (Baltimore, MD: The Johns Hopkins University Press, 1994) is exceptionally well written and balanced. Finally, James McLaird's essay on Calamity 's final year "Calamity Jane: The Life and Legend," *South Dakota History* 24 (spring 1994), is exhaustively researched, and his most recent essay, "Calamity Jane's Diary and Letters: Story of a Fraud," *Montana: The Magazine of Western History* 45 (autumn/winter 1995), proves that the so-called Calamity Jane diary is a spurious document.

Several full-length studies of Calamity are underway. James McLaird of Dakota Wesleyan University has nearly completed what should be the definitive biography of Calamity. Several years in the making, based on the widest research possible, and clearly and refreshingly interpretive, his biography-in-process will provide readers with the sound life story Calamity has lacked. This writer is greatly indebted to Professor McLaird for sharing several obscure sources and correcting misinformation in an earlier draft of this essay. Richard W. Etulain of the University of New Mexico is working on a brief study of Calamity's life and legends, and Professor Anna Bates has completed a book-length study of the cinematic treatments of Calamity.

For those who wish to undertake further research on Calamity Jane in manuscript and newspaper materials, several collections in the northern West are particularly useful. Much of the information Clarence Paine gathered for his projected biography of Calamity has been deposited in the Center for Western Studies at Augustana College, Sioux Falls, South Dakota. Another useful collection is the material Lloyd McFarling gathered for his unpublished life story of Calamity, now on file at the South Dakota State Historical Society in Pierre. A third such collection is that of J. Leonard Jennewein of Dakota Wesleyan University, who once considered writing an extended study of Calamity. His materials should be consulted at that university's library in Mitchell, South Dakota. Finally, ambitious researchers will also want to examine the extensive newspaper clippings and miscellaneous files at Montana Historical Society in Helena, the Western Heritage Center at the University of Wyoming in Laramie, the Wyoming State Historical Society in Cheyenne, and the Billings and Denver public libraries.

5

Annie Oakley:
The Peerless Lady Wing-Shot

GLENDA RILEY

IN ONE SENSE ANNIE OAKLEY FAILS TO BLEND with the other women portrayed here. Oakley was not born in the West, nor did she make her home there. In fact, she traveled only occasionally in the West with Buffalo Bill's Wild West Exhibition. But in another way, Annie Oakley's story is crucial to understanding the American West. Oakley, who possessed an abundance of grit and grace, used these qualities to shape people's beliefs about the West. Through dazzling athletic skill, consummate show business acumen, and a captivating femininity, Oakley strongly influenced how Americans and Europeans viewed the American West—and in turn how westerners often perceived themselves.

Between 1885 and 1902, the years when Oakley achieved fame with Buffalo Bill's Wild West as the peerless lady wing-shot, her interpretation of the West proved attractive to millions of people, at home and abroad, for she characterized the best of the West. She came from humble beginnings, maintained modesty throughout her meteoric career, and managed those mainstays of western life—the horse and the gun—with exceptional skill. Oakley's West was one of straight shooting, fair play, and the triumph of good over evil.

In addition, Oakley became the archetypal western woman. As the person who created the genre "cowgirl," Annie projected an image so feminine, ladylike, Victorian, and beguiling that most people found themselves drawn to a woman who shot and rode horseback in public. Rather than being repelled by Annie's version of a strong, achieving woman, viewers cheered her onward and often came to believe that women—especially those of the western variety—were fully capable of great feats and daring exploits.

MISS ANNIE OAKLEY,
THE PEERLESS LADY WING-SHOT.

A Buffalo Bill Wild West lithograph advertising Annie Oakley, "The Peerless Lady Wing-Shot," in 1890. (Courtesy of the Buffalo Bill Historical Center, Cody, Wyoming)

Annie Oakley might be surprised at this assessment of her legacy to the West, and to its women. She certainly did not set out to affect the world's image of the American West. Rather she simply tried to do her best at whatever task came to hand. After her rise to stardom, she expressed her homely philosophy in her motto:

> Aim at a high mark and you will hit it.
> No, not the first time, nor the second and maybe not the third.
> But keep on aiming and keep on shooting
>   for only practice will make you perfect.
> Finally, you will hit the bull's eye of success.

As a young girl, however, Annie would have worried more about survival than ultimate success. On August 13, 1860, she was born into a large family with the last name Moses. Because records differ, the spelling may have been Mosey or even Mosee. Although the family worked hard, they barely scratched out a living on their small farm in Darke County, Ohio. As the fifth surviving child, Annie could not expect a life of ease and plenty, but she encountered want, personal loss, and even physical abuse that forced her to draw upon all her resilience and resources.

When a baby brother and then a sister joined the family, Annie sacrificed schooling to help her mother, Susan, supplement the family's slim larder and to keep the critical supply of food, clothing, bedding, and medicine flowing. As Annie stood on the cabin's plank floor laboring next to Susan, their faces grimy from the greasy smoke of the fireplace and their backs aching from bending over a kettle of boiling laundry, Annie must have wondered about the whereabouts of some pencil sketches her mother had once drawn. Annie must have also pondered what her own future held.

The answer seemed to be one misfortune after another. In 1865, Annie's sixty-two-year-old father, Jacob, arrived home in a desperate condition from the postal route that brought in the family's only cash income. Rain and sleet froze him atop his horse, stole the mobility from his hands and the timbre from his voice, and plunged him into pneumonia. Late in 1866, Jacob finally succumbed to his illness, leaving thirty-two-year-old Susan to fend for herself and support seven children under the age of fifteen.

The bereft family barely coped. Susan sold the cow named "Pink" to pay medical bills and moved the destitute family to a smaller farm, which she cash-leased from a neighbor. Annie, who was not yet seven, remembered that she "donned" her homespun linsey dress "and started for the woods." With ingenious, homemade traps she bagged quail, squirrel, and grouse that she brought to Susan who fried, boiled, and even fricasseed them. During these years, Annie improved her hunting technique. She removed her father's cap-and-ball Kentucky rifle from over the fireplace and taught herself to shoot small game through the head so the shot would not spoil the meat.

When Susan's and Annie's efforts proved inadequate to keep the family afloat, Susan took employment as a nurse for $1.25 a week and farmed out most of her children to helpful neighbors and friends. Annie moved to the Darke County Infirmary where she knitted, darned, embroidered, and did odd jobs. From there Annie took a job as a hired girl with what she later termed "the wolf family." Although the family wrote to Susan about Annie's progress in school and her light workload at home, in reality Annie spent her days, which began at four in the morning, making breakfast, milking cows, washing dishes, skimming and churning milk, feeding stock, weeding the garden, gathering wild berries, getting dinner, and caring for the baby. In between Annie trapped and hunted wild game.

Not surprisingly, Annie eventually seized the opportunity to run away and to hitch a train ride back to Susan. Annie later wrote that "for years" she asked "God each night" to bless the stranger who had helped her escape the "wolves" by buying her train ticket. Although she never spoke directly of it, Annie also indicated that she had suffered physical mistreatment, and perhaps sexual abuse as well, at the hands of her employer.

Once home, Annie soon discovered that during her absence Susan's second husband, Daniel Brumbaugh, had died, leaving Susan with a baby girl. Susan had soon entered a third marriage with a widower named Joseph Shaw who welcomed Annie to their sparse cabin. During her teen years Annie alternated between living with her mother and working at the Darke County Infirmary. At home, she absorbed Susan's Quaker values; at the infirmary, she learned the rudiments of reading and writing.

Remarkably Annie later remembered these years as "happy" and described them as "wonderful days of simplicity." Perhaps Annie's own buoyant personality made her growing-up years tolerable, for she saw everything with a sense of humor and escaped to her beloved woods whenever possible with an old, single muzzle-loading shotgun in her hand. "Oh, how grand God's beautiful earth seemed to me as I glided swiftly through the woods," she effused.

During the 1870s, Annie became a market-hunter. In her early teens, she sold game to a local shopkeeper who resold it to Cincinnati hotels. As her family endured continuing poverty and her stepfather gradually descended into blindness, Annie put aside the nickels and dimes she earned. When the mortgage on the farm came due Annie placed her savings in Susan's hands. "Oh, how my heart leaped with joy," she wrote. "I handed the money to mother and told her that I had saved enough from my trapped game" to pay off the mortgage.

Annie Oakley with shotgun in the mid-1880s. No medals as yet adorn her chest. (Courtesy of the Buffalo Bill Historical Center, Cody, Wyoming)

Annie's prowess with weapons not only served her family well but led to a match with stage-shooter Francis E. Butler. Although legend has it that the contest took place on Thanksgiving Day, 1875, it may have occurred as late as 1881. Family records and documents are so few that Annie's early life is impossible to document exactly.

Reportedly, when Frank Butler saw the local favorite was a mere girl he chuckled. After Annie beat Frank twenty-five to twenty-four, he stopped smiling. Frank quickly recovered from his defeat, however, and invited Annie to be his guest at one of his performances at Cincinnati's Coliseum Theater.

Annie accepted Frank's invitation with thanks. Thus began a courtship that, in Annie's words, led her to tying "a knot so hard" it lasted "some 50 years." Whether they married in 1876 as some believe—or in 1882 as others argue—Annie found a husband and companion as well as a shooting partner, teacher, business manager, agent, and father figure. Frank proved to be genial, accomplished, wise, and patient. He also possessed the stage experience necessary to fashion the young, inexperienced shooter into a star.

At first Frank wanted Annie to travel with him when he played the theater circuit or to wait for him at home with Susan. Although Annie had little to say in her memoirs about this time, such enforced idleness can have hardly suited either her work ethic or her preference for activity. Soon fate—and Annie—took a hand in the situation. On May 1, 1882, Frank's shooting partner fell ill; Frank, or perhaps Annie, suggested that she assist Frank during a performance at Springfield, Ohio's Crystal Hall. "I went on," Annie recalled, "with Mr. B. to hold the objects as he shot, he thought. But I rebelled." To the audience's roaring approval, Annie insisted on taking every other shot.

After that initial performance, Annie chose the name Oakley and toured with Frank. The couple played vaudeville and circuses, especially the Sells Brothers Circus. In virtually every appearance, the 5-foot-tall, 110-pound Annie, wearing a long-skirted dress and allowing her hair to flow down her back, raised a rifle or shotgun to her shoulder. With every show she astounded her viewers. Meanwhile Frank helped Annie improve her reading and writing, which was rudimentary due to her lack of formal schooling. Frank also refined Annie's act and stage presence, and dropped increasingly into the background.

In 1884, Frank noticed an announcement in *New Orleans Picayune* that changed his and Annie's lives: Buffalo Bill Cody's Wild West Park planned to set up near the Sells Brothers lot on Canal Street. Although Frank soon learned that the Wild West was overloaded with shooting acts, Frank sold Annie's act to Cody and his partner Nate Salsbury the following season. In 1885, Annie and Frank put behind them third-class hotels, impossible theaters, and ragged circus lots when they signed with Cody's Wild West. "There was I facing the real Wild West," Annie reminisced, "the first white woman to travel with what society might have considered an impossible outfit."

For sixteen of the next seventeen seasons Annie and Frank traveled with Cody's Wild West. It proved a demanding life, including short stands primarily throughout the eastern, central, and middle-western states and Canada, and longer engagements in Europe. But the Wild West also provided numerous rewards. Cody and Salsbury paid on time, cared for their stock and equipment, and created a congenial atmosphere. Too, Annie did what she loved most—she trained daily, performed brilliantly, and hunted in between performances. Meanwhile Frank, who was devoted to Annie, managed contracts, generated publicity, invented new tricks, and arranged for guns, ammunition, and licenses.

During these halcyon years of the 1880s, Annie and Frank built an act and a persona for Annie that appealed to everyone in her audiences— young or old, male or female, conservative-minded or progressive. By the 1890s and early 1900s, Annie and Frank shaped an act and an image with universal appeal yet one that reflected their moral values. Although Annie's and Frank's show business acumen dictated the inclusion of dramatic elements—including using western clothing and tack, trying new tricks, and playing to the audience—their own personalities demanded a "clean" aura based on solid family values.

Foremost, of course, Annie's act and image included guns. That first season with Buffalo Bill in 1885 Annie began each performance by shooting clay pigeons sprung from a trap, then shot pigeons from two traps at a time, picked up her gun from the ground and shot after the trap was sprung, shot two pigeons in the same manner, and shot three glass balls thrown in the air in rapid succession, the first with a rifle, the second and third with a shotgun. During following seasons—until she left Buffalo Bill in 1902—Oakley practiced constantly and regularly added new tricks to her repertoire.

Unlike other shooters of the day who relied upon an accomplice to shatter targets by means of wires or other devices, Oakley never used tricks or illusion. Although temptations to employ artifice or cut corners must have existed, Annie and Frank strove to keep her act honest. On one occasion a circus performer who fired a rifle while swinging from a trapeze and hit the bull's eye every time attracted Annie's interest until she discovered that the woman fired blanks while a property man rang the bell behind the target. Similarly, in the cigar-ash trick a shooter need not come anywhere near the target; the smoker simply pulled a wire in the cigar's center and the ash dropped off at the appropriate moment. But when Annie shot the ash off Frank's cigarette she did so without any trickery.

Annie Oakley, Frank Butler, and poodle, George, in 1884. (Courtesy of the Annie Oakley Foundation, Greenville, Ohio)

Besides guns, Annie's act included horses, heroines, and, notably, a western ambience. Oakley's identification with the American West had begun as early as 1884, when Chief Sitting Bull saw Annie perform in St. Paul and promptly adopted her. Frank, who had no hesitation about identifying Annie with the West to attract people caught somewhere between the disappearing frontier and the emerging machine age, quickly recognized the tremendous advertising possibilities in the Sitting Bull incident.

Two weeks after the meeting between Annie and Sitting Bull, Frank placed an advertisement in the *New York Clipper* announcing that "the premier shots, Butler and Oakley" had made friends with the most fearsome Indian chief of all. Frank added that, in front of numerous witnesses, Sitting Bull had given them, along with other gifts, the pair of moccasins he had worn at the Battle of the Little Big Horn. Although the friendship was short-lived because Sitting Bull returned to the Standing Rock reservation in Dakota Territory and Annie turned eastward, first to visit her mother, then to join the Sells Brothers Circus for a season, Frank proved prophetic. The alliance of Sitting Bull and Annie Oakley initiated Annie's reputation as the "girl of the western plains," which many fans and reviewers liked to call her.

Sitting Bull and Annie reunited in 1885 after William F. Cody's press agent, John Burke, escorted Sitting Bull from the Standing Rock Reservation to tour with the Wild West. Annie welcomed Sitting Bull into the Wild West troupe. She marched up and asked him about coins and a red silk handkerchief she had sent him. Through his interpreter Sitting Bull replied that he had received the gifts but left them behind for safe-keeping. He added "I am very glad to see you. I have not forgotten you and feel pleased that you want to remember me."

During the following months on the road during the 1885 season Annie formed a fast alliance with Sitting Bull, especially by listening to his complaints. Some members of the troupe claimed Annie was the only one in camp who could lift Sitting Bull out of his frequent depressions. The chief's foremost grievance concerned Army troops who trespassed on the hay and timber lands of his home reservation, Standing Rock. He feared that in a few years his people would face utter poverty. He also told Annie that cattle ranchers encroached on the reservation and counted twice each cow intended for Sioux consumption. And the agents, Sitting Bull confided, gave Indians "half-and-half instead of sugar—the other half being sand."

Annie also sympathized with Sitting Bull when he gave away much of his salary to the poor urchins who haunted every show lot. She understood his desire to help others. Sitting Bull failed to understand the white people he met who, in his view, refused to take care of their own. He also feared for the Indian. Such stingy, selfish people would be unwilling to share their resources with Native Americans.

Oddly enough, John Burke failed to turn the chief's and Annie's friendship into a publicity gimmick. Neither did Oakley join the various publicity events that Burke staged for Sitting Bull that season. Since Burke never missed such an opportunity perhaps Annie, out of fondness for the chief, refused to cooperate.

After the final performance of the season on October 11, 1885, Sitting Bull told a reporter through his interpreter that, "The wigwam is a better place for the red man." He added that he was "sick of the houses and the noises and multitude of men" who stared and poked their fingers at him. Sitting Bull went to Annie to say good-bye. Before he departed, in appreciation of her friendship, he gave her invaluable Indian artifacts. In return Annie wrote to Sitting Bull after he returned to Standing Rock.

Unfortunately, because of the growing deterioration of Indian-white relations during the late 1880s, Annie never saw Sitting Bull again. On December 14, 1890, the Indian Police tried to arrest Sitting Bull and the chief's followers opened fire on them. In the subsequent melee, Sitting Bull lost his life, as did seven of his men and six police officers.

After Sitting's Bull's death, Oakley found herself caught in a dilemma: Should she trade on Sitting Bull's image, or should she let his memory rest in peace? No evidence exists that Annie protested or in any way objected to advertisements and posters billing her as "Little Sure Shot," "Watanya Cecilla," and "Sitting Bull's Adopted Daughter." She also frequently spoke with reporters about Sitting Bull, his adoption of her and the moccasins and other gifts he gave her, yet she did so with reverence and respect.

Besides Sitting Bull, the English people and press also proved instrumental in casting Annie as "the girl of the western plains." In 1887 Cody's outfit had sailed to London to help celebrate Queen Victoria's Golden Jubilee, the fiftieth anniversary of her coronation. The troupe played to forty or fifty thousand people a day and gave command performances for former prime minister William Gladstone; Edward, Prince of Wales; and, of course, the Queen herself who told Annie, "You are a very clever little girl."

Annie's tent overflowed with gifts, her tray with invitations, and the English newspapers with articles about her. One reporter described Oakley as a charming "western girl" and a "frontier girl" while the *Dramatic Review* enlarged Annie's emerging western image by claiming that, as a young woman, Annie had whipped a pistol from her purse to remove a would-be robber from the Greenville, Ohio, mail train. Yet another account lumped Annie Oakley with shooter Lillian Smith as "a couple of fine young Californianesses."

A London entrepreneur also published a small booklet about Annie in 1887. Titled the *Rifle Queen,* it ran sixty-four pages and sold for the bargain price of two cents. *Rifle Queen* described Oakley's supposed childhood in Kansas (rather than Ohio), including her trapping wolves, foiling train robbers, riding out a blizzard, shooting a bear, and defeating a desperado. Many readers took it as the truth. So did many reporters who then reported Oakley's fictional exploits as fact.

Four years later, when the Wild West returned to England in 1891, people welcomed the troupe and its star shooter by playing daily the "Wild West Waltz" dedicated to Annie Oakley, "Little Sure Shot," at the International Horticultural Exhibition. Clearly the English continued to see Annie Oakley as an authentic westerner. Fans and reviewers alike referred to her as a "frontier" girl. Some who had the opportunity to visit with her even thought she spoke with a delightful "western" accent. Thus did the Ohio farm girl become a symbolic western woman.

Americans also helped deify Annie into a western woman. On the one hand, Annie encouraged this identification by wearing western-style clothing, using western tack and guns, and eventually even twirling a lariat. In her early appearances during the mid-1880s, for example, Annie had skipped into the arena wearing a western-style blouse and calf-length, fringed skirt of a material resembling buckskin. She topped off her outfit with a western hat with an upturned brim accented by a silver star. In following years Annie routinely incorporated a western motif by wearing cowboy-style hats and dresses that, according to one reporter, "reminded one very forcibly of the wild West."

On the other hand, Annie never misrepresented her Ohio, farm origins. She always told reporters she came from Ohio and often talked about the family farm, the woods in which she first hunted, and her family still in Ohio. Even though the Census Bureau's frontier line had long since moved beyond Ohio and across the Mississippi River, and many Americans, especially Ohioans, realized that Ohio was no longer a "pioneer" state, reporters and fans alike saw Oakley as a frontier and western woman.

New Yorkers seemed especially fond of viewing Annie Oakley as a "true" westerner; from their perspective, Ohio probably seemed as far west as Colorado or Oregon. On May 13, 1894 *The Morning Journal* stated that Oakley was "a credit to the 'glorious country' beyond the Rockies from which she comes." Even reporter Amy Leslie, supposedly a close friend of Annie's, assured the public that Oakley had shot plenty of game—from coyote to buffalo—in the "high western mountains." Among the few American newspapers to counter this interpretation was the Portland *Sunday Times*, which in June 1900 emphatically declared Annie Oakley "not a western girl."

During the 1890s inventor Thomas Alva Edison also contributed to Annie's western image by capturing her in a motion picture. This film came about as a result of Buffalo Bill Cody's close connection with Thomas Alva Edison, who designed the Wild West's 600-horsepower electrical plant. Said to be the largest light producer in the world, the plant consumed two-and-a-half-tons of coal in twenty-four hours and frequently required Edison's attentive presence.

When Edison invented his battery-powered, moving picture machine he naturally turned to Cody and such performers as Oakley as subjects. In September 1894, Cody and fifteen colorfully dressed Native Americans went to Edison's "studio" in East Orange, New Jersey, to act before Edison's invention. The shoot took place in "Black Maria," a frame building covered with black tarpaper, later referred to as the first motion picture studio.

Later that fall Annie traveled to East Orange. Edison expressed particular interest in Oakley because he wanted to know if his invention could follow the flight of a bullet. Edison soon learned that his camera could reproduce Annie's shots, the smoke from her rifle, and the splintering of glass balls. He showed these early films, including those of Annie, in nickel-in-the-slot machines, called peep-show machines and later dubbed nickelodeons. Crowds lined up outside the kinetoscope parlors that had opened in New York in April 1894 to slip their coin in the slot, press their eyes against the slit, and watch a ninety-second "movie."

Thousands of people who saw Annie Oakley in a peep-show machine would remember her as one of the first "western" figures caught on film. One scene showed her repeatedly firing a Winchester rifle to demonstrate rapidity, and another pictured her shooting at composition balls tossed in the air. People who had never seen Annie in one of her many live appearances could now view her, courtesy of Edison's invention.

Thus, Annie became the first to create an image of the cowgirl. Although Oakley chose to characterize the cowgirl as a lady, her cowgirl was a strong woman with whom female viewers could identify. After all, the 1880s and 1890s witnessed a drastic change in thinking about women and their abilities, while the female workforce grew dramatically and women broke into virtually every professional field.

Even women who clung to the traditional female ethic of the Victorian era were curious about women who pushed at the bounds of that ethic. Although Annie shot and rode with unusual skill in a male-dominated arena, Oakley declared in 1888 her "highest ambition" was to be "considered a lady." Thus Annie captured first place in the public mind by personifying western women with unusual grace and charm.

Annie became a female cowboy, but her ladylike demeanor made her acceptable and appealing to all. For instance, throughout her career Annie refused to wear trousers or other masculine attire, even when riding a bicycle. Instead, she donned skirted outfits of fine broadcloth or tan gabardine that resembled buckskin but were lighter and easier to maintain. During the summer she switched to costumes of washable material, usually in blues or tans. When, by the 1890s, clothing styles relaxed among some women, especially arena "cowgirls," Annie still maintained her formal ladylike look. Although other women adopted bloomer outfits, split skirts, and even trousers, Annie wore skirts.

Oakley's feminine appearance fit in well with Cody's purposes. Buffalo Bill and his partner Nate Salsbury expressed the hope that the appearance of a woman shooter in the arena would reassure female viewers and calm their fears. Cody regularly reminded audiences that "ladies and children can attend my exhibition with Perfect Safety and Comfort." Thus, for eight of the sixteen seasons Annie spent with the Wild West between 1885 and 1902, management placed her in the number-two spot on the bill to help women relax during the frequent bursts of gunfire. In the words of publicity agent "Arizona" John Burke: "Women and children see a harmless woman there, and they do not get worried."

In the arena this "harmless woman" wielded potentially deadly weapons, yet she acted more like a charming ingenue than a sharpshooter. When she missed a shot, Annie stamped her foot on the ground and pouted in full view of the audience. When she hit her mark she gave a satisfied little kick. At the end of her act Oakley blew kisses to the crowd and gave a distinctive jump-kick as she exited.

Cody and Salsbury also capitalized on the emerging genre of cowgirls. As early as 1891 Cody's publicity used the term "cowgirls." Later, in 1898, the staff coined the term "rancheras" to describe women riders in the show. But as more women joined the Wild West shows, the graceful term rancheras lost ground to the more descriptive one, cowgirls. Even Annie Oakley's niece, Fern, came to think of her aunt as a cowgirl. She later wrote that as Annie rode into the arena, her long brown hair flying in the breeze, she "was typical of the Western cowgirl." Fern's words, of course, were inaccurate; her Aunt Annie, along with a few others, was only in the process of helping Cody *create* the typical western cowgirl.

At the same time, Annie demonstrated "female" characteristics in other ways as well. Throughout the 1890s and early 1900s, she adhered to prevailing standards of female decorum by refusing to ride a horse astride. In keeping with her ladylike beliefs, she declared riding astride a "horrid idea." Instead she performed horseback tricks from a sidesaddle, a contraption with a flat seat, upon which the rider sat sideways, and a thick, leather-covered hook, which the rider used to anchor herself by her leg to the horse's back. Using this device and wearing full, ankle-length skirts, Annie Oakley lay back against her horse while traveling at a gallop in special exhibitions. With her skirt draped gracefully over her legs she pointed her rifle in the air and almost always hit her target.

In the Wild West arena, however, Oakley refrained from shooting while riding, probably to avoid competing with Cody. She also refused to perform one of her most dramatic stunts—shooting while standing on her head, skirts buckled around her ankles—because to show one's undergarments was "not proper for a lady" in public. She would, however, retrieve a handkerchief or her hat from the ground by dangling off the side of her horse from the side-saddle or by draping herself across the horse's back and reaching down the other side. Using the sidesaddle to her advantage, she created the illusion, whatever her mount's speed and gait, that she floated on the horse's back.

Annie also projected a Victorian-style family impression. In an era of spiraling divorce rates during the 1880s and 1890s, Annie assuaged fears concerning the changing American family and supported traditional values by regularly including Frank and their current dog in her act. As her family, Frank and the dog helped establish a domestic aura and sent a message of family unity. When Annie shot a coin out of Frank's finger or an apple off the dog's head, she illustrated the trust that *should* exist between family members.

Outside the arena, Annie presented herself as a lady as well. When she first joined Cody's Wild West in 1885, Oakley had noted that she was the only Anglo woman in the troupe. She had no intention, however, of becoming a vaudeville-like, fast-living, or even a colorful, showgirl. Instead Annie explained that she never allowed anyone to curse or drink in her presence and that even the roughest roustabout should treat her with respect.

Annie's personal behavior reflected Victorian standards in another way— it assured women that, although independent and perhaps employed, they could still be domestic. Oakley furnished her tent/dressing room with a Brussels carpet, a rocking chair, and a parlor table. Between appearances Annie sat in the chair, her guns lining the walls, and did fancy embroidery. After shows Annie often entertained guests with punch, tea, cakes, and ices.

During the late 1890s and early 1900s numerous other cowgirls modeled themselves after Annie. Throughout these years most Wild West and rodeo cowgirls refused to ride astride and wore dresses or skirts and bodices, gloves, and hats with turned-up brims. Lucille Mulhall, who, like Annie, was five feet tall, also dressed and acted in a feminine manner. Mulhall even wore a white shirtwaist and a floor-length skirt to bulldog steers. And, again like Annie, Mulhall attracted numerous fans, garnered favorable reviews, and received hundreds of gifts.

For many people then, Annie constituted a nearly perfect heroine and role model. Still, she also developed other admirable attributes. For instance, Annie proved herself a crack competition shooter: "I was justly proud of my shooting," she later wrote. Well she should have been because during the early 1880s until her death in 1926 Annie Oakley triumphed in hundred of matches, routinely established new records, and opened the match-shooting circuit for other women shooters. Annie especially took satisfaction in providing an example for other women. Frank once stated that Annie counted "some of the best lady shots in the country" among her dearest friends. He added that "as she was the pioneer in that line she is always proud when they score well, for what better monument can she leave behind than lady shots and lady gun clubs."

Women flocked to Annie's matches. In 1899 one match attracted what a reporter termed "a large number of lady marksmen." Women also formed shooting clubs in Annie's honor. Yet Frank never allowed Annie's popularity on the field to mar her reputation as a lady. "No women with a shady past or doubtful reputation," he announced, "can ever enter into a contest with Annie Oakley while I am managing her, as she values her personal reputation far more than her shooting one." Frank had in mind such impostors and humbugs as dance-hall shooters and one he especially disliked who had three living husbands.

Besides match shooting, Annie gave exhibitions, often for charity, especially for orphans' homes. Her usual demanding program included shooting coins tossed in the air, firing in rapid succession at bull's-eyes, splitting a playing card held edgewise, using the blade of a table knife to see to shoot objects behind her, hitting five targets thrown up at a time, shooting off a potato held on a stick piece by piece, extinguishing cigars held in an assistant's fingers, and smashing tiny marbles into nothing but puffs of white dust.

Annie was also a skillful hunter in an age when Americans still applauded proficiency in shooting wild game. In between Wild West performances, Annie and Frank bagged prairie chickens, rabbits, ducks, grouse, and even deer. As Oakley's repute as a hunter grew so did the number of invitations to hunt increase. In 1888, for example, Annie and Frank hunted in Virginia. She brought down twice as many birds as her host and three times as many as Frank. It is little wonder that Annie Oakley was thought praiseworthy, especially by women who gloried in her adventures.

Throughout these developments, Annie remained incredibly unaffected by her accomplishments. She regularly visited her mother and sisters in Ohio, calling upon friends and neighbors as well. In addition, although frugal with herself, Annie proved generous with others. When on the road Annie sent her mother and other family members money, material for clothes, and a variety of other gifts. She also not only shot exhibitions for charity, but helped some twenty young women with schooling costs, and sent gifts to her many namesakes. When she visited Hot Springs, Arkansas, in 1896 the local society column described Annie as "an accomplished and intellectual lady ... known for her charity donations."

Thus by the early 1900s, especially because of Buffalo Bill's Wild West and its far-reaching publicity, Annie Oakley had become the western woman and cowgirl *par excellence.* From Wild West advertising, her performances in the arena, and her many imitators, Annie Oakley's feminine cowgirl was known throughout America and Europe.

In 1902, however, Annie's life changed dramatically; she left Cody's Wild West. Changes in the organization, especially the hiring of circus entrepreneur James A. Bailey, as well as Cody's drinking and domestic turmoil, encouraged Annie and Frank to consider a change in their future. After a 1901 train crash, which threw Annie out of her bed and slammed her back against a trunk, the couple formally resigned from the Wild West. Frank would travel as the northeastern representative for the Union Metallic Cartridge Company of Bridgeport, Connecticut, while Annie would pursue other enterprises.

Annie as star of The Western Girl *in 1902. (Courtesy of the Annie Oakley Foundation, Greenville, Ohio)*

Among those planned pursuits were shooting matches, charity exhibitions, and especially stage appearances. Although these performances have received far less notice than Cody's Wild West, stage vehicles were crucial in spreading Oakley's "western girl" reputation. In between seasons with Cody's Wild West, Annie and Frank had played vaudeville, especially Tony Pastor's variety show at the South Broad Street Theater in Philadelphia.

In addition to working with Cody's Wild West, Annie had played in melodramas designed to showcase her shooting talents and to capitalize on her western image. As early as 1888, Annie starred in *Deadwood Dick, or the Sunbeam of the Sierras.* Oakley portrayed a feminine heroine who wielded guns to save only those in need. Reviewers, however, were less than enthusiastic. Bombastic and unreasonable were among the terms applied to the show's plot. Other kinder critics lauded Annie's dramatic ability and predicted a brilliant future for her as an actress. But the show closed at the end of January 1889 after the show's manager decamped with the receipts.

During the fall of 1894, Annie and Frank had tried again with a play, *Miss Rora.* Publicity described *Miss Rora* as a drama illustrating "life on the frontier"; Annie played the role of a supposedly "wild, wayward Western girl."

On stage Annie wore what one viewer termed "picturesque North American attire" that was also very modest—its long skirt and sleeves exposed only Oakley's hands and face. Throughout the play Annie shot at a variety of targets, including glass balls, and rode her horse, Gypsy, even though the horse's hoofs sometimes broke through the stage floor.

But in November 1902, shortly after she left Cody's Wild West, Oakley turned to the stage full-time. She opened in her greatest hit, *The Western Girl,* written by the prolific and popular Langdon McCormick. The melodramatic plot featured Oakley shooting, riding, and defeating evil at every turn. Dressed in a long-skirted, fringed outfit, Annie shot a liquor bottle out of her drunkard father's hand and caused him to foreswear drinking; shot off the villain's hand just as he was about to plunge a dagger into the hero's back; won a prize at glass ball shooting in a barroom; and lassoed the villainess who was about to murder the heroine's blind sister.

Apparently no one questioned the authenticity of the play's representation of cowgirls. Audiences packed theaters to see Oakley as "the" western girl and often went wild with their applause, demanding as many as six curtain calls. The Wilkes-Barre *Record* understood the appeal of *The Western Girl,* saying it was a "dashing, sparkling, not to say sensational, melodrama" that remained "clean and wholesome throughout."

As she had in the Wild West arena, Annie proved herself a western girl on the stage. During one performance, for example, Annie's horse tripped, smashing Annie's head into the scenery. After a doctor in the audience hurried backstage to dress the deep gash and pull it together with adhesive, Oakley returned to the stage and, with what one viewer called "grit," continued the play, thus establishing herself as a courageous western woman in fiction and in fact.

During these post–Buffalo Bill's Wild West years Annie Oakley's reputation as a western woman also grew through her inclusion in a dime novel series. It began in 1908 with Prentiss Ingraham's *Buffalo Bill's Girl Pard; or, Dauntless Dell's Daring.* Ingraham's leading character, Dell Dauntless of the Double D Ranch, appeared on the scene dressed, much like Oakley in *The Western Girl,* in a knee-length skirt, "blouse-like waist," tan leggings, and "small russet shoes, with silver spurs at the heels." In one early scene, Dell chastises two cowboys because they have chased away the bandits who the intrepid heroine planned to lead into a nearby draw and capture. As Dell slaps at her brace of holsters she explains, much as Oakley might have, that she dislikes rowdyism: "I try to be a lady, both at home, on the ranch and when I'm abroad in the hills. But I don't think any the less of a lady because she's able to take care of herself."

Next, Dell sets out to rescue her kidnapped friend, Annie McGowan. She enlists the aid of Buffalo Bill and so impresses him with her abilities that he accepts her as his "pard." Watching her shoot and ride, Buffalo Bill asks himself, "Was there anything … in which Dell Dauntless did not excel?" Along the way, with the bowie knife swinging from her belt, Dell rescues a young Indian man named Little Cayuse. Cayuse rather rudely tells Dell that "squaws" are supposed to boil water, make fires, and sew beads. After Dell replies "I'm different from the ordinary run of squaws," Little Cayuse also accepts Dell as his "pard."

In subsequent chapters Dell shoots a rifle out of a villain's hand, carries important dispatches through armed Apaches, and breaks out of Fort Grant. Dell has indeed proven herself to Buffalo Bill, "the king of the scouts," who concludes that Dell ranks "Class A among Western girls."

But during the following year, 1911, when Oakley returned briefly to the wild-west arena by joining Vernon Seavers's Young Buffalo Show, she refused to follow this pattern. Although many Americans esteemed dime-novel heroines, Annie rejected such behavior. Instead, between 1911 and 1913 Annie continued to project the impression that had worked so well for her in the past; she wore her usual conservative clothing and acted like a Victorian lady. She drew audiences and received favorable reviews despite, or perhaps because of, the dress and actions of her competitors.

For two years Annie shot, rode, and acted her way into the hearts of Americans with Vernon Seavers's Young Buffalo Show. She not only wore her customary long-skirted, fringed outfits, but she stunned audiences by shooting down glass balls and smashing clay pigeons from a variety of positions and with a range of weapons. As gracious as ever, Annie and Frank claimed they were having an "enjoyable" time and thought the Young Buffalo Show a marvelous depiction of the Old West.

In 1913, however, Annie decided to leave what she called "the show business" for good. She gave a special farewell performance in Darke County that, along with most people in Darke County, her mother and sisters attended. Characteristically Annie provided the residents of the Darke County Children's Home with free tickets. Then, on October 4, 1913, Annie made her last arena appearance in Marion, Illinois. In retirement she and Frank intended to spend their leisure years in Cambridge, Maryland, where they would build a home, and there pass their days hunting and shooting.

As it developed, during the 1910s and early 1920s Annie and Frank divided their retirement time between their Cambridge home and resorts in Leesburg, Florida, and Pinehurst, North Carolina. In all three locales they continued to hunt, shoot, and enjoy a rich social life. Annie also gave

Principals of the Wild West troupe in London in 1887. Oakley on lower right; Cody on lower left. (Courtesy of the Annie Oakley Foundation, Greenville, Ohio)

shooting lessons, initiated women into the joys of hiking and camping, and gave charity exhibitions. Even after an automobile accident in Leesburg in November 1922 that resulted in Annie's wearing a steel brace on her leg, she soon returned to shooting and hunting.

When sixty-six-year-old Annie died (probably of injuries sustained during her recent accident) in her sleep in Ohio on November 3, 1926, thousands mourned. The *Springfield Republican* published an epitaph Annie would have especially liked; it described her as a "quiet, modest little figure" of a woman. Annie's friend Will Rogers wrote that Annie was a "marvelous" woman who taught him that, "It's what you are and not what you are in, that makes you."

Frank, seventy-six, followed Annie on November 21, 1926. Annie's niece Fern said Frank died of internal injuries he had sustained during the 1922 automobile accident and because "his heart was broken" from the loss of Annie, but his death certificate listed senility as the cause of his death.

On Thanksgiving Day 1926, Annie and Frank were buried in the family plot at the Brock cemetery near Greenville, Ohio. According to legend the container holding Annie's ashes lies in Frank's casket. Some family members, however, believe Annie and Frank lie in separate graves. These are marked with handsome red granite stones, one proclaiming "Annie Oakley, At Rest," the other "Frank E. Butler, At Rest."

Annie Oakley's life quickly became the stuff of legend and fantasy. From Barbara Stanwyck's 1935 film *Annie Oakley* to endless renditions of *Annie Get Your Gun,* which began with Ethel Merman in 1946, Annie's fame continues, although often in a misrepresented form. As a result of such myth-making, it is difficult to assess fully Oakley's contributions to the American West and its women.

Clearly, however, Annie Oakley played a major role in the world's great love affair with the American West. For example, among the numerous fan letters that Annie received before her death many identified her with the West. A California man who described himself as "an old Westerner" wrote Annie that he first went west in 1881. Now he too, he wrote, neared "the end of the trail." And a California woman, born in a covered wagon in 1851 during her family's way west, felt akin to Annie because they had both shared in "the era of the Wild West."

Other Americans remembered Annie as a model western women. Even after Oakley left the arena in 1913 her portrayal of the cowgirl as a lady continued to appeal to a number of other performers who emulated her style. During the 1910s, Prairie Lillie Allen excelled at riding broncs yet maintained a girl-like image. Some, like young Vera McGinnis, rode sidesaddle while others, such as trick-rider Tad Lucas, like Annie, made all her own costumes, feminine in style and excellent in quality. And Pearl Mason, who became the World Champion Bronc Rider in 1918, claimed that her behavior was always that of a "lady."

Annie also made it acceptable for women to ride, shoot, and hunt. Although a few people criticized Annie for performing and shooting in public, most thought of her as a ladylike monarch. In 1887, for example, a reporter had termed Oakley the "queen of the female wing-shots," whereas an 1891 letter labeled her the "Queen of the Lady Shooters." In addition, commentators repeatedly linked Oakley's skill at customary male pursuits with her ladyhood. After an 1887 match, which Annie lost, J.J. Walsh, editor of London's *Field* magazine, declared: "Miss Oakley, I certainly expected to find you a better shot than you are, but not to find you so much of a lady."

Ultimately, however, perhaps Annie's effect on perceptions of the West, and of western women, can best be seen through the location of her present-day memorials. Logically enough, an active Annie Oakley Foundation is based in Greenville, Ohio, while a bronze statue graces the city square, and Greenville's Garst Museum includes an Annie Oakley room. In Nutley, New Jersey, and Cambridge, Maryland, historical societies and other groups also remember Annie. But the major exhibits of Oakley's rifles and shotguns, clothing, and other memorabilia are in the West—one at the Buffalo Bill

Historical Center in Cody, Wyoming; another at the Autry Museum of Western Heritage in Los Angeles, California; and a lesser one at the Cowboy Hall of Fame in Oklahoma City.

The adults and children who crowd around Annie Oakley exhibits indicate that Oakley continues to have widespread appeal. She still personifies an appealing and attractive West, one that Americans are proud to claim as an important part of their collective past. For those Americans fascinated with the optimistic side of the American West, Oakley provides an ideal symbol. Although Annie became a westerner by affinity rather than by birth, she achieved an enduring role as a heroine of the Old Wild West.

Sources and Further Reading

This essay draws heavily from my earlier works on Annie Oakley, especially on the interpretive biography, *The Life and Legacy of Annie Oakley* (Norman: University of Oklahoma Press, 1994), and on "Annie Oakley: Creating the Cowgirl," *Montana: The Magazine of Western History* 45 (summer 1995):32–47.

An exceptionally accurate biography of Oakley is Shirl Kaspar's *Annie Oakley* (Norman: University of Oklahoma Press, 1992). Kaspar, a practicing journalist, makes extensive use of the Oakley scrapbooks and presents an outstanding narrative biography.

Other earlier biographers offer a wide variety of interpretations—and factual information—regarding Annie Oakley's life and career. Oakley's first biographer, Courtney Ryley Cooper, *Annie Oakley: Woman at Arms* (New York: Duffield, 1927), combines facts and legend to produce a picture of an achieving, successful woman. Oakley's niece, Annie Fern Campbell Swartwout, *Missie: An Historical Biography of Annie Oakley* (Blanchester, OH: Brown Publishing Company, 1947), incorporates many legends into her account and does best when giving her personal recollections of Annie and Frank. Walter Havighurst, *Annie Oakley of the Wild West* (New York: Macmillan, 1954), gives a fictionalized, highly readable account that is generally accurate. Edmund Collier, *The Story of Annie Oakley* (New York: Grosset and Dunlap, 1956), provides young readers with a fictionalized account that lionizes Oakley as a child of the frontier. Shannon Garst, *Annie Oakley* (New York: Julian Messner, 1958); Jan Gleiter and Kathleen Thompson, *Annie Oakley: Great Tales* (Nashville, TN: Ideals Publishing Company, 1985); and Charles P. Graves, *Annie Oakley: The Shooting Star* (Champaign, IL: Garrard, 1961), offer fictionalized accounts for young readers that characterize Oakley as a young woman with true grit. Clifford Lindsey Alderman, *Annie Oakley and the World of Her Time* (New York: Macmillan, Inc, 1979), analyzes Oakley in the context of her own era.

More thoroughly researched statements can be found in Isabelle S. Sayers, *The Rifle Queen—Annie Oakley* (Ostrander, OH: n.p., 1973), and *Annie Oakley and Buffalo Bill's Wild West* (New York: Dover Publications, 1981).

More recently, Robert Quakenbush, *Who's That Girl With the Gun? A Story of Annie Oakley* (New York: Prentice Hall Books for Young Readers, 1987), also ties Oakley to the frontier, whereas Ellen Levine, *Ready, Aim, Fire! The Real Adventures of Annie Oakley* (New York: Scholastic, 1989), interprets Oakley as a courageous, achieving woman, an admirable role model for girls of the late twentieth century.

In addition, a variety of popular articles characterize Oakley in differing ways. These include "Annie Oakley" in Stewart H. Holbrook, *Little Annie Oakley and Other Rugged People* (New York: Macmillan, 1948), 1–7; Louise Cheney, "Annie Oakley, Little Miss Sureshot," *Real West* 10 (November 1967):53–57; Mark Taylor, "Annie Oakley: A Shooting Legend," *American Rifleman* 131 (December 1983):44–46, 68–69; Patricia Croft, "Highlights of Annie Oakley," *Winchester Repeater* 1 (fall 1984):37–38; R. Douglas Hurt, "Annie Oakley: An Enduring Western Legend," *True West* 36 (July 1989):14–19; and *Cobblestone Magazine,* special issue on "Annie Oakley and the Wild West," 12 (January 1991). Also, Oakley's years in North Carolina are discussed in Claude R. Flory, "Annie Oakley in the South," *North Carolina Historical Review* 43 (1966): 333–43.

Unfortunately, primary sources are limited. Because Annie Oakley had little sense of her own historical significance, she kept few of her letters and personal documents. As a result, the two best sources for Annie Oakley's words and memories are Annie Oakley, "Autobiography," undated, copy in possession of the author, and Annie Oakley, *Powders I Have Used* (Wilmington, DE: DuPont Powder Company, 1914). In addition, Annie and Frank compiled invaluable scrapbooks of newspaper clippings. The originals are held by the Buffalo Bill Historical Society in Cody, Wyoming, along with documents, ephemera, vertical files, and artifacts. Copies of the scrapbooks are located in the Western History Collection of the Public Library in Denver, Colorado.

Several of Oakley's letters as well as Frank Butler's essay, "The Life of Dave," Bess Lindsey Walcholz's sketch, "Annie Oakley," 1909, and Hazel Moses Robertson's memoir, "Moses Memories," 1989, are held by the Annie Oakley Foundation in Greenville, Ohio (also copies in the author's possession). Other Oakley letters are in the Oakley Collection at the Nutley Historical Society in Nutley, New Jersey.

Irene Patterson Black (a niece), Beatrice Blakeley Hunt (a grand-niece), and Lela Border Hollinger (a neighbor) also retained many useful and interesting memories of Annie and shared them in interviews with the author. Notes from interviews, all conducted in January 1993, are held by the author.

For those who wish to go beyond Oakley herself, an overview of mid- and late-nineteenth-century show business and shooting can be found in Douglas Gilbert, *American Vaudeville: Its Life and Times* (New York: Whittlesey House, 1940); John and Alice Durant, *Pictorial History of the American Circus* (New York: A. S. Barnes, 1957); Jack Burton, *In Memoriam—Oldtime Show Biz* (New York: Vantage Press, 1965); Robert C. Toll, *On With the Show: The First Century of Show Business in America* (New York: Oxford University Press, 1976); Jaroslav Lugs, *A History of Shooting* (Felthma, Middlesex, England: Spring Books, 1968); and Joseph Durso, *Madison Square Garden: 100 Years of History* (New York: Simon & Schuster, 1979). Especially useful is the Amon Carter Museum and Don Russell, *The Wild West or, A History of the Wild West Shows* (Fort Worth, TX: Amon Carter Museum of Western Art, 1970).

Early rodeos and cowgirls are analyzed in Teresa Jordan, *Cowgirls: Women of the American West* (Garden City, NY: Anchor, 1982); Kristine Fredriksson, *American Rodeo: From Buffalo Bill to Big Business* (College Station: Texas A&M University Press, 1985); Joyce Gibson Roach, *The Cowgirls,* 2d ed. (Denton: University of North Texas Press, 1990); and Sarah Wood-Clark, *Beautiful Daring Western Girls: Women of the Wild West Shows,* 2d ed. (Cody, WY: Buffalo Bill Historical Center, 1991). Also useful is Jack Rennert, *One Hundred Posters of Buffalo Bill's Wild West Show* (New York: Darien House, 1976).

Books and articles on Buffalo Bill Cody and his Wild West abound. Among them are M. B. Bailey, ed., *Buffalo Bill's Wild West Route Book* (Buffalo, NY: The Courier Company, 1896); Richard J. Walsh, *The Making of Buffalo Bill: A Study in Heroics* (Indianapolis, IN: Bobbs-Merrill Co., 1928); Adolph Regli, *The Real Book About Buffalo Bill* (Garden City, NY: Franklin Watts, 1952); Henry Blackman Sell and Victor Weybright, *Buffalo Bill and The Wild West* (New York: Oxford University Press, 1955); Don Russell, *The Lives and Legends of Buffalo Bill* (Norman: University of Oklahoma Press, 1960); Louis Pfaller, "Enemies in '76, Friends in '85—Sitting Bull and Buffalo Bill," *Prologue: Journal of the National Archives* 1 (1969):16–31; Joseph J. Arpad, *Buffalo Bill's Wild West* (Palmer Lake, CO: Fetter Press, 1971); William E. Deahl, Jr., "A History of Buffalo Bill's Wild West Show, 1883–1913" (Ph.D. diss., Southern Illinois University, 1974), and "Buffalo Bill's Wild West Show, 1885," *Annals of Wyoming* 47 (fall 1975):139–51; Nellie Snyder Yost, *Buffalo Bill: His Family, Friends, Fame, Failures, and Fortunes* (Chicago: Swallow Press, 1979); Sarah J. Blackstone, *Buckskins, Bullets, and Business: A History of Buffalo Bill's Wild West* (Westport, CT: Greenwood Press, 1986); and Joseph G. Rosa and Robin May, *Buffalo Bill and His Wild West* (Lawrence: University Press of Kansas, 1989). For interpretations of Cody's image, see Wayne M. Sarf, *God Bless You, Buffalo Bill: A Layman's Guide to History and the Western Film* (Rutherford, NJ: Fairleigh Dickinson University Press, 1983).

Also worth perusing are William F. Cody, *Buffalo Bill's Life Story: An Autobiography* (New York: Rinehart & Co., 1920), and Stella Adelyn Foote, ed., *Letters from Buffalo Bill* (El Segundo, CA: Upton & Sons, 1990).

⁊ 6 ⁊

Mary Ellen Pleasant:
Entrepreneur and Civil Rights
Activist in the Far West

QUINTARD TAYLOR

⁊ WEALTHY ENTREPRENEUR, ABOLITIONIST, civil rights activist, confidante of the rich, powerful advocate for the weak and disfranchised—Mary Ellen Pleasant remains one of the most enigmatic figures of the nineteenth-century American West. For much of the twentieth century her remarkable life has been the focus of speculation by journalists, novelists, and folklorists. She appears anecdotally in numerous collections of notorious women in the West or in chronicles of the halcyon days of San Francisco's Barbary Coast. In almost every instance, Pleasant is portrayed as a sexually manipulative "madam" or a voodoo queen, more feared than loved because of the scandal she could produce at will. Perhaps biographer Sam Davis exaggerated when he wrote in 1902 that Pleasant knew, "the history of [San Francisco's] people better than any other living person. In her breast are locked the secrets of hundreds of leading families." Yet his comments reflected the real and imagined fears of many prominent people in the city.

Few professional historians, however, have examined Mary Ellen Pleasant's life. Their reluctance to reconstruct her saga is rooted in the difficulty of separating fact from fiction, history from myth. Through an autobiography as well as numerous interviews with the San Francisco press during the last years of her life, Pleasant continually attempted to refashion her public image. In a 1901 interview with San Francisco *Call* reporter Isabel Fraser, Pleasant allowed that, "some folks say that words were meant to reveal thought. That ain't so. Words were meant to conceal thought." Pleasant's comments were directed against her critics who had written of her penchant for the

MARY ELLEN ("MAMMY") PLEASANT AT 87 YEARS OF AGE
The first and only photograph taken since she was 13 years old

Mary Ellen Pleasant at eighty-seven years of age. This photograph appeared in The Pandex, *a magazine that was published briefly in San Francisco. (Courtesy of The Bancroft Library, Berkeley, California)*

"black arts." But Pleasant herself, through her own writing and public statements, generated a contradictory persona that contributed to the confusion regarding her life. As a consequence of her desire to "reinvent" herself in the West, huge questions remain unanswered, including her actual surname, her birthplace, her occupation, and the extent of her wealth.

But historians' reluctance to embrace Pleasant's story also stems from the difficulty of placing her in categories familiar to those who write about race, gender, or ninteenth-century African American women. By the 1870s Pleasant had accumulated mining stocks and valuable urban real estate, speculated on gold and silver prices, and derived a regular income from investments in one of the most successful accounting firms in San Francisco—hardly the economic experience of the vast majority of nineteenth-century African American women.

Pleasant's experience differed sharply in one additional area. During her half century in San Francisco from 1852 until her death in 1904, her personal history was intrically interwoven with the fortunes and prospects of San Francisco's rich and powerful white families, instead of with the city's struggling African American community. The wealthy Thomas Bell family resided in the mansion Pleasant claimed as her own for two decades. In 1884 she financed legal proceedings in *Sharon v. Sharon*, a celebrated divorce case that pitted former U.S. Senator William Sharon against his estranged wife Sarah Hill Sharon for control of a twenty-million-dollar fortune.

Pleasant's success flowed from three attributes almost unheard of among black women. First, she had the ability to advise and, on occasion, the courage to challenge the most powerful members of San Francisco's economic elite. She successfully cultivated a devoted following of young marriageable white women who trusted their futures to her ability to match them with wealthy husbands. But Pleasant also profited handsomely from "insider information" gleaned from her contacts with the city's most successful white males. That she effectively managed these separate objectives while ostensibly working as a "servant" illustrates her remarkable capacity to cross boundaries of race, gender, and class, which supposedly fixed a permanent place for black women in America. But the very qualities that made her exceptional for the era also generated fear, suspicion, and anger among her contemporaries and eventually cost her the fortune she had assiduously accumulated over five decades.

Like many nineteenth-century western women, Mary Ellen Pleasant's saga began outside the region. Pleasant claimed in her 1902 autobiography that she was born on August 19, 1814 in Philadelphia and that her father, Louis Alexander Williams, was a native of Hawaii. Her mother, of whom she recalled very little, was a "full-blooded Louisiana negress." But she also claimed Cincinnati, Ohio, as her birthplace whereas some of her African American contemporaries in San Francisco recalled her saying she was born on a plantation near Augusta, Georgia. It seems clear from these various accounts that Pleasant camouflaged her origins for unknown reasons. It was entirely possible that if Pleasant was in fact a fugitive slave, the subterfuge was necessary. Her work as an abolitionist would have reinforced the need for secrecy. But unlike ex-slaves who after 1865 eagerly recalled their actual histories, Pleasant continued to advance conflicting stories about her birthplace long after they were no longer necessary to protect her from slavecatchers.

Mary Ellen Williams's childhood is more easily reconstructed. From the age of six, most of her formative years were spent on Nantucket Island with a Quaker family named Hussey. It was in the shop of this family that she learned business practices from "Grandma Hussey." "Mrs. Hussey ... sold everything from fish hooks to a ton of coal ... " recalled Pleasant. "I was finally placed in the store as a clerk, and I could make change and talk to a dozen people all at once and never make a mistake, and I could remember all the accounts and at the end of the day [Mrs. Hussey] could put them down, and they would always be right as I remembered them."

Mary Ellen's business acumen included a sharp wit that attracted customers.

> I was a girl full of smartness and quick at coming back at people when they
> tried to have a little fun [with] me. I was a good-looking girl, too, and people
> used to come in to hear what I had to say .... All of this brought customers to
> the shop, and I would ... get people to buy things of me. I was always on the
> watch, and few people ever got by that shop without buying something of me.

Nonetheless Williams felt compromised by her lack of formal education
even though Thomas Gardner, the Hussey grandson, taught her to read and
write. In her 1902 autobiography she wrote, "I often wonder what I would
have been with an education. I envy, as I always did, children who can write
a good hand and spell correctly, and [I] blame the Husseys for not giving me
an education." Like many nineteenth-century Americans, however, Pleasant
seized opportunities to develop her writing and reading skills and eventually
had no problem expressing herself in oral or written form. "I have always
noticed that when I have anything to say people listen. They never go to
sleep on me."

Williams left Nantucket in her early twenties and moved to Boston where
she soon met her first husband, James W. Smith. Despite his claim to be
"Cuban," Smith was in fact a successful mulatto foreman and contractor in
the Boston area. Smith was also an abolitionist who introduced his new wife
to New England antislavery activity. When he died in 1844, Smith left Pleasant $15,000—the basis for her subsequent investment activity in California
and her future fortune.

Mary Ellen Smith was soon attracted to another mulatto, Virginia-born
John James Pleasant, a waiter and cook in New Bedford, Massachusetts, in
the late 1840s. Pleasant's most recent biographer, Lynn Hudson, believes that
Smith and Pleasant may have been drawn together by their mutual interest
in abolitionism. They married in 1847 and lived together intermittently
for the next thirty years. Both John's work as a cook on various ships and,
through the early 1860s, their activities as abolitionists prevented the couple's
residing together permanently. Their only child, Elizabeth, was born in Boston in 1851.

In 1852 Mary Ellen Pleasant arrived in San Francisco, the city that would
be her home for most of the next five decades. The decision to move west for
her, as for thousands of other African Americans, was primarily economic.
Most free African Americans who entered the state in the Gold Rush era
pursued the promise of quick wealth in the gold fields or in the rapidly
growing cities of San Francisco and Sacramento. But many black migrants,

including Pleasant, subscribed to the quintessentially American belief that anyone, including African Americans, could improve one's life by migrating west. A determined minority of blacks faced the grueling physical hardships of overland or transoceanic travel to California because they believed their lives would be better in the Far West.

Ninety percent of the nation's blacks were slaves and thus could not freely choose to migrate to California (or anywhere else). Moreover the costs associated with the migration ensured that only free African Americans with considerable means, with access to credit, or with prosperous whites accompanying them, would undertake the arduous journey. Four thousand African Americans joined nearly four hundred thousand people from the United States and numerous other nations in emigrating to California in the 1850s.

Surviving accounts reveal the dogged determination of some African Americans to reach the Golden State. Margaret Frink, for example, described a black female emigrant she encountered in 1850 near the Humboldt Sink, the desert just east of the Sierra Nevadas. Frink recalled the woman was alone "tramping along through the heat and dust, carrying a cast iron bake stove on her head with her provisions and a blanket piled on top—all she possessed in the world—bravely pushing on for California."

For those who reached California, the effort seemed well worth the dangers. The New Bedford (Massachusetts) *Mercury* in September 1848 described an encounter between a black man walking near the San Francisco docks and a white gold-seeker who had just disembarked from a ship. When the newcomer called on the black man to carry his luggage, the African American responded with an indignant glance and then walked away. After having walked a few steps he turned toward the newcomer, drew a small bag from his bosom and said, "Do you think I'll lug trunks when I can get that much in one day?" The sack of gold dust was estimated by the newcomer to be worth over one hundred dollars.

Such reports of equal opportunity in the gold fields, at a time when economic restrictions were increasing daily in other free states, ensured that some fortunate African Americans would continue to seek out California. Peter Brown, a gold miner wrote in 1851 to his wife in St. Genevieve City, Missouri, "I am now mining about 25 miles from Sacramento City and doing well. I have been working for myself for the past two months ... and have cleared three hundred dollars. California is the best country in the world to make money. It is also the best place for black folks on the globe. All a man has to do is to work, and he will make money."

Two years before Pleasant arrived in California the black population in the state stood at 962 with only 9 percent of them women. That population would quadruple in the next decade to 4,086 inhabitants with black women comprising 31 percent of the total population. Although the Mother Lode was the destination of the majority of all emigrants, about half of California's African Americans in the early 1850s migrated to the state's cities. By 1860 San Francisco had 1,176 blacks, a 243 percent increase from the 484 who resided there in 1852. On the eve of the Civil War, San Francisco's African Americans comprised 2 percent of the city's total population but 29 percent of the state's African American inhabitants.

Pleasant entered San Francisco at a time when the boundaries of race and capitalism were not yet fixed. Thus, she was able to seize a series of economic opportunities in the growing bayshore metropolis. Antebellum, urban California blacks pursued menial occupations similar to those available in eastern cities, but in the gold-enriched economy these jobs paid significantly higher wages. Black stewards on river steamers, for example, earned $150 per month during the 1850s. In overwhelmingly male San Francisco, cooks stood at the top of this employment hierarchy and commanded impressive salaries. When a ship captain asked a black San Francisco cook to join his crew, extending what he considered a lucrative offer of $10 a day, the black man laughed and made the captain a counteroffer of a job in his restaurant as a cook for $20 a day. One of San Francisco's earliest restaurants, the Battery House, generated in the early 1850s an income of $100 a day, primarily on the reputation of its two African American cooks.

Pleasant, one of the first black women in the city in 1852, capitalized on the local shortage of cooks and possibly the ethnic stereotyping that suggested African American women were particularly skilled in culinary arts. She was, according to one account, "besieged by a crowd of men, all anxious to employ her, before she had so much as left the wharf at which her ship had docked." Pleasant auctioned off her services with the stipulation that she "should do no washing, not even dishwashing," ultimately selecting an employer who promised $500 a month. Thus, her first job in the Far West netted Pleasant an income more than twice as much as any other San Franciscan cook and equal that of many gold miners.

Given her business background, her small inheritance of $15,000 from her first husband, and extensive contacts with New England businessmen–abolitionists (some of whom had relocated in California), Pleasant began looking for investment opportunities to augment her already lucrative income as a cook. Within a year of her arrival, Pleasant invested her $15,000 inheritance in the accounting firm of West and Harper, which guaranteed her a 10 percent annual return. She also speculated in precious metals, exchanging gold and silver at fluctuating prices through agents at the Wells

Fargo Bank. Finally, recognizing the demand for laundry services in the city, Pleasant, by 1855, established three laundries, all of which employed recently arrived African Americans. Thus Pleasant combined her obligation to help fellow blacks with a profitable business venture. Three years after relocating in San Francisco, Mary Ellen Pleasant was already one of the most successful businesswomen in the Far West.

Pleasant's entrepreneurial achievements came, however, against a growing background of restrictions on the liberties of all people of color. As she and other recent African American arrivals in California would soon note, California's eastern- and southern-born political leadership seemed determined to recreate in the Far West the racially based political and economic restrictions common in their former states. Successive California legislatures in the 1850s devised what one historian has called "an appallingly extensive body of discriminatory laws" that denied voting rights, prohibited African American court testimony, and banned homesteading, jury service, and marriage with whites.

Despite their small numbers, California's African Americans challenged these restrictions. The state's 4,000 African Americans in 1860 comprised 75 percent of the free black population west of Missouri. Moreover, with newcomers from both north and south of the Mason-Dixon line as well as Afro-Latin Americans from Mexico, Peru, and Jamaica, California's black population was the most diverse population in North America. Only in antebellum California could free-born women and men from northern states such as Massachusetts, New York, Illinois, and Ohio rub shoulders with slaves from Georgia, Alabama, Tennessee, and Texas. That mix, particularly with its leadership drawn disproportionately from New England abolitionist circles, produced a community willing and capable of protecting its interests.

The community's major interest was to end California slavery. In 1849 California adopted an antislavery constitution and, less than one year later, was admitted to the Union as a free state. Yet California officials were unable or unwilling to challenge slaveholders who continued to bring their bond servants to the state until the outbreak of the Civil War. By 1852 an estimated 300 slaves worked in the gold fields and an undetermined but sizeable number were house servants in California cities, giving the state the largest number of bond servants west of Texas.

Slaveholders in California, however, did not anticipate the role that a dedicated group of black and white abolitionists would play in undermining the institution. The free African American community quickly united in its opposition to local slavery. The close proximity of slaves and abolitionists exposed the bond servant to direct contact with his champions—a position virtually impossible in the eastern United States—and heightened the sense of urgency for antislavery activists who, on a daily basis, witnessed the horrors of the servile institution. Black abolitionist Peter Lester, a former member of the Pennsylvania Anti-Slavery Society, invited slaves into his San Francisco home to lecture them on their rights. "When they left," he declared, "we had them strong in the spirit of freedom. They were leaving [slavery] every day." The active role of blacks in challenging slavery prompted one contemporary German observer to remark, "The wealthy California Negroes … exhibit a great deal of energy and intelligence in saving their brethren."

With over a decade of antislavery work in New England, Pleasant's abolitionist credentials were beyond dispute when she arrived in San Francisco. Her antislavery activity between 1852 and 1860 added immeasurably to her stature among local abolitionists. Pleasant assisted accountant William West, an abolitionist and business associate, in establishing a boardinghouse that was actually a refuge for runaway slaves. In the mid-1850s Pleasant and livery stable owner George Washington Dennis hid a fugitive slave named George until the California Fugitive Slave Act expired in 1855. Pleasant also financed various legal challenges to slavery, including, most notably, the successful effort to free eighteen-year-old fugitive slave Archy Lee in 1858.

Unsatisfied with her antislavery efforts in California, Pleasant and her husband, John, left San Francisco in 1858 for Chatham, Canada West (Ontario), a gathering point for abolitionists who supported John Brown. In May 1858, Brown convened what he called a "provisional constitutional convention" while secretly developing his plan to raid the arsenal at Harper's Ferry to initiate the wholesale liberation of millions of southern slaves. For the only time in their lives the Pleasants resided in an area that was home to thousands of fugitive slaves and free black refugees from the United States. This was also the longest time they lived together as husband and wife. Mary Ellen and James Pleasant joined the Chatham Vigilance Committee whose members included Mary Ann Shadd, Martin R. Delany, and Osborne Anderson, one of the five black members of Brown's ill-fated raiding party. The Pleasants also participated in the upstate New York rescue of fugitive slave Sylvanus Demerest.

Decades later Mary Ellen Pleasant would claim that she financed John Brown's raid on the arsenal at Harper's Ferry in 1859 and, moreover, that she traveled through Virginia ahead of Brown, warning black slaves about their impending liberation. There is no evidence to substantiate those claims. Nonetheless, Pleasant invested enormous personal significance in her trip to the East "to meet John Brown." Forty-two years after the episode she crafted an image as a background participant in the dramatic event that plunged the United States into civil war and ultimately liberated four million black slaves. Beginning in 1901 she related in a number of interviews her role in the Harper's Ferry raid and requested that the inscription on her tombstone read, "She was a friend of John Brown."

In 1860 Mary Ellen Pleasant returned to San Francisco to resume her entrepreneurial activities and to participate in the local civil rights campaign. She and other black political activists soon had reasons to be optimistic that the political disabilities affecting their community would soon end. In 1862 Leland Stanford became California's first Republican governor. Whatever their limitations and compromises on race, the state's Republicans were far more sympathetic to black civil rights than previous California Democratic administrations. The following year the Republican-dominated legislature removed or weakened discriminatory barriers in education and public transportation. Sensing growing popular support, San Francisco area blacks in 1862 created the Franchise League, the first avowedly political organization of African Americans in the West. The league agitated for the end of testimony restrictions, which came one year later when in 1863 the mostly Republican legislature repealed the antiblack provision of the testimony statute.

The 1860s marked the apex of Mary Ellen Pleasant's "civil rights phase." Her involvement in local civil rights and black community development efforts began a decade earlier with her support of *Mirror of the Times,* which, in 1856, became the first African American newspaper west of St. Louis. In 1862 Pleasant was a founding member of the Franchise League, and by the mid-1860s she supported efforts to build black churches and establish a school for African American children after they were excluded from the city's public school classrooms. But her legal challenges to streetcar exclusion in the late 1860s proved the most enduring legacy of Pleasant's civil rights activities.

Nineteenth-century African American women frequently led streetcar exclusion protests. Working-class black urban women often depended upon public transportation to deliver them to employment sites. Middle-class black women who took streetcars to shop or attend social events, however, were more frequently at the center of exclusion protests. Given the gender and class conventions of the era, their exclusion by working-class, white male streetcar drivers or conductors was seen as a greater affront to African American community sensibilities than a similar rebuff of working-class black women or of any black men. In March 1863, the *Pacific Appeal,* San Francisco's second African American newspaper, described how "two of our most respectable females were denied seats in one of the city railway cars." The newspaper declared that middle-class black women should not be insulted by "coarse threats of ejectment [sic]." Two months later the *Appeal* reprinted the decision of a New York judge in an 1855 exclusion case under the heading "The Right of Colored Persons to Ride in the Railway Cars." "The law justifies no person," concluded the newspaper, "in committing an assault upon another, especially a defenceless [sic] female."

The first lawsuit against streetcar exclusion in San Francisco came in April 1863. Charlotte Brown, daughter of local entrepreneur James Brown, was ejected from a streetcar operated by the Omnibus Company. Brown filed suit in county court for $200 in damages. In June the case came before Judge Maurice C. Blake who reminded the jury that California law prohibited such discrimination. Still, the jury awarded Brown only $25 and court costs. Three days after the trial Brown was again ejected from an Omnibus streetcar, and she filed suit in Twelfth District Court for $3,000 in damages. Her second suit ended on January 17, 1865, with a jury awarding her $500 in damages.

Brown's victory did not permanently end streetcar exclusion. Consequently in 1866, fifty-two-year-old Mary Ellen Pleasant entered what the San Francisco press called "the war between the Negroes and the Railroad Company" when she became the most prominent litigant against exclusionary streetcar companies. Carriage-owning Pleasant had long ceased taking streetcars. Nonetheless she decided to utilize the public transportation system to focus attention on the continuing exclusion of black riders. She at first sued the Omnibus Railroad Company for removing her from one of it cars. Dramatically, in October 1866 Pleasant appeared in police court and withdrew her suit against the company. In a front page article in the city's largest newspaper, the *Alta California*, Pleasant revealed that agents of the company had informed her "that negroes would hereafter be allowed to ride on the car" regardless of its potential impact on the company's business.

On the same day that Pleasant dropped charges against the Omnibus Company, she testified against the North Beach & Mission Railroad Company in a separate lawsuit for excluding her from one of its cars. This case proceeded far differently from the Omnibus Company incident. The North Beach & Mission Company (NBMRR) steadfastly refused to change its policy and appeared eager to argue its position in court.

Pleasant's lawsuit charged that the driver refused to stop for her even though there was room on the car and she had a ticket. "I hailed the driver of the car—his name is James Doyle—and he looked at me, and instead of stopping, he passed on." As the car moved by, Pleasant signaled the conductor who stood at the back of the street car. She reported him as saying, "We don't take colored people in the cars."

Pleasant won her case before a jury that determined she was "willfully and purposely deprived by the defendant of the exercise of a plain legal right ..." and awarded $500 in punitive damages. The railroad appealed the case to the California Supreme Court, which ruled in 1868 that the damages were excessive since "there was no proof of ... malice, or ill will, or wanton or violent conduct on the part of the [railroad]."

Pleasant gambled that her notoriety among the city's elite families—as evident in the front page article about her in the *Alta California*—would prompt railroad officials to end their exclusionary policies. Certainly her victory in the lower court, along with similar victories for Charlotte Brown and Emma J. Turner (whose $750 award in 1867 was also overturned by the California Supreme Court) indicated considerable support for the principle of equal access to public transportation. But complete relief for Pleasant and other African Americans would not come until 1893 when the California legislature passed a statute prohibiting racial discrimination in public accommodations and conveyances.

The California Supreme Court decision in *Pleasants [sic] v. North Beach & Mission Railroad* marked the last instance Mary Ellen Pleasant was publicly involved in civil rights activity of significance to the African American community. After 1868 her name appeared far less in San Francisco's African American newspapers, the *Pacific Appeal* and the *Elevator,* and she was no longer associated with philanthropy specifically directed toward local black organizations or institutions. Pleasant concentrated on her business activities, which propelled her into the world of powerful white men.

Pleasant left no indication of the reasons for her shifting focus. She may have become disillusioned following the California Supreme Court's 1868 reversal of her lower court lawsuit victory. Perhaps other black activists in the city objected to her role or challenged her leadership of San Francisco's African American community. At the age of fifty-four, Pleasant may have decided that three decades of activism in the cause of abolitionism and black civil rights was sufficient and that younger leadership should emerge to continue the campaign. Since we know little of her thinking on this subject, Pleasant may not have consciously decided to abandon civil rights activism. Instead, her business activities and associations mainly with white males, her growing wealth, her residence in a mansion in the city as well as a summer cottage south of town, and her eventual ownership of a Napa Valley ranch, simply pulled her out of the orbit of most African Americans and their concerns.

It is misleading to suggest that Pleasant "returned" to entrepreneurship after 1868. Even during the height of her civil rights phase Pleasant never relinquished her wide-ranging business activities. Upon her return from

Canada in 1860 Pleasant worked in the home of wealthy merchant Selim Woodworth and lived in his mansion with family members and other servants. Her employment as a domestic servant when she already was a prosperous businessowner and investor invites explanation. Despite her success, gender and racial restrictions in San Francisco allowed no place for a black woman other than as a domestic servant. Pleasant simply could not have worked in any other capacity. The majority of the 1,100 adult black San Franciscans, including its most successful citizens, labored in menial positions. Richard Barber, whose $70,000 in real estate made him the wealthiest African American in the city (census records show his estate as officially twice the value of Pleasant's holdings), was a porter nonetheless. Salina Williams, the second wealthiest black woman in the city with some $12,000 in real estate, continued her job as a steamer stewardess.

But Pleasant continued to work in the homes of wealthy San Franciscan families precisely because it placed her in proximity of political and financial decision making in the city. From the mid-1850s when she was a housekeeper and cook in a boardinghouse (which was established as a residence for commission merchants) until the death of her confidante and business advisor Thomas Bell in 1892, Pleasant always worked for the city's most successful entrepreneurs and politicians. Later her fortune would be attributed to her ability to "blackmail" powerful but scandal-prone businessmen. Yet most of her business "advantages" came from her knowledge of "insider information" gleaned from overhead conversations that she coupled with sharp trading and negotiating skills acquired from her childhood of clerking in the Hussey general merchandise store in Nantucket.

In 1868, the same year *Pleasants v. North Beach & Mission Railroad* reached the California Supreme Court, Mary Ellen Pleasant purchased a boardinghouse at 920 Washington Street—the first of three such apartment houses she would eventually own in San Francisco. Boardinghouses, common throughout the nation, were particularly important in rapidly growing, predominantly male San Francisco. Some of the city's houses catered to miners or laborers, others to white-collar employees of banking houses such as Wells Fargo and the Bank of California. Pleasant's boarding houses, however, were expensive and exclusive lodgings which, at a time before luxury hotels were built in the city, attracted some of the city's most successful white politicians and businesspeople.

The Washington Street boardinghouse was located close to Portsmouth Square, the city's central business plaza. Also nearby were major banks, retail stores, the stock market, the courts, and City Hall. Locating her establishment near the center of the city's economic and political activity, as well as its night life (the opera and largest gambling house were also nearby), ensured Pleasant high visibility among San Francisco's elite. The Washington Street boardinghouse soon became known for its "fine food and wines and its … lavishly furnished upstairs rooms which were set up as combined private dining and bedrooms."

California governor Newton Booth was the most famous resident of the Washington Street boardinghouse. In 1871 Booth won the statewide election by a slim majority of 4,000 votes with San Francisco's African Americans providing 1,700 of those ballots. Mary Ellen Pleasant called Booth a personal friend and threw an elaborate postelection gala where she proudly proclaimed "This is Governor Booth who has been elected from my house." The governor-elect in turn gave an impromptu speech to an interracial crowd gathered in front of Pleasant's boardinghouse declaring that he stood squarely for political equality, a theme he reiterated at his Sacramento inaugural address when he said, "All badges of distinction that are relics of the slave-holding era of our national history should pass away with the system they commemorate."

In 1877 Pleasant moved her home and financial headquarters from Washington Street to a hill overlooking the city center. At the corner of Octavia and Bush Streets she built a multi-storied, ten-room Victorian mansion on a property that encompassed two city blocks. Worth $100,000 at the time of construction, Pleasant's home was one of the largest black-owned residences in the nation. Although she derived a steady income from her boardinghouses, the capital for the Octavia Street mansion came primarily from the profits she made during the Comstock silver mining boom in Nevada in the 1860s and 1870s. Her fortune was also tied to the success of Scottish-born banker Thomas Bell, a co-founder of the Bank of California. Pleasant and Bell met soon after they both arrived in San Francisco in the early 1850s. It is unclear as to how the two became linked, but by the 1870s Bell was the millionaire vice president of the state's largest bank. By the early 1870s Bell and Pleasant had become financial partners and, in 1878, Thomas Bell moved into the newly built mansion on Octavia Street. Most San Franciscans presumed Bell employed Pleasant as a servant—an assumption she did little to dispel. But in fact Bell resided in Pleasant's home. Pleasant, however, did arrange a marriage with Teresa Clingan, and eventually she shared the house with Thomas and Teresa Bell and their six children.

With property in both San Francisco and Oakland, and a sizeable fortune in mining stocks (estimated at three hundred thousand dollars), Pleasant by the 1870s finally felt confident enough to acquire some of the trappings of wealth. She spent lavishly on the Octavia Street mansion and by 1880 was seen around the city in a carriage with "a coachman dressed in a livery of a long black coat, white breeches, and a top hat [and] a footman dressed the same." Still, Pleasant remained mindful of the white public's demand that African Americans occupy acceptable roles as servants and menials. During her numerous courtroom appearances in the 1880s and 1890s she always wore the uniform of a housekeeper—a modest dark dress partly covered by a white cotton apron.

Mary Ellen Pleasant's family began to disintegrate at the moment she was rapidly ascending in power. Elizabeth, her only child, remained in the care of Boston area families until she arrived in San Francisco in the early 1860s. In 1865 fourteen-year-old Elizabeth married James Peck in San Francisco in a ceremony financed by her mother. Elizabeth and her husband, and occasionally James Pleasant, lived at 920 Washington Street through the 1870s. Then in 1877 James Pleasant died. Two years later, twenty-eight-year-old Elizabeth passed away as well, leaving Pleasant with no living relatives. Thomas and Teresa Bell and their children became Pleasant's surrogate family for the next two decades, a relationship that would later be cited as evidence of her role as household "mammy."

In 1884 Pleasant became a central figure in the case of *Sharon v. Sharon*, a legal imbroglio that generated the first public vilification of her character. Twenty-four-year-old Sarah Althea Hill shocked San Francisco society when, after claiming she and sixty-four-year-old former Nevada Senator William Sharon were secretly married in 1880, had him arrested at his personal suite in the Palace Hotel on September 8, 1883. Senator Sharon had, she charged, committed adultery with at least nine women. The adultery charge was dismissed on a technicality and Hill promptly filed for divorce. William Sharon responded that Hill, far from being a wronged wife, was nothing more than a manipulable prostitute who forged marriage documents in a sinister plan hatched by Pleasant to wrestle his $20 million fortune from his control.

Although the unfolding charges and countercharges raised images of a comic-opera, the financial stakes in the trial were enormous for both sides. Under the laws of California, Sarah Hill Sharon could gain half of the estate of one of the West's wealthiest men. During the 1860s William Sharon reaped a fortune from Nevada mining stock speculation, and by 1875 he controlled the Comstock Lode, the richest silver mining region in the nation as well as Nevada's most influential newspaper, the *Territorial Enterprise*. In 1875, the year he was elected to the U.S. Senate from Nevada, Sharon built the Palace, San Francisco's first luxury hotel and lived there, rather than in the state he represented during his senatorial term. Three years into that term, Sharon gained control of the Bank of California from rival Thomas Bell, prompting some observers to speculate that revenge by Bell, or his confidante, Pleasant, underlay this "divorce case."

Although she certainly was not as wealthy as the former Nevada Senator, Pleasant invested sizeable capital into the case. She reluctantly admitted in court to contributing $5,000 "to Sarah's cause" and as the only public supporter of Sarah Hill capable of assuming responsibility for legal costs, may have spent from $65,000 to $100,000 on attorneys' fees. As with other aspects of her life, Pleasant was notably silent on her motivation in Sarah's cause other than her desire for justice for an aggrieved, vulnerable friend. However the amount Pleasant spent on legal fees represented a considerable portion of her accumulated fortune, suggesting that she invested in the case expecting compensation far beyond her stated objective of preserving Sarah Hill Sharon's honor. Whatever her motives, it is clear that *Sharon v. Sharon* would not have occurred without Pleasant's emotional and financial support of Sarah Hill Sharon.

The trial began on March 10, 1884, in San Francisco's City Hall and lasted for the rest of the year, becoming in the process, one of the nation's most publicized civil cases. Mary Ellen Pleasant, as the "sponsor" of Sarah Hill and as the financier of her case, soon became a central figure in the proceedings. In their attempts to represent their respective clients, six attorneys for the plaintiff and ten for the respondent helped fashion the contradictory images of Mary E. Pleasant that would follow her for the remainder of her life.

William Sharon's lead attorney, William Barnes, portrayed Pleasant as a ruthless madam who employed voodoo to control Sarah Hill. He also charged Pleasant was a blackmailer and devious dealer in "black market" babies. Indeed much of the Sharon case rested on the unusual relationship between seventy-year-old Pleasant and twenty-five-year-old Sarah Hill. Barnes hammered away at what he contended was the preposterous idea of a friendship that crossed racial boundaries. "Will anybody tell me why it was," Barnes pleaded before the court, "that this unfortunate woman [Hill] never confided the secret of her marriage to one respectable person of her own color, class, or rank in life? … [Pleasant's] intimacy with Miss Hill … was one that ought not to have existed."

Sarah Hill Sharon's lead attorney, George Washington Tyler, countered the image of Pleasant as scheming manipulator by casting her in an acceptable gender role as nurturer and servant. Calling up the "selfless mammy" as a familiar icon of an earlier era, Tyler argued that Pleasant did no more than attempt to protect naive Sarah from sexual exploitation by a wealthy, powerful, and heartless husband. When asked to testify, Pleasant embellished the image, describing how she sheltered Sarah at her Octavia Street home when Senator Sharon evicted her from the apartment he maintained at the Grand Hotel. Pleasant then, upon hearing of the marriage contract, confronted the senator on Sarah's behalf with no other intent than to protect her new charge. Finally she related how a chastened William Sharon promised to pay the bills for a small house Pleasant intended to provide for his estranged wife.

On Christmas Eve 1884, Judge Jeremiah Francis Sullivan awarded Sarah Hill Sharon $2,500 a month and $55,000 in attorney fees. Sarah had little time to savor her legal triumph; William Sharon initiated *Sharon v. Hill* in Federal Court where he countersued Sarah Hill, claiming he had paid for "her services" and that the marriage contract she presented in the previous litigation was a forgery. The federal case lasted eleven months, ending on December 26, 1885. Federal Judges Matthew Deady and Lorenzo Sawyer ruled the marriage contract invalid. Judge Deady took special aim at Pleasant, writing that she was a "shrewd old negress of considerable means." He then concluded "this case, and the forgeries and perjuries committed in its support, have their origin largely in the brain of this scheming, trafficking, crafty old woman."

Seventy-five-year-old Mary Ellen Pleasant endured the greatest humiliation of her life as a result of these highly publicized trials. Newspaper and magazine articles across the nation vilified her name, and a federal judge blamed her for the entire episode. Numerous creditors, now aware of both her wealth and her vulnerability, crafted schemes to wrest her fortune away much like, they assumed, she had planned to do with Senator William Sharon's estate. For the remainder of her life Pleasant mortgaged property or borrowed funds to pay mounting legal fees as she reentered the courtroom either as plaintiff or defendant to protect her dwindling assets.

In 1891 Mary Ellen Pleasant purchased the last piece of property she would ever own—a sprawling 985-acre ranch in the Napa Valley she called Beltane. Soon afterward a series of events conspired to shatter her personal life and finances. On October 15, 1982, seventy-two-year-old Thomas Bell died at the Octavia Street mansion. The cause of death was officially listed as a twenty-foot fall from a staircase railing. But given the recent reputation of Pleasant, rumors soon appeared in the press that she was responsible for his death. Moreover, Bell's death precipitated a power struggle between his oldest son, Fred Bell, and Pleasant, which forced her to return to court. In 1897 seventeen-year-old Bell asked that his mother, Teresa, be removed as head of household and guardian of the children because she was controlled by Pleasant. Bell claimed his mother knew "absolutely nothing about business affairs," and was manipulated by Pleasant, "a negro woman … of eighty-three years [who is] neither a fit or a proper person to guide, control, or direct any person other than herself." During the proceedings, Bell's attorney declared in court that his client's "prime object ... is not to strike at his mother at all, for he believes she is ... an innocent party. He wants to destroy the power of 'Mammy' Pleasant and show her up to people in her true colors."

Although Fred Bell lost his lawsuit, he immediately filed a new legal action forcing Pleasant to undergo yet another round of fundraising and court battles. More distressing, however, was Teresa Bell's decision in 1899 to oust Pleasant from her own Octavia Street mansion, which the women had shared for twenty-one years. Teresa Bell also sued for control of Beltane. The origins of the rift between Pleasant and Bell can be traced to 1894. Under pressure from creditors, Pleasant signed the deed for Beltane over to Teresa Bell while continuing to manage the property. Five years later Pleasant regained control of the ranch to protect it from Bell's creditors, prompting many observers to conclude that the women may have repeatedly engaged in an elaborate ruse of deed swapping on both Beltrane and the Octavia Street mansion to protect their individual and mutual assets.

If that was the case, Bell ceased cooperating in the ruse in March 1899. She accused Pleasant of squandering Thomas Bell's life savings and forced her out of Beltane. Confiding in her diary, Bell wrote "MP has had such success in working this whole family that she believes she is the absolute owner of everyone and everything here, her constant gobble is how ... it's all hers." On April 20, 1899, Mary Ellen Pleasant "passed out the door after her two trunks, snarling like a mad dog." After two decades of sharing a San Francisco mansion and eight years a Sonoma County ranch, Teresa Bell and Mary Ellen Pleasant would never again live under the same roof.

Pleasant retreated to the last piece of property she had clear title to— Geneva Cottage, her summer home on San Jose Road south of San Francisco. The cottage was to be her residence for the last five years of her life. Impoverished, enfeebled, and abandoned, Pleasant spent much of her time granting interviews and supervising the dictation of her last "autobiography." In November 1903, Pleasant moved to the home of friends Olive and Lyman Sherwood. Two months later, on January 11, 1904, eighty-nine year-old Mary Ellen Pleasant died there and was buried in the Sherwood family cemetery plot in the Napa Valley.

Mary Ellen Pleasant left an ambiguous legacy. She achieved what biographer Lynn Hudson called a "visibility ... unprecedented for a black woman in any region of the United States." Yet her name became synonymous with financial scandal and sexual manipulation. She was probably the first African American woman to become a millionaire although we will never know the exact extent of her estate because much of what she owned was placed in other people's names. During the first half of her life, Pleasant used her wealth to contest in the courts for her own citizenship rights and those of other African Americans. Oral history recollections of other black San Franciscans place Pleasant at the center of virtually every abolitionist and civil rights campaign in the Bay Area between 1852 and 1868. By the 1870s, Pleasant the philanthropist and civil rights activist had given way to the Gilded Age capitalist, preoccupied with her own financial success.

Pleasant embraced the tactics of the bonanza mining kings and railroad barons of her era. She engaged in leveraged acquisitions, real estate speculation, and insider trading on the San Francisco stock market—practices routinely admired among the wealthiest white men in the nation but greeted with disbelief and disdain when exercised by an African American woman. Thus it was easier for the public to accept Pleasant as the scheming, manipulative madam and voodoo queen who parlayed sexual secrets into financial gain than to acknowledge her entrepreneurial acumen as responsible for her remarkable success.

Pleasant herself was trapped by these restricting gender and racial conventions. Wearing a white apron, bonnet, and shawl to project the "servant" facade or the intermingling of her property with white friends and employers to protect it from racially inspired creditor harassment suggests that she understood well the limits of her "success." Toward the end of her life she rebelled against the faithful servant image, "Listen … I'm not mammy to everybody in California" she wrote in a 1901 interview. "I got a letter from a minister in Sacramento. It was addressed to Mammy Pleasant. I wrote back to him on his own paper that my name was Mrs. Mary E. Pleasant … . That letter wasn't in the house fifteen minutes. I sent it back to him unread."

Yet Pleasant never fully understood her role in generating the very image she detested. The decisions she made at crucial junctures of her life, the silences she embraced, the mysteries she encouraged, and the varied personal histories she chose to advance, all ensured that contradictory images of pliant servant and scheming manipulator would continue to fashion the enigma of Mary Ellen Pleasant long after her death.

The saga of Mary Ellen Pleasant was a uniquely western episode. Her economic success was clearly tied to the expanding regional mining industry as well as to a growing urban economy in San Francisco that allowed any property owner who arrived early enough to reap the enormous profits in the rapidly growing city. Pleasant also exploited the still largely evolving western societal norms between the 1850s and 1870s to push the limits of racial and gender boundaries. It is not coincidental that her power and influence would begin to wane by the 1880s. San Francisco's period of spectacular growth ended in that decade, and societal values, including racial boundaries, became much more pronounced. The young, raw western metropolis serving the gold miners had given way to the staid, increasingly conservative center of western finance capital. Mary Ellen Pleasant was now marginalized in the city she loved. The story of Mary Ellen Pleasant is a biography of individual success and failure. But it is also an example of past and future possibilities in the West where race and gender do not curtail individual aspiration.

SOURCES AND FURTHER READING

The literature on Mary Ellen Pleasant is varied and uneven. Primary sources include Pleasant's interview titled "Memoirs and Autobiography" in a January 1902 issue of the San Francisco publication, *Pandex of the Press*. But other sources include J. Lloyd Conrich, "The Mammy Pleasant Legand," unpublished manuscript, no date, California Historical Society, and the series of interviews of Pleasant's contemporaries in the Mary Ellen Pleasant Collection, San Francisco History Room, San Francisco Public Library.

By far the most important secondary sources are Lynn M. Hudson's, "When 'Mammy' Becomes a Millionaire: Mary Ellen Pleasant, An African American Entrepreneur" (Ph.D. diss., Indiana University, 1996); "A New Look, or 'I'm Not Mammy to Everybody in California': Mary Ellen Pleasant, A Black Entrepreneur," *Journal of the West* 32 (July 1993):35–40; and Sushell Bibbs, "Mary Ellen Pleasant: Mother of Civil Rights in California" *Historic Nantucket* 44 (1995):9–13. Hudson's dissertation may finally elevate Pleasant from colorful folklore character in early San Francisco to a subject worthy of study by professional historians. Helen Holdredge, *Mammy Pleasant* (New York: G.P. Putnam's Sons, 1953), remains the only booklength study of Pleasant, but it is riddled with inaccuracies and suffers from the author's penchant for embracing negative stereotypes of Pleasant (madam and voodoo queen) while downplaying her considerable business abilities and attributing her commitment to black civil rights to a crass attempt to control gullible black San Franciscans. The revision of Pleasant's unsavory image began with Lerone Bennett's "An Historical Detective Story," *Ebony* (April/May 1979):90–96, 71–86.

Other secondary sources provide information on selected episodes of Pleasant's life and activities while portraying her as a "colorful" and often "exotic" character in San Francisco's lurid past. See for example Herbert Asbury, *The Barbary Coast: An Informal History of the San Francisco Underworld* (New York: Alfred A. Knopf, 1933), and Ronald Dean Miller, *Shady Ladies of the West* (Los Angeles: Westernlore Press, 1964). Pleasant is portrayed sympathetically if simplistically in three works by black California historians, Delilah L. Beasley, *The Negro Trail Blazers of California* (Los Angeles: Times Mirror Printing, 1919); Sue Bailey Thurman, *Pioneers of Negro Origin in California* (San Francisco: Acme Publishing Company, 1971); and James Adolphus Fisher, "A History of the Political and Social Development of the Black Community in California, 1850–1950" (Ph.D. diss., State University of New York at Stony Brook, 1972).

A number of sources provide rich background information on nineteenth-century black California and San Francisco. For the former, see Rudolph Lapp, *Blacks in Gold Rush California* (New Haven: Yale University Press, 1977), which, to date, remains the best work on the initial period of Pleasant's residence in the Golden State. But see also Douglas Henry Daniels, *Pioneer Urbanites: A Social and Cultural History of Black San Francisco* (Philadelphia: Temple University Press, 1980); Albert Broussard, *Black San Francisco: The Struggle for Racial Equality in the West, 1900–1954* (Lawrence: University Press of Kansas, 1993); and Malcolm Edwards, "The War of Complexional Distinction: Blacks in Gold Rush California and British Columbia," *California Historical Quarterly* 56 (spring 1977):34–45; Eugene H. Berwanger, *The Frontier Against Slavery: Western Anti-Negro Prejudice and the Slavery Extension Controversy* (Urbana: University of Illinois Press, 1967); and Leon Litwack, *North of Slavery: The Negro in the Free States, 1790–1860* (Chicago: University of Chicago Press, 1961). On San Francisco history, see William Issel and Robert Cherny, *San Francisco, 1865–1932: Politics, Power, and Urban Development* (Berkeley: University of California Press, 1986), and Roger W. Lotchin, *San Francisco, 1846–1856: From Hamlet to City* (New York: Oxford University Press, 1974).

Jacqueline Jones's *Labor of Love, Labor of Sorrow: Black Women, Work, and the Family from Slavery to the Present* (New York: Basic Books, 1985) remains the most comprehensive history of black women during the period, but for specific treatment of western African American women, see Lawrence B. de Graaf, "Race, Sex and Region: Black Women in the West, 1850–1920," *Pacific Historical Review* 49 (May 1980):285–313; and Glenda Riley, "American Daughters: Black Women in the West," *Montana: The Magazine of Western History* 38 (spring 1988):14–27. Loren Schweninger, "Property-Owning Free African American Women in the South, 1800–1870," *Journal of Women's History* 1 (winter 1990):13–44; and Juliet E.K. Walker, "Racism, Slavery, and Free Enterprise: Black Entrepreneurship in the United States Before the Civil War," *Business History Review* 60 (autumn 1986):342–82, describe black women as nineteenth-century entrepreneurs and property-owners. Willard B. Gatewood's *Aristocrats of Color: The Black Elite, 1880–1920* (Bloomington: Indiana University Press, 1990) describes nineteenth-century wealthy blacks but fails to mention Pleasant.

On the fight against streetcar segregations, see *Pleasants v. North Beach & Mission Railroad,* 34 *California Reporter,* 586, and Willi Coleman, "Black Women and Segregated Public Transportation: Ninety Years of Resistance," in Darlene Clark Hine, ed., *Black Women in United States History* vol. 5 (Brooklyn: Carlson Publishing Company, 1990); whereas the Sharon divorce case is described in *Sharon v. Hill,* 26 *Federal Reporter,* 337; and Robert Kroninger, *Sarah and the Senator* (Berkeley: Howell-North Books, 1964). For background on Senator Sharon, see Richard H. Peterson, *The Bonanza Kings: The Social Origins and Business Behavior of Western Mining Entrepreneurs, 1870–1900* (Norman: University of Oklahoma Press, 1991).

7

Iron Eye's Daughters: Susette and Susan LaFlesche, Nineteenth-Century Indian Reformers

VALERIE SHERER MATHES

It is a little thing, a simple thing, which my people ask of a nation whose watchword is liberty; but it is endless in its consequences. They ask for their liberty, and law is liberty.

—Susette LaFlesche, 1879

It has always been a desire of mine to study medicine ever since I was a small girl, for even then I saw the need of my people for a good physician ... . I feel that as a physician I can do a great deal more than as a mere teacher.

—Susan LaFlesche, 1886

※ TWO SISTERS WITH DREAMS AND GOALS—not necessarily uncommon for nineteenth-century women, although the pursuit of a medical career and the luxury of liberty were not always easily accessible to their gender. That they were Omaha Indian women who ultimately achieved part if not all of their goals at a time when Indians were not yet considered citizens and had few rights, was extraordinary.

Late-nineteenth-century Indian reformers emphasized the shift from a communal way of life to one of Christianization, assimilation, and individualization. Reformers focused on turning Indian men into yeoman farmers and the women into skilled practicers of Victorian-era domesticity. For many Indians this reform movement failed; their land base was eroded, and they were forced deeper into poverty. For some, however, the acculturation process was more successful. One such family was the LaFlesche family, who lived on the Omaha Indian reservation in Nebraska. The patriarch of the family was Joseph ("Iron Eye") LaFlesche, son of a French fur trader and an Indian woman and the last recognized chief of the Omaha tribe. Joseph had eight children, five with Mary Gale, the mixed-blood daughter of army physician, John Gale, and his Omaha wife; and three with Tainne (Elizabeth Esau), an Omaha woman. The four daughters from his first marriage—Susette (1854–1903), Rosalie (1861–1900), Marguerite (1862–1945), and Susan (1865–1915)—and a son, Francis (1857–1932), from his second marriage, all successfully navigated the treachous path of assimilation and, in varying degrees, lived successfully as part of the dominant culture. Francis become a leading ethnologist with the Bureau of American Ethnology and author of *A Dictionary of the Osage Language* (1932). He also collaborated with ethnologist Alice Cunningham Fletcher on *The Omaha Tribe* (1911).

Three of Francis LaFlesche's sisters joined the ranks of Indian reformers in varying capacities. Susette became an outspoken critic of injustice to the Indian people and, working closely with her reformer husband, became a lecturer and campaigning journalist advocating other causes as well. Although Rosalie did not become a reformer, she did become a businesswoman, handling the family's stock-feeding business as well as managing any monies that Susette raised for the Omaha tribe during her speaking tours in the East. Marguerite served as a field matron from 1896 to 1900 for the Office of Indian Affairs, a position created in 1890 by the federal government to aid in the assimilation of Indian women. Field matrons promoted Christianity and instructed Indian women in housekeeping chores, the care of the sick, and child rearing. And finally Susan, the first American Indian woman to graduate from medical college, became a medical missionary as well as a political advocate for the Omaha tribe.

Although their father embraced Christianity, lived in a frame house instead of the traditional Omaha earth lodge, and farmed a quarter section of land, he did not abandon all Omaha traditions. He raised his children to respect their Indian heritage, but he was also aware that his people would have to adjust to the ways of the dominant white society. Concerned about their future welfare, he refused to have his daughters tattooed and his sons' ears pierced because he wanted them to be able to move freely within white culture. But the most enduring legacy to his children was a strong emphasis on education. His children all learned to speak as well as to read and write English. In addition to attending local schools, all but Rosalie went east for further education.

The LaFlesche children's education began at the white stone mission boarding school built and run by the Presbyterian Board of Foreign Missions above Blackbird Hills. When it closed, they attended the government day school at the Omaha Agency that in 1869 had been assigned to the Hicksite Friends, one of two branches of the Society of Friends, or Quakers. In an effort to improve the quality of Indian agents, as part of his "Peace Policy," President Ulysses S. Grant accepted civilian agents recommended by the nation's

Susette LaFlesche Tibbles.
(Courtesy of the Nebraska State
Historical Society)

religious leaders. The Quakers had been assigned to the northern superin-
tendency that included the Omaha Agency.

After the Presbyterian boarding school closed, Susette, too old to attend
the agency day school, educated herself from the small library of the Reverend William Hamilton, a Presbyterian missionary. Fortunately, one of her
former teachers, Nettie C. Read, headmistress at Elizabeth Institute for Young
Ladies in Elizabeth, New Jersey, arranged with friends in 1872 to finance
Susette's education at the institute. The young Omaha woman graduated
with honors in 1875 and returned to the reservation. Realizing that she had
to help her family financially and also bored with reservation life, she wrote
the commissioner of Indian affairs requesting a teaching position. Initially
turned down, Susette informed him that reservation rules provided that a
qualified Indian had preference over a white person for Indian service positions. The civilization process was a "farce," she remarked to him, "after we
educate ourselves, … [you] refuse us positions of responsibility and leave us
utterly powerless to help ourselves." As an afterthought, she added, "perhaps
the only way to make ourselves heard is to appeal to the American public
through the press. They might listen." How prophetic. As part of an eastern
lecture tour several years later, her speeches were carefully recorded by reporters, and they listened.

Susette's persistence paid off. From 1877 to 1879 she taught at the Omaha
Agency school, although at a salary half that of a white teacher. To bring
the Omaha children closer to Christianity, she also opened a Sunday
School and from her own salary, bought an organ so the children in both
schools had music.

The fall of 1879 was an important turning point in the lives of Susette and Susan. Susan and her sister Marguerite left the Omaha reservation for the first time and traveled to New Jersey to attended their older sister's alma mater, Elizabeth Institute. While Susan was engaged in her studies, Susette was almost instantaneously thrust onto the public stage where she gained a national reputation in the field of Indian reform and inspired numerous eastern philanthropists to take up the Indian cause. The catalyst that launched Susette's public career was the forced removal in 1877 of the small, peaceful Ponca tribe from their Missouri River Reservation in present-day South Dakota to Indian Territory. More than 160 members of the Ponca tribe died, many from malaria. Two years later, Ponca Chief Standing Bear, with the body of his only son and a small party of followers, left Indian Territory and headed for their former home and burial grounds. By March 1879 they had traveled as far as the Omaha Reservation in Nebraska. The Ponca and Omaha, both members of the southern Siouan linguistic group, were closely related. Joseph LaFlesche's half-brother, White Swan, for example, was a Ponca chief. Therefore Joseph, Susette, and other Omahas welcomed their Ponca kinsmen and visitors, giving them lands to settle on and cultivate.

Susette had been involved in the plight of the Poncas from the very beginning, having, with her father, consulted numerous times with them over which course to follow to prevent removal. She and Joseph had even visited with the Ponca during the actual removal process. Therefore Susette was greatly concerned when soldiers from General George Crook's garrison in Omaha arrested Standing Bear and his party for leaving Indian Territory without permission. The Poncas were subsequently freed by a decision in *Standing Bear v. Crook*, won with the help of Thomas Henry Tibbles, assistant editor of the *Omaha Daily Herald*, who had hired two white lawyers, rallied supporters, and helped organize the Omaha Ponca Relief Committee composed of local Nebraska ministers and interested citizens.

Susette and her father attended the two-day trial of Standing Bear and the other defendants and participated in one of the Omaha Committee meetings. In May 1879, at the request of the committee, they visited Joseph's brother, White Swan, in Indian Territory to learn if the government was correct in its assertion that the Ponca were happy in their new home. Susette discovered that the Ponca were unhappy, and although uninformed yet about the outcome of the trial, many were ready to follow in Standing Bear's footsteps. The agent, aware of the Indians' displeasure, was awaiting the arrival of more soldiers to keep the Poncas on the reservation. As Susette traveled with her father throughout the new Ponca reservation, she saw numerous graves, no roads, scattered groups of tents, six crude little houses,

Dr. Susan LaFlesche Picotte.
(Courtesy of the Nebraska State
Historical Society)

and various agency buildings, which were much more substantial than the Indians' buildings.

With a successful verdict behind them, Tibbles resigned his position at the *Daily Herald* and, sponsored by the Omaha Committee, organized a multicity lecture tour to acquaint the public with the plight of the Ponca and other tribes and to raise money. Tibbles and Standing Bear hoped through lawsuits not only to recover lost lands, but to return the Indian Territory part of the tribe to their original reservation in South Dakota, and to determine the Indians' legal status. Chicago, Pittsburgh, Boston, New York, Philadelphia, Baltimore, Washington, D.C., and various smaller American cities were selected and prominent local leaders contacted. Susette, accompanied by her brother Francis as her guardian and chaperone, was selected to serve as Standing Bear's interpreter. The poignant picture of the dignified elderly chief and the pretty, young, Omaha Indian woman moved audiences, who not only gave their money but their hearts to the cause. One supporter was Henry Wadsworth Longfellow, who called Susette "Minnehaha," after the heroine in his poem *Hiawatha*.

Longfellow was not the only prominent citizen who became involved with the Ponca cause and acquainted with Susette. Numerous philanthropists and humanitarians, as well as local, state, and federal officials, were swept up in the Ponca crusade. Organizations were formed in major cities, articles and books written, senate hearings held, and congressional legislation passed. Two of the best-known crusaders were Henry Laurens Dawes, junior senator from Massachusetts, who would serve on the Senate investigative hearings on Ponca removal, and Helen Hunt Jackson. Jackson, a noted New England poet and author, then living in Colorado, was visiting in Boston when she attended one of Tibbles's public meetings, heard Standing Bear, and befriended Susette. In a November 20, 1879, article in the *Independent,* entitled "Standing Bear and Bright Eyes," Jackson described the young Omaha woman as "a graceful, winning, lovely girl ... eager, interested [and] observant," whose English was "stately in its very simplicity." Incensed with the injustice of the Ponca removal as intrepreted by Susette, Jackson began her one-woman campaign to elicit public support. The information she uncovered while researching in the Astor Library in New York was initially written as letters to the editors and later included in her book *A Century of Dishonor* (1881), which included a chapter on Ponca removal.

Others who were caught up in the Ponca cause were journalists and editors who continually covered Standing Bear's movements throughout the host cities. The newspaper accounts of the various meetings enabled the public to read Standing Bear's speeches that Susette had ably translated. Interested citizens also learned about the young Omaha woman's personal feelings from her eloquent speeches. In a revealing October 30, 1879, statement in the *Boston Daily Advertiser,* readers were informed that "had it not been for the memory of the noble Christian women with whom" Susette had once lived, she "should have been an utter disbeliever in God and humanity" because of the mistreatment of the Ponca. This comment followed her recitation of the hardships that her uncle, White Swan, and other Ponca chiefs had endured after being deliberately left in Indian Territory with no food or transportation and forced, because they had refused to select a new reservation, to find their way back to the Dakotas. Such heart-felt sentiments on the part of Susette played not only on the emotions of those who heard her speak in public but upon those who read parts of her speeches in the newspaper. Thus continual sympathetic reporting gained a large following for the Poncas and for Susette. A *New York Herald* reporter on December 9, 1879, described her as "a cultivated young lady" of above average ability with a "strong sense of her people's wrongs."

But not all reporters were as sympathetic to the Ponca cause and to Susette; some sided with Secretary of the Interior Carl Schurz and other government officials who had ordered the Ponca to remain in Indian Territory. In early January 1881, the Washington reporter for the *Springfield Daily Republican,* noting with relief that the Ponca tour was over, had trouble comprehending how the people of New England "came to swallow everything they said as gospel truth." He also described Susette as a "phenomenal liar." Other papers had carried her story that twice she had been denied the right to see her uncle, White Swan, when she went to the Globe Hotel in Washington. The

Republican reporter, giving the Interior Department's version of the story, noted that it was Christmas Day and the Indians were getting ready to visit Secretary Schurz's home when Susette arrived. She was told they were going out but was given ample time afterward to talk with her uncle.

During the hectic six-month tour, Susette and the others often gave daily public lectures, and participated in a continual round of receptions, teas, luncheons, banquets, and gatherings in private homes and churches. They remained in the Boston area for more than a month, and during the last meeting on December 3, 1879, Susette became the first woman to make a speech in Faneuil Hall before a large group, many of whom were women. The *Boston Daily Advertiser* reported that Longfellow watched her from the gallery as she spoke about the Indians' lack of legal rights. "Did our Creator who made us all intend that men created in his own image should be ruled over by another set of his creatures?" she asked her audience. "I think not," she answered. Quoting from the Fourteenth Amendment, she reminded her listeners that all persons born in the United States were citizens, and that for the first time in the history of the United States "justice ... [had] been accorded to an Indian" as a result of the successful decision by Judge Dundy.

Audiences in New York City; Elizabeth, New Jersey; Carlisle and Norristown, Pennsylvania; and Wilmington, Delaware listened to Susette and read her various speeches on Ponca removal, about her two years teaching on the reservation, and on numerous injustices against the Indians. Then in mid-Feburary of 1880, the Ponca tour traveled to Washington, D.C., to testify before a special Senate committee investigating the tribe's removal. The committee, chaired by Senator Samuel Jordan Kirkwood of Iowa but with Massachusetts Senator Dawes conducting much of the questioning, concluded that the removal, carried out without Ponca approval, had resulted in great suffering for the Indians and recommended not only restoration of their lands but also monetary restitution.

After months of hectic traveling, Susette and her companions finally returned home. During the tour, Susette, who wrote all of her own speeches, had been encouraged by Helen Hunt Jackson to write children's stories for publication. She had already written a short introduction to Tibbles's book, *The Ponca Chiefs: An Indian's Attempt to Appeal from the Tomahawk to the Courts,* which had been published in the winter of 1879. Once home, Susette decided to follow Jackson's advice. She wrote an Indian story entitled *Nedawi* and sent it to *St. Nicholas,* a children's magazine. It was accepted for publication in the January 1881 issue. Thus began a writing career that included an introduction to *Ploughed Under, the Story of an Indian Chief,* a novel by William Justin Harsha, son of the pastor of the Omaha First Presbyterian

Church who had been active in the Ponca cause, and various other articles or editorials on Indian as well as non-Indian issues in numerous newspapers. In the fall of 1880, Susette, Tibbles, and members of the Boston Committee for the Protection of the Ponca began another tour of eastern cities with a similar round of teas, receptions, lectures, and luncheons. This tour coincided with the appointment in December by President Rutherford B. Hayes of a special commission to confer with the Poncas living in Indian Territory and with those who had returned to the Dakotas with Standing Bear. Susette, who testified before the commission, also had an opportunity to visit again with her uncle White Swan. In January 1881, the Ponca commission recommended that the Indians be allowed to choose the reservation they preferred. In March, Congress appropriated $165,000 as reparations for losses sustained during removal. Thus Susette, her brother Francis, Standing Bear, and Tibbles had not only brought the plight of the Ponca before the public, but had succeeded against great odds in righting a grievous wrong.

That summer, on July 23, Susette LaFlesche married Thomas Henry Tibbles, a widower. Reaction to this marriage was mixed. Her brother Francis never liked "T. H.," as the family always called him, because he believed that Tibbles, whose first wife had died in 1879, had been much too familiar with his sister on the tour. The rest of the LaFlesche family's opinion of the marriage is unknown, but they often disagreed with T. H.'s reform ideas regarding the Omaha, possibly because of his abrasive, as well as paternalistic, manner.

One of the most interesting reactions to the marriage came from Alonzo Bell, assistant secretary of the interior under secretaries Carl Schurz and Samuel Kirkwood. In an August 5, 1881, letter to Schurz, Bell rejoiced that "Bright Eyes had capitulated to Tibbles, and that Tibbles had surrendered to Bright Eyes." Although personally fearing that Susette had made a mistake, he noted, "I am willing to forgive her if the act has effectually disposed of Tibbles." He concluded that "even so great a sacrifice may be rare economy if it gives the Nation a rest from the vexatious borings of the Tibbles school of philanthropy." Obviously Tibbles's tour and the resultant antigovernment publicity had been extremely trying for Secretary Carl Schurz and his staff.

Susette and her new husband settled into a house near the Omaha reservation agency and later, after the Omaha land was allotted, moved to Susette's quarter section and began farming. During the next two winters Susette and T. H. lectured in eastern cities on behalf of the Indians and, in between, she wrote and illustrated a children's story for the June 1883 issue of *Wide Awake*. In May 1887 they sailed for a year of lecturing in England and Scotland. Staying mostly in private homes, sometimes with the nobility, they kept a hectic schedule. It was not uncommon for them to be on the lecture platform as many as five times a week. In the summer of 1888 they returned to their homestead near Bancroft, Nebraska, during a grasshopper plague. The plague and various other aspects of farming were distasteful to Susette's husband, who leased the farm and accepted a job on the editorial staff of the Omaha *World Herald* in 1888. In late 1890 Susette and T. H. were sent as special "war correspondents" for the *Herald* and the *Chicago Express* to the Pine Ridge Agency on the Sioux Reservation in South Dakota to report on the Ghost Dance sweeping the reservation. One day Susette had an opportunity to witness the actual ceremony, which in itself was harmless. Several days later she found herself nursing wounded women and children, all victims of the Massacre at Wounded Knee. Altogether, an overly concerned agent, who had requested additional military support, the death of Sitting Bull at the hands of agency policemen while being arrested, and the flight of frightened Sioux Indians under Chief Big Foot ultimately led to the massacre on December 29, 1890. Returning home, they remained in Omaha until 1893, when once again Susette followed her husband as he pursued his quixotic crusades, this time to Washington, D.C., on behalf of Populism and its demands for free silver and pro-farmer, pro-labor legislation. The People's or Populist Party had emerged full blown in 1892, holding its national convention in Omaha where it presented its reform platform and nominated candidates for the presidency and vice presidency. Years later, in 1904, Tibbles ran as the party's vice presidential candidate. But in the meantime, in 1893, they had been offered a position as reporters for the *Nonconformist,* an Indiana weekly, and for a syndicate of other weeklies published by the Farmer's Alliance, one of the sponsoring founders of the Populist Party. Tibbles's job was to report on actions in the House of Representatives while Susette reported on Senate actions.

In the summer of 1894 Susette and T. H. returned to Nebraska where he edited the *Weekly Independent* (later the *Lincoln Independent*), a Populist newspaper in Lincoln. Susette wrote articles and editorials for the paper and in 1898 illustrated a small book titled *Oo-mah-ha Ta-wa-tha*, which included Omaha Indian stories. Because of Susette's health problems, the couple moved back to the farm in 1900 so she could be closer to her family. T. H. continued to edit the newspaper by mail with frequent trips to Lincoln. Susette's health continued to fail, and she died on May 26, 1903.

Susan LaFlesche's career followed a very different road from that of her older sister. While Susette and her husband were touring and editing various newspapers, Susan continued her studies. After graduation from the Elizabeth Institute, she entered Hampton Normal and Agricultural Institute in Virginia. Founded in 1868 by General Samuel C. Armstrong to educate Negro freedmen and women, the institution enrolled its first Indian student a decade later. Susan graduated from Hampton on May 20, 1886, and more than likely would have returned to her reservation except that Alice Cunningham Fletcher, a prominent ethnologist, and the Women's National Indian Association (WNIA) arranged for her to attend medical college.

Fletcher had suffered a severe bout of inflammatory rheumatism in 1883 while working on the Omaha Reservation. Susan had cheerfully nursed her back to health. That following fall while attending her first Lake Mohonk Conference, where government officials and reformers gathered annually to discuss Indian policy, Fletcher met Sara Thomson Kinney, president of the Connecticut Indian Association, an auxiliary of the WNIA. The Connecticut Association, like other WNIA branches, sometimes singled out capable young Indian women for advanced education. Remembering Susan's healing abilities, Fletcher made arrangements with Kinney for her education. In October of 1886, tired and suffering from motion sickness, the young Omaha woman arrived in Philadelphia to attend the Woman's Medical College of Pennsylvania. Most of Susan's expenses, with the exception of the $167 a year provided by the government for Indian students at boarding schools, were financed by the Connecticut Indian Association. In an association pamphlet, Kinney had appealed to the residents of the state for donations to support Susan, who she described as gentle, refined, and unselfish.

Susan was immediately placed in suitable YWCA housing and provided with supplies and necessary clothing and began her studies as a "beneficiary student" at the medical college, which had opened its doors in 1850. This institution was chosen in part because Hampton Institute resident physician Dr. Martha M. Waldron was a graduate, but also because Philadelphia was a center for Indian reform. Both the WNIA and the male-dominated Indian Rights Association were headquartered in Philadelphia. For the next three years Susan's lively and colorful letters to her sister Rosalie reflected the acculturation she was experiencing. At Hampton her daily contact had been only with Indian girls, but at the medical college all her classmates were white. She was accepted by them, dressed like them, participated in all social gatherings, lived with a white roommate, and was chosen corresponding secretary of the Young Women's Christian Association.

Susan's letters also described a hectic round of activities, academic and social. She took the streetcars everywhere, often visited the Philadelphia Academy of Arts, and attended numerous musical and theatrical events. She also participated in various church services with school chums, noting in a letter how "grand" the music was during one Catholic service.

During her first year, Susan attended lectures in chemistry, anatomy, physiology, histology, general therapeutics, and obstetrics and participated in daily clinics at the Woman's Hospital of Philadelphia. Continuous note-taking, weekly examinations, and classes in dissecting cadavers completed her busy schedule. One day male students from Jefferson Medical College joined the female students at the Woman's Hospital. Just as the surgeon was preparing to operate, a young man passed out and was carried from the room. "I wasn't even thinking of fainting," wrote Susan to Rosalie, nor for that matter were any of the female students. "I am going to wield the knife tonight," she wrote in another letter, but she reassured her sister by qualifying, "not the scalping knife though."

Although family members were probably bemused by some letters, her correspondence was helpful in another way. Susan often dispensed medical advice. To Rosalie she prescribed plenty of exercise, fresh air, and sleep, and to Ed Farley, Rosalie's husband, she prescribed less quinine and more leisurely meals. Susan graduated on March 14, 1889, at the head of her class of thirty-six young women and was selected as one of only six graduates to serve as an assistant to the resident physician in the local Woman's Hospital. In August she returned permanently to the Omaha Reservation as government physician at the Indian agency school, a position she had requested from the commissioner of Indian affairs. In December, when Omaha Agent Robert Ashley requested that she be allowed to treat adults as well as children, Commissioner Thomas Jefferson Morgan agreed. Susan was soon in charge of the health care of 1,244 Omahas.

For the next four years she served as tribal physician and lived at the government school where her sister Marguerite was principal teacher. Her office, amply supplied with various medicines, games, scrapbooks, picture books, and magazines donated by various branches of the WNIA, was often full of school children and adults who came for advice, personal and legal, or merely to pass a pleasant hour visiting with Susan or looking through the magazines.

The thirty- by forty-five-mile reservation with its network of poor dirt roads was a physicial challege to the young, energetic, although frail, Omaha doctor. Susan walked to patients living within a mile of her office and hired a team and buggy to reach the more distant homes. Her day, which began at eight in the morning, often dragged on until ten in the evening as she treated cases of consumption, influenza, dysentery, malaria, cholera, and conjunctivitis, an eye ailment spread by unsanitary conditions. Between October 1891 and the spring of 1892 she attended to more than six hundred patients, sometimes in freezing weather.

Susan not only cared for the physical well-being of her people, but she nurtured their souls as well. Christian Endeavor meetings were held for the young people on Sunday evenings, prayer meetings were held on Wednesdays, and Sunday school was attended by the children in the schoolhouse before the regular church service. When schedules allowed, Susan and Marguerite sang and interpeted during Sunday service. They encouraged couples to marry legally and with church sanction and advocated that tribal members perform Christian services for the dead. Susan's devotion to Christian work was an ever-present dimension in her life. She had become a model of Victorian era Christianity for her people. A strong evangelical movement pervaded nineteenth-century America. Religion was not only a civilizing element in the Indian reform movement, which had sponsored her medical education, but was part of "True Womanhood," which regulated the lives of upper and middle class American women. The philanthropic work of the WNIA extended the concept of "True Womanhood" to native American women as well. Because of Susan's commitment to medicine and to Christianity, it was only natural that WNIA appoint her as medical missionary to the Omaha in 1891 at a salary of $250 annually. In return for writing annual reports and speaking before various WNIA auxiliaries, Susan won from the national association boxes of clothing, gifts, supplies, and gifts of money.

Susan's piety was recognized by the Presbyterian Church as well. In 1905 the Presbyterian Board of Home Missions appointed her their missionary to the Omaha tribe and provided her with housing and a small stipend. With the Blackbird Hills Presbyterian Church as her headquarters, Susan held church services, read the Bible in her native tongue, interpreted hymns, and held simple Christian services for those who had died. Later when she moved to the newly established town of Walthill, Nebraska, which had been carved out of Indian land by the railroad, she became a major organizer of the local Presbyterian Church where she also taught Sunday school.

Between 1893 and 1894 Susan's life took a different direction. In early January 1893 she was bedridden, complaining of severe earaches and neck and back pain. This disabling health condition forced her to resign as government physican at year's end. However in the following summer, the twenty-nine-year-old Omaha doctor surprised her friends and family by announcing her forthcoming marriage to Henry Picotte, a Sioux Indian from the Yankton Agency and brother of Marguerite's late husband, Charles. The young couple moved into a house across from the Presbyterian Church in Bancroft, Nebraska, and Susan practiced medicine among Indians and whites while keeping house for her husband and, later, two young sons, Pierre and Caryl. Totally committed to the assimilationist education program of which she was a product, Susan eventually enrolled her sons in the Nebraska Military Academy in Lincoln, a private institution for young white boys that made "individualization their aim."

In 1897 her health again declined dramatically, with family members fearing for her life, but she recovered and threw herself into various public health issues. She helped organize the Thurston County Medical Association, served several times on the health board of the town of Walthill, and joined the state medical society. As chair of the State Health Committee of the Nebraska Federation of Women's Clubs for three years, she effectively worked to get health-related bills through the state legislature. She also lobbied for required medical inspection of schools, for sanitary ice cream dishes and spoons, for school drinking fountains, and for the establishment of a playground for Walthill children.

Susan was also involved in several other activities. For example, she vigoriously campaigned against tuberculosis, shared drinking cups, and the house fly. She lectured on the health problems of tuberculosis at the Indian church and before local townspeople and wrote to Indian Commissioner Cato Sells in 1914, suggesting that children at the government school be examined monthly for the disease. She wrote an article on the "evils of the drinking cup," which was published in the local newspaper; eventually, legislation was passed that abolished its use. And finally she designed an attractive anti-housefly poster encouraging people not to allow flies in their homes or near food. She urged them to sprinkle lime or kerosene where flies collected, thus eliminating their breeding grounds, to buy fly traps, and to use screens for doors and windows.

But Susan's most determined health-related crusade was against "demon rum." In 1905, her husband Henry died after years of hard drinking, leaving her the sole support of an invalid mother and two small boys. The battle Susan joined to keep liquor off the reservation was a long-range one. Prior to her father's death in 1888, very little liquor had been present on the reservation, in part because of the watchfulness of his police force, but in subsequent years alcoholism had reached epidemic proportions. "At first I went everywhere alone, at any time of night or day and felt perfectly safe among my people," she wrote on January 27, 1900, to Indian Commissioner William A. Jones. But increased alcoholism was now threatening everyone's safety. In her letter she recounted stories of street brawls, bizarre deaths, and increased poverty as a result of drink. Women pawned their clothing, men spent rent money on liquor, and even little children reeled down streets in drunken stupors. Requesting honest agents and removal of all bootleggers, she reminded Jones, "It is in your power to help us."

Although Susan failed to keep her people from liquor-related deaths, she did succeed in getting a hospital for Walthill. An $8,000 donation from the

Home Mission Board of the Presbyterian Church, additional funds raised by a benefit concert, and a $500 donation from the Society of Friends (Quakers) built the structure on an acre of land that Marguerite and her husband donated. The Walthill Hospital opened in January 1913. In 1915 alone a total of 448 patients were admitted, 126 of them Indian. Later, following Susan's death, the hospital was renamed the Dr. Susan Picotte Memorial Hospital by the Home Missions Board. In 1989, renovated and placed on the National Register of Historic Places, it was rededicated as the Susan LaFlesche Picotte Center.

The health care of her people was not the only concern for Susan. She was also forced into the volatile world of politics for the sake of her people when the federal government in 1909 arbitrarily extended the trust period for protecting Omaha land an additional ten years. This extension was based on the belief that Indians were uneducated and backward, incapable of protecting their land rights. This conclusion, of course, was not true of the Omaha, who had a higher literacy rate than most tribes. In June, Susan began a letter-writing campaign to government officials calling for the final allotment of Omaha lands.

The concept of allotment, which broke up Indian reservations and allotted land in severalty to tribal members, was a cherished goal of nineteenth-century reformers. They believed assimilation would best be achieved by turning nomadic as well as horticulturalist Indians into small farmers. The Omaha Severalty Act, with a twenty-five-year trust period, during which time Indian land was inalienable, had become law on August 7, 1882. Alice Fletcher, who had lobbied actively for this legislation, was appointed to implement the allotment process, which took until June 1884 to complete. Final allotment papers were delivered in 1885, with the trust period expiring in 1910.

Unfortunately, unanticipated problems arose as a result of the newly imposed ten-year extension—problems dealing with the disposal of tribal funds, the legal rights of allottees (they were not yet citizens), and the leasing of lands. Unanimously chosen by the Omaha to head a delegation to try to remove the extension, Susan traveled to Washington, D.C., and appeared before high-ranking government officials on February 7, 1910. The delegation was successful, and subsequently most of the Omahas were declared competent to rent or lease their lands and to receive their share of tribal monies.

In the fall of 1906 Susan, along with Marguerite's second husband, Walter Diddock, bought house lots in Walthill. Susan built a modern home, complete with fireplace, furnace, windows for light and fresh air, and an indoor bathroom. She and Marguerite became charter members of a new chapter of the Order of the Eastern Star, which supported community projects, lectures, concerts, and special events at the county fair. Finally, Susan helped organize the Presbyterian Church in Walthill while remaining active in the Omaha Agency's Blackbird Hills Presbyterian Church as spiritual adviser and physician.

Susan's diary between September 20, 1910, and January 19, 1911, reflected her fast-paced schedule of visiting home-bound patients, writing letters to government officials for illiterate Omahas, reading leases, and interpreting for a local attorney as he drew up wills or other legal documents. She also served on the Cemetery Association Board, raised money for church windows, and held prayer sessions for the sick. But her entries also reflect her increasingly poor health. Her ear infection steadily worsened, making her increasingly deaf, and in 1914 it was diagnosed as "decay of the bone," probably cancer. Sinking rapidly, Susan died on September 18, 1915, and was buried beside her husband at the Bancroft Cemetery. Three clergymen performed the simple service, the pastor of the Walthill Presbyterian Church, the pastor of the Blackbird Hills Mission, and a member of the Presbyterian Home Mission Board. That afternoon a graveside service was performed by members of the Amethyst Chapter of the Order of the Eastern Star.

Time has not diminished the many important contributions of Susette and Susan LaFlesche. These remarkable women's lives spanned not only the decades of the new femininity for middle and upper class women, but also decades of reform that emphasized the forced assimilation of the Indians. Although the sisters did not directly challenge the concept of the Victorian woman's sphere, they moved beyond it. And in the realm of reform, Susette and Susan benefited from the ideals of the reformers. They assimilated, and became reformers in their own right.

For instance, Susette's role in the Standing Bear tour gained the attention of prominent Bostonians and New Yorkers who organized, raised money, and supported the tour. Helen Hunt Jackson was definitely drawn to the Ponca cause, in part because of Susette. Furthermore, the young Omaha Indian woman's testimony before congressional hearings lent credence to the injustice of the Ponca removal and probably was a factor that helped prompt Congress to pass legislation for reparations. And finally, those familiar with her introduction to *Ploughed Under* were presented with a powerful sentiment when they read "the huge plough of the 'Indian system' has run for a hundred years, beam deep, turning down into the darkness of the earth every hope and aspiration which we have cherished." The key, Susette wrote, was simple; recognize the Indian as a person, a citizen, an individual with legal rights.

Meanwhile, Susan, although never part of a public lecture tour like Susette, nevertheless lectured locally on health issues or to various auxiliaries of the WNIA and continually wrote letters to government officials. She, too, expanded her sphere by shifting her doctoring skills from her family to the extended tribe, to neighboring white residents, and eventually to the state at large. Her fight against tuberculosis, the shared cup, the common household fly, and alcoholism benefited not only the Omaha Indians but all Nebraska residents.

The chain of events that propelled Susette and Susan into prominence obviously had certain common denominators. With similar backgrounds, educational experiences, and strong parental guidance, they also benefited from the federal government's assimilationist policy that emphasized education and Christianization. Furthermore, both sisters were sponsored by well-to-do white women interested in furthering their educations, yet the sisters remained loyal to their Indian culture, promoting and preserving it through their writings and teachings. Susan spoke publicly about her childhood, wrote articles on the home life of the Indian for readers of the Women's National Indian Association's magazine, *The Indian's Friend,* and published Omaha stories and legends in local newspapers. Susette, who had promoted the Indian way of life while on the lecture platform, had also continued to publish Indian essays in *St. Nicholas* and other magazines.

There were differences, however, in the two sisters' roles. Susette's prominence came at the very beginning of the late-nineteenth-century Indian reform movement, before any national organization had been established. Her appeal and personality may have helped spawn reform organizations, such as the Boston Indian Citizenship Committee, which strongly supported the Ponca. On the other hand, Susan, who came along a half dozen years later, became prominent after the establishment of the first national Indian organization, the Women's National Indian Association, founded in 1879. Susan could not have become a physician without their monetary support. She was therefore a beneficiary of the movement, not a catalyst.

Probably the greatest difference between Susette and Susan was in their choice of spouses. By marrying Tibbles, Susette became estranged at times from her family because her husband disagreed with them on several issues dealing with Indians. Since Susette was unable to focus entirely on Indian issues, she often had to support Populism, Free Silver, and other non-Indian issues that her husband championed. Furthermore, the estrangement from her family was also exacerbated when, after marriage, Susette moved off the reservation, living in Omaha, Lincoln, and Washington, D.C., for extended periods. Meanwhile, Susan's marriage to an Indian enabled her to remain an active part of the reservation and close to her family—a daily reminder to her patients of the advantages of acculturation to white ways.

Susette and Susan LaFlesche walked with dignity and grace in a world that encompassed both their reservation and American cities and towns. They were at home on the Nebraska prairie as well as in the halls of Congress. They were not reluctant about writing to government officials when injustices or critical situations arose. They attained positions in reform and medicine that few contemporary white women reached. By any cultural standards, they were remarkable nineteenth-century women. Their story may be one of the few positive achievements of the myopic Indian reform movement that saw little value in Indian culture and intended, through the process of assimilation, to replace it completely.

SOURCES AND FURTHER READING

The LaFlesche Family Papers, located in the Nebraska State Historical Society, include correspondence of various family members as well as letters from Alice Cunningham Fletcher and Sara T. Kinney.

For information on Joseph LaFlesche's children, see Norma Kidd Green, *Iron Eye's Family: The Children of Joseph LaFlesche* (Lincoln, NE: Johnsen Publishing Company, 1969). For information on Joseph's daughters from his first marriage, see Green, "Four Sisters: Daughters of Joseph LaFlesche," *Nebraska History* 45 (1964):165–76; Anne P. Diffendal, "The LaFlesche Sisters: Victorian Reformers in the Omaha Tribe," *Journal of the West* 33 (1994):37–44; and Lisa E. Emmerich, "Marguerite LaFlesche Diddock: Office of Indian Affairs Field Matron," *Great Plains Quarterly* 13 (summer 1993):162–71.

Dorothy Clarke Wilson's *Bright Eyes: The Story of Susette LaFlesche, an Omaha Indian* (New York: McGraw-Hill Book Company, 1974), although lacking in primary source material, is the standard biography of Susette. Margaret Crary, *Susette LaFlesche: Voice of the Omaha Indians* (New York: Hawthorne Books, 1973), is a juvenile biography with invented scenes and incidents.

There are numerous articles on Susan. See, for instance, Valerie Sherer Mathes, "Susan LaFlesche Picotte: Nebraska's Indian Physician, 1865–1915," *Nebraska History* 63 (winter 1982):502–30; Mathes, "Dr. Susan LaFlesche Picotte: The Reformed and the Reformer," in *Indian Lives: Essays on Nineteenth- and Twentieth-Century Native American Leaders,* ed. L. G. Moses and Raymond Wilson (Albuquerque: University of New Mexico Press, 1985), 62–90; and Mathes "Susan LaFlesche Picotte, M.D. Nineteenth-Century Physician and Reformer," *Great Plains Quarterly* 13 (summer 1993):172–86; Laurence M. Hauptman, "Medicine Woman Susan LaFlesche, 1865–1915," *New York State Journal of Medicine* 78 (1978):173–88; Peggy Ann Pascoe, "The Search for Female Moral Authority: Protestant Women and Rescue Homes in the American West, 1874–1939," (Ph.D. diss., Stanford University, 1986), 199-330, published as *Relations of Rescue: The Search for Female Moral Authority in the American West, 1874–1939* (New York: Oxford University Press, 1990); and Jerry E. Clark and Martha Ellen Webb, "Susette and Susan LaFlesche: Reformer and Missionary," *Being and Becoming Indian: Biographical Studies of North American Frontiers,* ed. James A. Clifton (Chicago: Dorsey Press, 1989), 147–59.

No full-length scholarly biography has been written on Thomas Henry Tibbles; however, some of his interesting life can be found in Thomas Henry Tibbles, *An Account of the Trial of Standing Bear,* ed. with introduction by Kay Graber (Lincoln: University of Nebraska Press, 1972), and Tibbles, *Buckskin & Blanket Days* (Lincoln: University of Nebraska Press, 1969). The Ponca tour was a media event, covered extensively during the fall and winter of 1879 in newspapers, such as the *Boston Daily Advertiser, New York Daily Tribune, New York Times, Washington Evening Star,* and *Philadelphia Public Ledger.* Newspaper coverage continued sporadically during 1880 and 1881 as a government commission met and congressional legislation was enacted.

The following are the citations for the quotes: Susette LaFlesche's 1879 quote, from Tibbles, *An Account of the Trial of Standing Bear,* 3; Susan's 1886 quote, from *Lend-A-Hand.* Susette to the Indian Commissioner in Wilson, *Bright Eyes,* 131–32; Alonzo Bell to Carl Schurz in Schurz, *Speeches, Correspondence and Political Papers of Carl Schurz,* ed. by Frederick Bancroft (New York: G.P. Putnam's Sons, 1913), 4:147–48; Susan's comments about the woman's clinic in Susan LaFlesche to Rosalie Farley, [probably] January 1888 and November 5, 1886, La Flesche Family Papers; Susan to Commissioner William A. Jones in Hampton University Archives, Hampton, Virginia; and Susette's sentiments on Indian rights in Inshta Theamba ("Bright Eyes"), "Introduction," *Ploughed Under: The Story of an Indian Chief* (New York: Fords, Howard & Hulbert, 1881).

8

Elinore Pruitt Stewart:
The Adventurous Woman Homesteader

SUSANNE K. GEORGE

In OCTOBER 1913, the *Atlantic Monthly* began publishing a series of letters by "The Woman Homesteader," Elinore Pruitt Stewart. These writings, which promoted the myths of the West as a Garden of Eden and of homesteading as a means to achieve the American Dream, spoke to the hearts of early-twentieth-century Americans twenty years after Frederick Jackson Turner had declared the frontier "closed." Stewart wrote, "any woman who can stand her own company, can see the beauty of a sunset, loves growing things, and is willing to put in as much time at careful labor as she does over the wash tub, will certainly succeed; will have independence, plenty to eat all the time, and a home of her own in the end."

Stewart's life not only personified this belief but revealed her courage and self-reliance in overcoming incredible odds to take control of her life. She stands today as the archetypal woman homesteader, the mythic Earth Mother of the Plains, who not only nurtured her own family and her neighbors with her undaunting energy and her selfless toil, but who hoped by her own example to serve as a model to raise women out of poverty to a more fulfilling life.

Stewart's various writings document the realization of her goal as well as her physical and emotional regeneration in the New West. After the publication of her letters from Wyoming in *Atlantic Monthly*, Houghton Mifflin published them in *Letters of a Woman Homesteader* in 1914. The following year, editor Ellery Sedgwick commissioned her to write another series for the *Atlantic Monthly*, which Houghton Mifflin published as *Letters on an Elk Hunt*. Stewart only published seven more stories after that. Two appeared in the *Atlantic Monthly*, four in the *Youth's Companion*, and one in *Folk-Say*. Many of her stories and letters were not published during her lifetime but

Describing herself as "an expansive old lady with four chins and not much lap," Stewart avoided having her photograph taken. In this one, taken around 1925, she tries to hide behind a pine tree. (Courtesy of the University of Nebraska Press)

were simply sent to entertain her various correspondents. Although the realities of her homesteading experiences often contradicted the optimism with which she described them in these letters and stories, her persona of the "Woman Homesteader" became her ideal as she turned hardship into "adventure" on the last of the American frontiers.

Born on June 3, 1876, in White Bead Hill in the Chickasaw Nation, Indian Territory, Stewart learned early that life would grant her no favors. After her father died while serving in the military on the Mexican border, her mother married his brother, Tom Pruitt, and Stewart soon had eight half brothers and half sisters from this union. The family lived so precariously poor, she related, that she did not even own a pair of shoes until she was six years old. Teaching herself to read and write, she questioned the local storekeeper about the letters, words, and numbers she found on pieces of paper. When an opportunity arose to attend school, it was short-lived, for one day a band of men rode up to the school, dragged her teacher out of the room, and hanged him from a nearby sycamore tree for stealing a horse. Although no stranger to violence, she wrote that she was ten years old before she "knew that any one could die without being shot." Living during turbulent times in the lawless West, she also remembered a bloody shoot-out between her father, who barricaded himself in their house, and a drunken band of thirty men of Indian and Negro blood.

Life did not relent for Stewart. In 1893 when she was seventeen, her mother died shortly after giving birth to her ninth child, who also did not survive. The deaths were traumatic for Stewart, who huddled with her brothers and sisters in the moonlight, wondering "how the moon *could* shine when the end of our world had come." To lessen his burden, Pruitt found husbands for his daughters Laura, thirteen, and Maggie, twelve. Later that same year, Stewart's stepfather died in an accident at work, leaving her, at eighteen, responsible for five of her siblings: Lucius, ten; Joseph, eight; Josephine, six; Tom, four; and Susie, two. Although relatives offered to divide up the children among them, they refused to be separated and arranged to live with their blind grandmother, Mary Ann Courtney, in Davis, Oklahoma. Unfortunately, this decision proved to be too much of a burden on the old woman, and around 1900, Stewart and her siblings found themselves once more on their own.

To survive, Stewart, now twenty-four, found work for herself, her sister, Josephine, and her brothers with the Santa Fe Railroad, which was constructing new bridges and branch lines in the area. The boys drove mules that pulled scrapers for building the railroad bed, and Stewart and her sister helped prepare the crew's meals and washed their laundry. At night they all slept on the floor of the commissary tent. Because of the hardships and danger of their situation, Susie, eight, had to be sent back to live with their grandmother.

In 1902, an opportunity for escape and a better life for Stewart, Josephine, and Susie arrived when Harry Cramer Rupert, who was about forty-eight years old, asked her to marry him, and they filed on a homestead in the Indian Territory. Again, security eluded her. By 1906, she was living in Oklahoma City with her sisters and working as a domestic, but Rupert was curiously absent. On February 10, Stewart gave birth to her first child, Mary Jerrine Rupert, and began training as a nurse in Bethany Hospital, west of the city.

Approximately ten months later, Stewart, her daughter, and her sisters boarded a train for Colorado, ostensibly so that she could write an article about the Mesa Verde cliff dwellings for the *Kansas City Star*. She was, however, more probably escaping to another state to avoid losing custody of Jerrine, as was often the case for women in nineteenth-century divorces. Supposedly, a police matron had warned Stewart that legal proceedings were being filed that would take Jerrine away from her. The woman gave her travel funds and asked not to be told of the destination.

No record has been found of Stewart's divorce, but since record-keeping in the Indian Territory was not systematic and courthouse fires were frequent, speculations are tempting. Because Stewart knew poverty and hard work on a first-name basis, one can assume that homesteading would not have daunted her as it did some new brides. As her future experiences would prove, she was not a quitter. Perhaps the fault lay with Rupert. That he wrote to wish her a "Happy Christmas" two years later in Denver probably rules out desertion, a common cause listed in nineteenth-century divorce suits. Revealingly, however, Stewart's stories frequently condemn alcohol and drinking. In her *Homesteader* series, Stewart's persona refused to confront a character, Greasy Pete, her neighbor and Mrs. Louderer's hired man, when she heard that he had been drunk for two days. She knew enough to stay away from the Louderer place. Stewart also writes of several women married to men who drank excessively, women like Ma Gillis and Mrs. Pond, who were eventually forced to survive on their own. Her literary characters continuously hunted down moonshiners, destroyed their stills, and called in the revenuers, thus unconsciously revealing her negative attitude toward liquor. Stewart, pregnant and with two sisters and a daughter to support, may have chosen to make it on her own rather than remain with Rupert and endure abuse.

When Stewart arrived in Denver, she had no job, no friends, no money, and a family to feed and clothe. Inventing a story about her husband's death in a railroad accident, she assumed the role of a widow, more acceptable in Victorian society's eyes, and began looking for work. Denver, at the beginning of the twentieth century, had become a haven for people hoping to enlarge their prospects in the new cities of the West. Without special skills or an education, however, Stewart could only find jobs requiring manual labor, such as washing laundry, scrubbing floors, and stoking coal furnaces.

Stewart's sisters decided to try their luck in California, lessening Stewart's responsibilities, but her prospects remained dismal until she found employment with the genteel Mrs. Juliet Coney, a retired schoolteacher from Boston. Although Stewart labored for the kindly widow seven days a week as a nurse, cook, and housekeeper for two dollars, out of which she had to pay child care, Stewart found in Mrs. Coney a compassionate friend, who shared her books and encouraged Stewart to read and study to better her life. Help, too, came from the Sunshine Rescue Mission on Larimer Street where the Rev. Father Corrigan began tutoring her in preparation for the Civil Service examination.

By 1909, discouraged and physically ill, Stewart confided in the minister that what she really wanted to do was to homestead—to escape the stress and poverty of the overcrowded city and to raise Jerrine herself, instead of leaving her child in the daily care of strangers. Perhaps influenced by the news of the Enlarged Homestead Act, the Mondell Act of 1909 that granted 320-acre tracts in semiarid lands, Stewart wanted her part of the American Dream, and she was willing to work hard to obtain it. Corrigan suggested that she obtain a position where land was still available so that she could learn about the area and homesteading while earning money to help her start a new life.

At the same time, Clyde Stewart, a Wyoming rancher and widower, decided that he needed a housekeeper and placed an ad in the *Denver Post,* perhaps this one published on March 7: "*Wanted*—Young or middle-aged lady as companion and to assist with housework on Wyoming ranch; a good permanent home for the right party." Stewart courageously responded to the advertisement, and soon she and Jerrine, accompanied by Mr. Stewart, began their journey to Burntfork, Wyoming, a tiny community nestled in Henry's Fork valley just north of the snowy Uinta Mountains.

Stewart's determination to take control of her life was finally beginning to pay off. One month after she arrived in Wyoming, she began writing letters to Coney, describing her new situation. Ebullient over the eggs and cream that her Plymouth Rock hens and milk cows would provide, she delighted in her good fortune. More significantly, Mr. Stewart, as she always referred to him, was "absolutely no trouble."

By May, Stewart had realized her dream and filed on 147 acres of land adjoining Mr. Stewart's homestead, boasting that she was now a "bloated landowner." She had wanted land in the forest reserve, but she told Coney that she had chosen land in the valley because it was better suited to ranching. The mountains had but three seasons, she joked, "winter and July and August." In reality, Stewart had decided to homestead the neighboring land because she and Mr. Stewart planned to marry. On May 5, 1909, one week after her homestead filing, the couple were married by the justice of the peace, neighbor William Pearson, in the family's living room. Although she was chagrined that she had forgotten to remove her apron and old shoes before the ceremony and seemed somewhat ashamed at the haste in which she married, she never regretted her choice of marital partner, even though the marriage was partly one of convenience. She did not even know where to begin telling Coney about "my Clyde," for her friend would think she "could do nothing but brag."

For the first time since her parents had died, Stewart not only had a home, but she even enjoyed a room of her own. In order to meet federal regulations and "prove up" on her homestead, she needed to build and occupy a residence on her claim. Creatively interpreting the law, Mr. Stewart, whose own house had been built two feet from the edge of his property, built his wife's cabin next to her boundary line and then added a long room connecting the two buildings. Stewart could then "hold down" her land and live with her husband. Except for the four years the family spent in Boulder to facilitate

The Stewart home in Burntfork, Wyoming, consisted of several additions. Her husband's original cabin is on the far right, and Stewart's homestead building is on the far left. Her garden encompassed the area in front of and beside the house. This photograph was taken in 1987 by the author.

the children's schooling, from the fall of 1921 to the spring of 1925, Elinore never left her homestead.

Pride in her cabin overflowed in Stewart's letters to Coney. Built snugly into a hillside and on the sunny south end of the house, the room measured approximately twelve-by-sixteen feet. "Every log in my house is as straight as a pine can grow," she boasted. Decorating the room required ingenuity. Stewart had only two rolls of wallpaper, so she cut out each of the red, pink, and yellow roses and pasted them around the room on the heavy gray building-paper that covered the logs. Then she made a screen from broken bamboo fishing rods and old blue curtains to make a private corner for Jerrine to arrange her own little treasures. For the floor, Stewart braided a blue and white rug made from old sheets and Jerrine's old dresses. No ornate Victorian parlor could have been more beautiful to its owner than this humble room was to Stewart.

"This has been for me the busiest, happiest summer I can remember," wrote Stewart in her glowing letter of September 11, 1909, to Mrs. Coney. She had been working hard in her garden and on the ranch, but after struggling all of her life simply to shelter and feed her family, the abundance of food now available to her from the small ranch made the myth of the West as a Garden of Eden a reality. Having tasted the bitterness of hunger, she stockpiled her food and relished each meal.

Every year Stewart planted more than an acre of produce in her garden in front of the house and continuing around to the south. She only had to walk a few feet out her kitchen door to gather fresh vegetables and fruit for the family table. By fall, they had all of the vegetables they could store. She boasted to her friends that her large stone cellar northwest of the house was filled with more than two tons of potatoes, a half a ton of carrots, and nearly one hundred heads of cabbage as well as large bins of beets, turnips, and squash. Stewart planted a variety of vegetables and often had witloof, endive, celery, Bermuda onions, carrots, and salsify in her cellar. Disappointed at first because her tomatoes would not ripen before the early frost in the mountains, she soon discovered that she could store them, and they would ripen after they had been harvested. Soon she was growing six varieties of tomatoes that would last the family through November. Tempted by the colorful seed catalogues, guided by horticultural pamphlets from the Department of Agriculture, and driven by necessity, Stewart's zeal for gardening and experimenting with new plants was only restrained by the mountain altitude and the limited growing season.

Stewart also raised more than enough chickens to eat as well as to renew the flock, and she had plenty of turkeys for all of the birthdays and holidays. Jars of preserved pickles, fruits, jams, and jellies lined the shelves of the small cellar under the kitchen. The indefatigable Stewart also made butter from milking ten cows twice a day, which paid for a year's supply of flour and gasoline. The hay she helped mow wintered the cattle and horses. Stewart's immense energy and long hours of hard work not only provided sustenance for her loved ones but also enriched her own sense of self-satisfaction and self-worth.

Even nature provided Stewart with ample bounty. She hunted the countryside for sage chickens, combed the mountains for wild fruit and berries, and caught all of the trout she could eat in a few minutes using a simple birch rod cut from beside the stream and a few grasshoppers as bait. Deer hunting was likewise a community activity, as were elk-hunting expeditions in the mountains north of Green River. In her second book, *Letters on an Elk Hunt,* Stewart described such a hunt on the Bridger Reserve near Pinedale. Although the hunt itself constitutes only a few chapters of the narrative, the trip was undertaken primarily to secure meat for the winter. Everyone, including Stewart, bagged her or his limit, and "an imposing row of game hanging in the pines" behind the tents at Camp Cloudcrest testified to nature's goodness.

With sensory delight, Stewart detailed the food she prepared. She enjoyed baking and described the treats in tempting detail. To the blind Mr. Zaiss, one of her regular correspondents living in New England, she explained that she had been working in the kitchen all day and had prepared "eight loaves of bread, two coffee cakes and three dozen doughnuts." In another letter to Miss Woods, a correspondent in the South, she asked, "Do you smell my bread baking? Shall I send you a piece of my coffee cake? We like it with cinnamon, raisins and sugar and it is raising fine and soon will be ready for the oven."

Stewart especially loved food prepared outdoors—"pork and beans heated in a frying pan on a camp-fire for breakfast … with coffee *boiled* in a battered old pail and drunk from a tomato-can." No one would ever again desire "iced melons, powdered sugar, and fruit, or sixty-nine varieties of breakfast food" after having sampled this repast. However, she warned, "you must be away out in Wyoming, with the morning sun just gilding the distant peaks."

Stewart shared her ample supplies with others less fortunate. During her first winter in Wyoming, while visiting the widow Louderer, the two women decided to take boxes of food to the lonely sheepherders as a Christmas treat. They roasted geese, baked meat loaves, boiled hams and hens, and prepared cakes, cookies, doughnuts, and jams to take to the isolated camps. Remembering her own poverty and ignoring her cattleman husband's differences with the sheepmen, Stewart did her part to brighten the holidays wherever she could. "It would have done your heart good to see the sheep-men," she wrote to Coney. "They were all delighted, and when you consider that they live solely on canned corn and tomatoes, beans, salt pork, and coffee, you can fancy what they thought of their treat."

Even during World War I and the Depression when the Stewarts had no money, there was always enough food for the family with provisions left over to share with neighbors and the needy. Not satisfied with the relief work the local Red Cross accomplished, Stewart and her neighbors decided to coordinate their own efforts, tithing their supplies of produce and garden seeds and visiting the needy families through planting and canning seasons. Calling the family a "valiant army," Stewart, her husband, and her children "fought the depression with hoes, plows, rakes, mowers, hayrakes, pitchforks, milk pails and mason jars." The flowers that she planted in the garden served to boost family morale.

When Stewart and her husband read a call for help from drought victims in their daily paper, they still were not content that they were doing all they could for others less fortunate. Stewart sent a letter to the newspaper offering aid, and within two weeks, a young couple and their baby arrived at Burntfork, all very sick and nearly starving. The Stewarts nursed, fed, clothed, and housed them and then helped them to a new start on their own homestead.

Firm in the belief that "Homesteading is the solution of all poverty's problems," Stewart informed Coney and, subsequently, the readers of the *Atlantic Monthly,* where her letters were first published, that if a woman wanted to homestead, she would not starve. She offered herself as proof that "a woman could ranch if she wanted to." Well-housed and well-fed, Stewart had journeyed a long way from her struggles to survive in the Indian Territory and the Denver slums to the Arcadian bounty of the frontier.

Stewart's success at homesteading rejuvenated her soul as well as her body. Because of her strong sense of humor, her positive outlook on life, and her delight in the natural world, she thrived emotionally in the wilderness. Stewart claimed, "I am a firm believer in laughter. I am real superstitious about it. I think if Bad Luck came along, he would take to his heels if some one laughed right loudly." Alluding to herself as a tenderfoot, even after many years of residence in Wyoming, she laughed at incidents that might have upset others less resilient.

In a chapter from *Homesteader* entitled "A Charming Adventure and Zebulon Pike," Stewart detailed how a heavy snow surprised her and her three-year-old daughter the second night out in the mountains. "Such a snow-storm I never saw!" she exclaimed. "I began to think how many kinds of idiot I was. Here I was thirty or forty miles from home, in the mountains where no one goes in the winter and where I knew the snow got to be ten or fifteen feet deep." Undaunted, she laughed at her foolishness and declared, "I could never see the good of moping." Fixing a hearty breakfast to give them strength for the treacherous journey, she checked her supplies of food and ammunition so that she could ration them carefully, and then considered her options. While waiting for the snow to cease, she went hunting to provide food for the day and saw smoke. Knowing help was near, she broke camp, rode toward it, and discovered a neighbor, who accompanied her out of the mountains the next day. Her courage and backwoodsmanship averted disaster, and in losing her way, paradoxically, she found a new friend. More important, she laughed about it afterwards. She did not need to be rescued by her husband and "be powerfully humble afterwards." Although this tale may have been imaginatively enlivened, Stewart undertook such camping expeditions regularly.

Stewart could also see the humor in everyday situations by putting problems into the right perspective. In "Among the Mormons" in *Homesteader,* Stewart displayed this talent. During her absence while visiting a Mormon settlement nearby, Mr. Stewart hired the "Tackler" to paper a room. The man decided to reverse every other strip of wallpaper so that some roses grew right side up and others stood on their heads. When Stewart returned and viewed the disaster, she laughed and remarked, "A little thing like wall-paper put on upside down doesn't bother me; but what *would* I do if I were a 'second' [wife of a Mormon]." Later, when she overheard her husband making plans with a neighbor to travel the sixty miles to Green River without her if she wasn't ready, she made a game of it and surprised him by being prepared—never telling him how she found out. "That only added to the fun," she said.

Foolish people bore the brunt of Stewart's light-hearted satire. In her *Homesteader* account of "The Contented Couple," Stewart poked fun at a neighbor's wife who was tight with her money. When Stewart and the woman rented rooms in Green River in which to freshen up and wait for the midnight train to Rock Springs, the neighbor wanted half of her money back since she was only staying half of the night. When the hotel owner refused to refund the money, the woman stubbornly stayed in the room to get her money's worth, thus missing the train and the shopping trip. To add to the injury, the neighbor had asked for such a high price for her eggs that she did not sell any and had to carry them the sixty miles back home in the loaded wagon.

Homesteading required more than a strong body and the courage to dream, however. An active sense of humor was as essential to Stewart as her hoe and her Mason jars. Stewart laughed out loud, both at herself and at society, which helped her survive the hardships and isolation of her little corner of the West. In addition to dealing with apparent catastrophes with humor, Stewart viewed misadventures as adventures. She theorized that "when we become sorry for ourselves we make our misfortunes harder to bear, because we lose courage and can't think without bias." Following Pollyanna's lead in searching "for something to be glad about," Stewart learned to view life's unexpected or unwanted detours with more tolerance.

An example of this positive attitude can be discovered in Stewart's Febru-

Stewart playfully peeks out from behind her husband in her garden in this 1921 photograph. Although the marriage could be considered "mail order," the couple worked together as equal partners in both good times and hardship. (Courtesy of the University of Nebraska Press)

ary 1912 letter to Coney, entitled "The 'Stocking-Leg' Dinner" in *Home-steader*. According to the tale, the Stewarts and their neighbors had been invited to a bachelor's house for a special dinner that featured foods de-scribed in James Fenimore Cooper's *Leatherstocking Tales*. On the way to the cabin in the mountains, not only did Mr. Stewart discover that he had for-gotten to bring the mess-box, but an avalanche halted the group's progress. Stranded high in the mountains at nightfall, hungry and cold, they were rescued by Manuel Pedro Felipe and his wife, Carlota Juanita, who warmed them, fed them, and housed them for the night. The next morning they continued in high spirits with a "merry, laughing party" arriving in time for the unusual repast of porcupine, beaver-tail, antelope, sage hen, and mack-erel. Rather than dwell on the hunger, cold, and danger of the expedition, Stewart concentrated on the new friends she had made and the good food she had eaten. The eventful excursion, one of several that the couple took, reassured her that "life held something new and enjoyable after all."

Many years later in the spring of 1925, after the family had moved tempo-rarily to Boulder for the children's schooling, Stewart's husband returned early to Wyoming to help with the spring calving. Stewart was to journey home in the spring across the Rocky Mountains in an open wagon with the family's possessions. Jerrine and her Grandmother Stewart were to follow later by train. Although Stewart had made the trip with Clyde in 1921 when they moved to Boulder, she would be on her own this time, her only help coming from her three boys, ages eleven, twelve, and thirteen. None of the roads were paved, and some places permitted only one lane of traffic, a haz-ard for a team of horses with the growing number of cars and trucks com-manding the roadway. Twelve to fourteen feet of snow lay in the passes, and, as it thawed in the May sunlight, the road became slippery and dangerous.

At first, the journey was uneventful with only "a series of small adven-tures, most of them pleasant." When Stewart reached the foot of Berthoud Pass, she decided to wait until morning to make the trek, so they found a splendid camping spot near Clear Creek where the boys caught trout for supper. A young man, his food box empty, his wagon in disrepair, and his knowledge of traveling faulty, camped next to them. Suddenly, Stewart had an adventure on her hands. No longer focusing on the next day's ordeal, she concentrated on helping the unfortunate young man, whom she called Goof, and learned his story. Both wagons eventually made it through the pass, with a lot of help from Stewart. She had made a new friend, and she had an "adventure" to embellish when she arrived home rather than just the memory of a difficult and frustrating climb.

Stewart was afraid that the friend to whom she had addressed the letter,

Mrs. Florence Allen, would think the event untrue, so she added, "You say I have an unusual knack of meeting extraordinary people; Miss Harrison once wrote me that she didn't like a letter because she didn't like the fiction. So I had a session with myself to determine whether I do fictionalize or how it happens that others do not see what I do in those we meet in passing." Stewart concluded that her ability to mingle with everyone and her fearless disregard of "manners," especially in the matter of questioning people about their lives, was to blame. Because of her innate curiosity and her unflagging optimism, Stewart looked for adventure in life, and she always found it.

Clearly, Stewart's appreciation of nature fueled her optimism and provided her with mental and spiritual revival. Beginning with her April 18, 1909, letter written to Coney when she had just arrived in Wyoming and continuing to her last journal entry written to Josephine Harrison, her Denver, Colorado, friend on June 26, 1933, Stewart's writings glorified the beauties of nature.

As Stewart traveled to Green River to file on her homestead, she experienced her first night camping under the Wyoming stars. The night was too beautiful to sleep, she recounted. She could hear the sound of a coyote and the whir of the wings of the sage chickens; she could see the violet shadows slowly encompass the snowy peaks as the stars "flirted shamelessly" with the hills; and she could feel the dry coldness of the snow that she shook off her blanket when she arose in the morning. Wyoming, she decided, didn't have any particular wonders of which to boast, but taken as a whole, it was inspiring. "Everything," she declared, "even the barrenness was beautiful."

Stewart especially gloried in the early morning sunrises in the mountains where the "amber light of the new day [chased] violet and amethyst shadows down the canyons," and the snow-covered peaks wore crowns of burnished gold. During her first year in Wyoming, she described the dawn as "a big jewel-box of dark green velvet lined with silver chiffon, the snow peak lying like an immense opal in its center and over all the amber light of a new day." At this hour wildlife abounded, with deer and their fawns carefully stealing out of the underbrush to nibble the lush grasses in the mountain meadows or to sip clear water from the rushing streams. The gold in the sunrises and the jeweled mountains became Stewart's wealth.

More than fifteen years later, while the family was residing in Boulder in 1924, Stewart still felt this same awe toward the sunrise. She slipped out of the city early in the morning, past the crystal frosted flowers and the golden leaves of the poplars, and climbed to the top of the hills not far from her home. There, she and "all nature waited reverently for the miracle." Trains whistled and trucks rumbled in the distance until in a "breathless minute the sun popped up. It hung like a red ball for a moment and then shot shafts of rosy gold after the fleeing, purple shadows." Stewart extended her arms to greet the new day: "I had gone wild," she said, and "eloped with the morning." In one of her last writings in 1933, she described the moment of sunrise even more reverently: "A little herald breeze rippled past warning every thing of the moment, just as the accolyte [sic] strikes the gong. A holy hush—then the golden day." The dawn, for Stewart, was a time of spiritual rebirth.

Stewart often viewed nature transcendentally, and it evolved into a spiritual source in her life. In *Homesteader*, she declared that when she was among the grandeur of the mountains, she felt insignificant and realized "how foolish is human endeavor, except that which reunites us with the mighty force called God." She later theorized that if the Garden of Eden had been in the mountains rather than in the lowlands, the serpent never would have tempted Adam and Eve. After all, hadn't Jesus resisted Satan's temptation on the mountain top? Even the irascible Mrs. Pond, in one of Stewart's stories, sermonized, "If every one lived on a hill there would be no sin. No one could live this high up, this near God and not love him and all the world too much to even think of doing Wrong."

Although Stewart was raised a Catholic, her family lived far from any churches, so her faith became a blend of philosophies garnered from visiting clergy of various denominations, from her readings, and from her fundamental belief in a benevolent God, good works, and the Golden Rule. Stewart worshipped God in her garden, on the mountain tops, and among the small stand of spruce and willows near the creek south of her home that she called her "cathedral." She even dabbled a little in Theosophy, an eclectic doctrine that emphasized brotherhood among all humanity, reincarnation, and the importance of the individual rather than an organized religion in communing with God. H. P. Blavatsky, in his book, *Key to Theosophy*, made the beliefs more appealing to Stewart when he employed horticultural images in his explanation of the doctrine.

Stewart wanted to share the beauty and spiritual enlightenment of nature with her friends. When Miss Woods was grieving, she wrote to her crippled Missouri friend: "My poor, dear you. How I wish I could bring you here right now, while my curtains are fresh and my company room clean and while the quaking aspens are so golden. From the window of what would be your room you could look out upon Mount Phillipeco, a big mountain near. High upon its side is a perfect cross, now flaming gold, where the quaking aspens are. It rest[s] me to look at it and it would you."

The realities of Stewart's world often presented a stark contrast to her optimistic portraits of it. During the years of World War I, with hired help hard to find and money even more scarce, Stewart's active involvement with the haying and ranch work, along with her garden and daily household chores, increased dramatically. Although professing that she was "having a perfectly lovely time helping" with the mowing, raking, and stacking of hay in the fall and with the planting and calving in the spring, Stewart really had no choice. The shortage of labor was felt nationwide, and especially in her remote corner of Wyoming. In addition, the children were all reaching the age when more formal schooling was becoming critical. Basically self-taught, Stewart realized the importance of a good education, so she determined that the children must stay with their Grandmother Stewart in Boulder during the school term. Taking on the children's chores added to Stewart's work load.

In the fall of 1919, the family had a good crop of steers as well as a fine herd of horses. They were looking forward to finally freeing themselves from debt in the spring. Unfortunately, the market price for cattle dropped, so the Stewarts decided to wait for better prices in the spring. But the winter of 1919–1920 proved especially severe, and Mr. Stewart had to borrow money to buy feed for the livestock. By spring, only about eight to ten cattle from an original herd of about one hundred survived.

To complicate matters, Stewart went to Boulder to spend the winter months with her children where they all contracted the flu. The virus affected Stewart so seriously that the doctor hospitalized her and warned Clyde, who had rushed from the ranch to Boulder to help his stricken family, that "the valves of [her] body had given out." Strenuous exercise could cause her death. The doctor consigned her to a wheelchair, a frustrating and depressing experience for the active homesteader. After her first outing, however, she returned home, true to her character, pushing the wheelchair!

That spring, when the family returned to the ranch, Jerrine fell from a horse and dislocated her shoulder, limiting her ability to help on the ranch. Stewart, still weak from her own recent illness, was so disconsolate that she couldn't even write letters to her friends. She admitted to Miss Woods that "the cattle died in piles and horses in other piles and I didn't want to write to any one." Attempting to find something about which to be "glad," she could only profess feeling relief when events reached "their worst." She rationalized, "You know what the worst *is* then and can plan for better things."

At this point, hoping that she could again publish to relieve the financial crisis, Stewart began a novel she entitled "Sage and Sand," set in the Wyoming ranch lands. She completed the adventure story about cattlemen, sheepmen, Indians, and rustlers in the summer of 1921, hiring one of their summer visitors to type the manuscript for her. That fall, the family decided to lease their ranch and live year-round in Boulder since they could not afford residences in both Colorado and Wyoming. Mr. Stewart did not want

In addition to her household tasks, Stewart worked in the garden, carried out the barnyard chores, and frequently helped with the haying—a task she especially enjoyed. In this 1926 photograph, she is driving one of the mowers that royalties from her books helped purchase. (Courtesy of the University of Nebraska Press)

to leave Burntfork but agreed with his wife that the children needed a good education. Packing all of their belongings and provisions into a wagon and hitching up the family horses, they made the five-hundred-mile journey across the mountains to Boulder.

Once settled in their house in Boulder, Stewart concentrated on finding a publisher for her book as well as other short stories that she had written. She asked for help from Ellery Sedgwick, editor of the *Atlantic Monthly*. In his reply he noted, "I am ever so glad to have your letter, for even though the news is not particularly cheerful, at least it shows that nothing very disastrous has happened." Evidently, both *Atlantic Monthly* and Houghton Mifflin had rejected "Sand and Sage," along with some short stories, but Sedgwick suggested other New York publishers for Stewart to contact.

Remembering F. N. Doubleday's interest in her writing years earlier, Stewart mailed the manuscript to Doubleday, Page, and Company. By the spring of 1923, when no news arrived from Doubleday, a disconsolate Stewart returned to Wyoming to help with the spring work on the ranch. Sometime later, the publisher wired Stewart in Boulder that they would buy the manuscript for five thousand dollars, but the telegram, which had been slipped through the mail slot in the seldom-used foyer, went unnoticed for some time by the children. When Stewart finally received the telegram in Burntfork, the deadline for a response had passed. Jerrine found her mother trying to stuff the novel into the stove, but intervened in time to save the charred manuscript. Stewart did not pursue its publication further, however. Between 1919 and 1923, Stewart's only audience was her friends although she continued to write with hopes of publication.

Finally, *Atlantic Monthly* accepted "Snow: An Adventure of the Woman Homesteader" for its December 1923 issue. The story describes an incident that occurred when the Woman Homesteader, Stewart's creative persona, had gone to a neighbor's home to assist in the delivery of her baby and on her return home became stranded in a deserted shack during a blizzard. The story added seventy-five dollars to the family's resources and fueled Stewart's hopes for future publication. During her stay in Boulder, relieved from the responsibilities of ranching, Stewart had more time to write and added more names to her list of correspondents to whom she sent letters and drafts of her stories.

In 1925, when the Stewarts stopped leasing their Wyoming land and once again lived there year-round on the ranch, their financial problems climaxed. Clyde, in his desperation to save the homestead, had made unwise financial decisions—co-signing for a neighbor's notes, mortgaging land, and buying what Stewart considered "worthless things." To add to what she termed their nightmarish "siege of horror," Clyde had became seriously ill with what the family later learned was hypoglycemia, an abnormally low blood-sugar level. She feared that her husband was losing his sanity, but her pride would not allow her to seek help. Finally, one night when her husband awoke raving and incoherent, Stewart fled to the barn where she "gave way" to her surpressed emotions. "I don't know what foolish things I did," she commented. "I was thankful that I had sense enough to get far enough away so that Mother would not be disturbed." As she walked back to the house, the stars once again twinkled in the early morning stillness.

Stewart's emotional release, with only the cows as witnesses, signaled a turning point in the family's affairs. Realizing that someone had to act, she took control of the business and started rebuilding. She nursed her husband back to health and encouraged him to go to neighbors to collect debts. They slowly began acquiring a herd of milk cows. Eventually, Mr. Stewart was able to work on road construction for the county, with his wages adding nine more cows to the herd.

The children, meanwhile, worked in the hay fields for the neighbors before returning to school in Boulder. Jerrine entered the newly opened art school at the University of Colorado, thanks to a scholarship. The four children continued to support themselves, attend school, and work at paying off the mortgage on their house in town. Although the bank eventually repossessed the house, the children were still able to afford rent on a little place on University Hill and to continue their schooling during the winter, returning to Wyoming during the summers to help with the work.

Stewart pursued her gardening, milking, and ranching activities until the fall of 1927. While Stewart was helping with the hay mowing one day, an owl flew up beneath the horses and frightened them. When they bolted, the mower struck an irrigation ditch, and Stewart was thrown from the metal seat. Afraid that the horses would run away and break the valuable mower, she clung to the lines. This caused the animals to back the eight-hundred-pound mower over her, and the horses stepped on her in the process. The accident broke three ribs, cracked her shoulder blade, spread her thorax, and bruised her entire body. The doctor told her that she must not do any lifting for a year or the breast bones would not unite properly. Stewart's response was typical: "All of this is foolishness, of course. I cannot possibly lay off for a year … . So that's that!"

Stewart's health remained troublesome. Her injuries from the mowing accident did not heal quickly, and an ulcerated sore on her leg, varicose veins, and sciatica continued to bother her. Although she continued her gardening, canning, and milking, rarely complaining, she had to take a chair to lean on while she worked, and she often resorted to a cane when she walked. Her letters and stories, however, flowed unabated even though her adventures now were more imaginary than lived.

In December 1931, when Stewart was fifty-five, her health failed again. She spent the holidays confined in bed: "I went to sleep. Just like a big, fat, old bear, hibernating for the winter. Seems like I slept for weeks and was never fully awake tho' I was often aware of hushed sounds, of the smell of medicine and of the great comfort of clean, smooth sheets and of everybody's being so kind, so kind." By spring she was able to entertain guests again and work out of doors, but she could not recover her stamina.

Hoping to regain her health and her spirits as well as refresh her creativity, Stewart retreated in the spring of 1933 to the mountains to camp and to write. The family helped her erect a large tent in the "Cedars" where she began a journal and planted an experimental garden. In her first journal entry of May 16, 1933, Stewart admitted her ill health and her depression: "My health has begun to fail. I arose in the morning just as tired as when I went to bed, everything any one said hurt me, even their very kindness enraged me. I had to watch myself every minute to keep from doing or saying something regrettable." She added, "It has been a terrible cold, hard winter, hard on stock and hard on people." Recounting all of her pleasures in life, she confided to Miss Harrison that even the joys of nature no longer encouraged her. "I suddenly lost courage," she wrote. That was why she needed this rest.

The family visited Stewart regularly, for her camp was only a few miles from the homestead. She faithfully recorded her daily events and reflections in her journal and began work on a reminiscence of her childhood days in the Indian Territory. One day, however, when her son Clyde stopped by to visit his mother, he found her delirious, and the family brought her back to the ranch. Stewart still had not regained her health by fall, so in September she was admitted to the hospital in Rock Springs where she had surgery to remove her gall bladder. Although the operation went well, she died during recovery on October 8, 1933, from a blood clot to her brain. Stewart was buried in the Burntfork Pioneer Cemetery located a few miles northwest of her home. Appropriately, the sandstone slab that once served as the front step to her homestead now stands as her monument.

Many readers believe that Stewart's letters and stories are primary historical documents of the settling of the frontier. Although much of the information she revealed about life in Wyoming was based on her own experiences and acquaintances, she never, reported her son Clyde Jr., "let facts get in the way of a good story." We have no way of knowing which of her adventures did or did not occur. We do know, however, that as the years progressed, Stewart's writing became more and more self-conscious; her style became more polished, her world expanded, and she grew more introspective. More importantly, her writings increasingly reveal her perception of the homesteading experience, her positive attitude toward life, and her belief in the American Dream and its fulfillment in the lands of the West.

One way to sift historical fact from fiction in Stewart's writings is to classify them loosely into three categories: everyday letters, which record real people and events in her life; "embroidered" letters, which describe people and events that she has enlivened with creative imagination; and local color fiction or formal short stories employing popular romantic and sentimental literary traditions.

Although most of the information about Stewart's childhood and her Denver experiences, the ranch, her home, her garden, and her family has been verified as true, Stewart was never above rearranging facts to her advantage. In *Homesteader,* for example, she claimed credit for placing the advertisement in the *Denver Post* when, in truth, Mr. Stewart had taken the initiative, and she held to the story of her widowhood as long as she lived. During her later years, however, in her more personal letters to Josephine Harrison, Maria Wood, and Mr. Zaiss, when her stories became more formal and no longer an integral part of her letters, Stewart's scenes of daily life disclosed a realistic view of a woman's ranching experiences.

Other Stewart tales appear to be based on true experiences that were creatively embellished, or "embroidered," to make a better story. The accounts of a cowboy named Lige and the doctoring of his rupture, the Stewart wedding tour and Elinore's adventure on the glacial ice, the selling of war bonds to neighbors, the camaraderie with Goof on the journey through Berthoud Pass in the Rockies, and the meeting with a consumptive World War I veteran in Boulder all seem to be based on actual events. Life, unfortunately, does not always provide romance or tidy endings, so in Stewart's stories, although she admitted that one relationship might only last as long as the groceries held out, lovers are united, mothers and sons reunited, and struggling families blessed by an opportune benefactor.

Stewart's more formal short stories, most of them written to commemorate Coney's birthday or penned explicitly for publication, describe local or regional happenings and personalities known to most inhabitants of Burntfork. Her stories about moonshiners, cattle rustlers, and wild-horse hunts seem to derive from such local events. At one point she actively sought information about Butch Cassidy's activities, a robbery at Point of Rocks Pony Express station, and information on Rawlins, supposedly a local outlaw. Remaining true to her narrative pattern, however, the Woman Homesteader always appeared in the right spot at the right time to take part in the adventure.

Above all, Stewart enjoyed telling a good story. Whether her tales are true accounts of a woman homesteader or local-color fictions, the flavor of the West revealed in her writings fed the appetites of her contemporaries across the United States. In them, and in her persona of the "Woman Homesteader," we can see several myths operating: a belief in the American Dream; the conviction that all people could achieve a good life in the democratic West; an acceptance of the Bootstrap doctrine, the assumption that personal perseverance and hard work would affect the achievement of that dream; and the idea of the West as a Garden of Eden, the presumption that one had only to till the free lands of the frontier, and nature would provide a living.

Readers today still appreciate Stewart's stories, not only for their entertainment value and the historical and cultural information they can discover in her texts but also for attitudes foundational to American culture. Nearly one hundred years later, audiences are still drawn to the Woman Homesteader's optimism, energy, and independence as well as the alluring belief that health, happiness, and the American Dream can still be realized if they simply have "the courage and determination to get them." This is what keeps readers coming back to Stewart's works, generation after generation after generation.

Throughout her life, Stewart fretted that she had so little to give those for whom she cared. So she gave what she had—joy, hope, courage, and love. Stewart wrote to Coney in 1913, "I am so glad when I can bring a little of this big, clean, beautiful outdoors into your apartment for you to enjoy, and I can think of nothing that would give me more happiness than to bring the West and its people to others who could not otherwise enjoy them. If I could only take them from whatever is worrying them and give them this bracing mountain air, glimpses of the scenery, a smell of the pines and the sage,—if I could only make them feel the free, ready sympathy and hospitality of these frontier people, I am sure their worries would diminish and my happiness would be complete." Stewart's happiness surely must still be overflowing.

SOURCES AND FURTHER READING

Material for this biography is based my book, *The Adventures of The Woman Home-steader: The Life and Letters of Elinore Pruitt Stewart* (Lincoln: University of Nebraska Press, 1992). Other information about her life and experiences can also be found in her two published collections of letters, *Letters of a Woman Homesteader* (Boston: Houghton Mifflin, 1914), and *Letters on an Elk Hunt* (Boston: Houghton Mifflin, 1915). Readers should be wary, however, of expecting complete biographical accuracy in her texts. Both works are currently in print with the University of Nebraska Press. Other unpublished letters and stories as well as an annotated listing of literary allusions in her work and an expanded critical analysis of her literary background are included in my Ph.D. dissertation (Susanne Kathryn Lindau), "My Blue and Gold Wyoming: The Life and Letters of Elinore Pruitt Stewart" (University of Nebraska, 1988).

Several articles have been published about Stewart, including Sherry L. Smith's "Single Women Homesteaders: The Perplexing Case of Elinore Pruitt Stewart," *Western Histori-cal Quarterly* 22 (May 1991):163–83; Peter C. Rollins, "Literature to Film: Why Is the Arcadian Vision of E. P. Stewart's *Letters of a Woman Homesteader* (1914) Absent from the Film Version *Heartland* (1979)?," *Literature/Film Quarterly* 20.1 (1992):25–32; and Susanne K. George, "A Patchwork of Friends: The Female Community of Elinore Pruitt Stewart" *Platte Valley Review* 17 (winter 1989):51–59; and "The Journeys of Elinore Pruitt Stewart," *Nebraska Humanist* (winter 1989):32–37. Stewart is also included in Cathy Luchetti and Carol Olwell's collection of women's histories, *Women of the West* (St. George, UT: Ante-lope Island Press, 1982); and in Elinor Lenz's "Homestead Home" in *Women, Women Writers, and the West,* edited by L.L. Lee and Merrill Lewis (Troy, NY: Whitston Publish-ing Company, 1979).

Those interested in other first-hand accounts by pioneer women may want to read the following works: Susan Armitage, et al., *Women in the West: A Guide to Manuscript Sources* (New York: Garland, 1991); Elizabeth B. Custer, *Following the Guidon* (Lincoln: University of Nebraska Press, 1966); Christiane Fischer, ed., *Let Them Speak for Them-selves: Women in the American West, 1849–1900* (Hamden, CT: Archon Books, 1977); Philip

L. Gerber, ed., *Bachelor Bess: The Homesteading Letters of Elizabeth Corey, 1909–1919* (Iowa City: University of Iowa Press, 1990); Kay Graber, ed., *Sister to the Sioux: The Memoirs of Elaine Goodale Eastman, 1885–1891* (Lincoln: University of Nebraska Press, 1978); Elizabeth Hampsten, *Read This Only to Yourself: The Private Writings of Midwestern Women, 1880–1910* (Bloomington: Indiana University Press, 1982); Kenneth L. Holmes, ed., *Covered Wagon Women: Diaries and Letters from the Western Trails, 1840–1890* (Lincoln: University of Nebraska Press, 1995); Janet Lecompte, ed., *Emily: The Diary of a Hard-Worked Woman* (Lincoln: University of Nebraska Press, 1987); Ruth B. Moynihan, Susan Armitage, and Christiane Fischer Dichamp, eds., *So Much to Be Done: Women Settlers on the Mining and Ranching Frontier* (Lincoln: University of Nebraska Press, 1990); Sandra L. Myers, ed., *Ho for California!: Women's Overland Diaries from the Hunington Library* (San Marino, CA: Huntington Library, 1980); Lillian Schlissel, *Women's Diaries of the Westward Journey* (New York: Schocken Books, 1982); and Joanna L. Stratton, *Pioneer Women: Voices from the Kansas Frontier* (New York: Simon and Schuster, 1981).

Biographies about pioneer women are finding wide publication throughout the West. A few of them include: Anne M. Butler and Ona Siporin, *Uncommon Common Women: Ordinary Lives of the West* (Logan: Utah State University Press, 1996); Susanne K. George, *Kate M. Cleary: A Literary Biography with Selected Works* (Lincoln: University of Nebraska Press, 1997); Ada Morehead Holland, *Brush Country Woman* (College Station: Texas A&M University Press, 1988); Julie Roy Jeffrey, *Converting the West: A Biography of Narcissa Whitman* (Norman: University of Oklahoma Press, 1991); Shirley A. Leckie, *Elizabeth Bacon Custer and the Making of a Myth* (Norman: University of Oklahoma Press, 1993); Carol Miles Peterson, *Bess Streeter Aldrich: The Dreams Are All Real* (Lincoln: University of Nebraska Press, 1995); Grace Ernestine Ray, *Wily Women of the West* (San Antonio, TX: Naylor, 1972); and Anne Seagraves, *Soiled Doves: Prostitution in the Early West* (Hayden, ID: Wesanne Publications, 1994).

9

Abigail Scott Duniway: Mother of Woman Suffrage in the Pacific Northwest

RUTH BARNES MOYNIHAN

❧ "MRS. DUNIWAY ... AROSE, stroked down the folds of her dress, walked to the middle of the platform as independently as a queen and began her address in an offhand manner that at once delighted her audience ... . They were especially struck with her unique comparisons, the incidents of Western life that she related. I [was] proud of Mrs. Duniway and Oregon."

So wrote a reporter for Oregon's leading newspaper, the *Oregonian,* in 1886 when Abigail Scott Duniway spoke at the National Woman Suffrage Association convention in Washington, D.C. The reporter also noted that she spoke with "force" rather than "excessive polish," while "the audience cheered lustily."

This once barefoot country girl, born Abigail Jane Scott in frontier Illinois, had traveled many long roads during the more than fifty years before that convention. By 1884, when she was elected to be the national vice president of the NWSA, Duniway was perceived as the representative of all western women—a first among equals in the burgeoning suffrage movement. She hobnobbed pridefully with "refined" eastern ladies who extolled her accomplishments as a successful writer, newspaper editor, lecturer, and woman's rights champion. By the time she died in 1915, her lifetime epitomized the changing history of western development and of western women in America.

Abigail Jane Scott was born early in the morning on her parents' fourth wedding anniversary, in a small log cabin in Groveland, Illinois. She was their third child. It was October 22, 1834.

*Abigail Scott Duniway in 1861
when she first opened her school.
(Courtesy of University of
Oregon Library)*

Fanny Scott was Abigail's seventeen-month-older sister; her older brother—the Scotts' first born—had died when he was four months old. According to Abigail's frequently repeated story, her father stormed and her mother wept because she was a girl. Their sorrow, she said her mother told her, "was almost too grievous to be borne." Frontier farmers wanted boys, not girls, to help clear land and do heavy field labor. Frontier farmers' wives knew all too well the burdens of being women at the "edge of civilization." "Poor baby," Jenny's mother sobbed when a younger sister arrived, "A woman's life is so hard." It was no accident that Abigail "Jenny" Scott spent a lifetime trying to justify and improve the condition of girls and women.

"Dreamy, untaught and imaginative," hot-tempered and frequently ill, young Jenny Scott grew up with eight more siblings, five of them girls, on the frontier Illinois homestead. Her mother's twelfth baby died at birth. The family lived in a log cabin throughout most of her childhood, and even spent one difficult year housed on a river boat.

Younger brother Harvey Scott, the apple of his parents' eyes, grew up to be Abigail's chief supporter—and her chief opponent. Harvey edited the influential Portland *Oregonian* for more than forty years, encouraging and helping his sister to establish and expand her own paper, *The New Northwest,* even as his undercut the suffrage vote at every crucial juncture over the years.

Their mutual affection, and their mutual rivalry, was established in early childhood—she rescued him from falling into the open fireplace; they planted ten-acre cornfields together; he got the educational advantages she was denied.

Groveland was still a frontier village in the 1830s, recently established by Abigail's grandfather, Sheriff James Scott, and her father, John Tucker Scott, at the northern edge of the current white settlement. Fort Peoria was six miles to the west, across the Illinois River, while Chicago had only just been incorporated in 1830, on the site of a fort on Lake Michigan, about 140 miles to the northeast.

Most of the other local settlers were Scott relatives and friends, all from Kentucky, moving northward in search of land, political opportunity, and freedom from the southern slave society that they deplored. Sheriff Jimmy Scott had provided free papers to several family slaves when he made his move in 1824; opposition to slavery and commitment to the dignity of hardworking men and women were part of Abigail Scott's heritage. So was her interest in land development and entrepreneurial enterprise.

Late in the 1830s, settlers from the northeastern states began to move into Illinois—people of financial, cultural, and educational means who looked down on the "primitive southrons" and began to take over the Illinois frontier's commercial and political opportunities. Then, along with the years of depression and widespread bankruptcies that followed the Panic of 1837, came tales of great opportunities in the Oregon Territory—the "Eden of the West."

The Scott family was one among many who were intrigued by such tales, especially as friends and relatives themselves began to move and send back their stories. Neill Johnson (Abigail's circuit-riding, preacher uncle), along with his wife and twelve children, who were among her favorite cousins, took the Oregon Trail west in 1851. He had circulated a "constitution" for a "colony" of like-minded Cumberland Presbyterian relatives and friends in Oregon—a form of group migration that had been typical of America's western movement ever since the Pilgrims landed at Plymouth Rock. By 1852, John Tucker Scott was also ready to go.

The Oregon Trail migration of 1852 was the largest mass movement in America's history. It was also one of the most devastating. Thousands of people, wagons, horses, mules, cattle, and sheep traveled together—polluting the rivers and campgrounds, eating the ever sparser grass. Cholera stalked the travelers all through the six- to seven-month journey. Makeshift graves lined the dusty, rutted tracks; death and dying were everyday events.

Many emigrants were heading west to escape the endemic malaria, and its attendant ills, which midwesterners had suffered for generations. Like Tucker Scott, they brought their folk remedies, patent medicines, and whiskey: an all-purpose disinfectant and anesthetic as well as an "oh-be-joyful" nourishment. And, like Tucker Scott, some of them tried to seek uncontaminated water and safe campgrounds despite the hundreds of wagons that surrounded them.

But cholera struck the Scott family anyway. Ann Roelofson Scott, Abigail's mother, still an "invalid" after the birth of her still-born twelfth child the previous September, visited a sick fellow traveler one day in June. Within a few hours, early on a beautiful Sunday morning, she too got sick with the debilitating diarrhea and died by five that afternoon. The family buried her in a shallow grave chiseled out of sandstone, heaped with stones to protect her from the wolves, and covered with wild roses. This was in eastern Wyoming, two-and-a-half months' journey from the Scott's Illinois home. Three months' arduous journey over deserts and mountains still lay ahead.

Abigail's cousin and close friend, Miranda Goudy, also recovering from the recent birth of a baby, was soon another victim of the family's ill-fated journey, along with Abigail's own three-year-old brother. In addition, she watched a young man she had fallen in love with being swept to his death in the Snake River as he helped ford the cattle across. The overland trail crossing in 1852 was a pivotal traumatic event in Abigail Scott's long life. It was certainly one of the many reasons why she and all of her sisters became committed suffragists.

Ann Scott had not wanted to leave her Illinois home and had often remarked that she did not think she would make it to Oregon. Abigail and her siblings would never forget their loss and their helplessness in the face of disaster. Again and again Abigail would speak of the difficulties and injustices of frontier housewifery that her mother had suffered, using them as the foundation of her campaign for women's equal rights and freedom from drudgery. "The debt that each generation owes to the past it must pay to the future," she said. Men made the decisions and women suffered the results, she claimed, and she was determined to right that wrong.

That overland journey was also the foundation of her writing career. It was to seventeen-year-old Abigail Jane, notoriously inept at domestic tasks like cooking and sewing, that her father entrusted the duty of keeping a daily journal of the trip. Such journals were intended to be a record not only for the family, but also to be sent back home to guide or warn future travellers. Often these journals only recorded miles and deaths and hazards, but Jenny Scott, like many other women diarists, also recorded interesting events, meetings, personal details, and emotions.

Some months after arriving in Oregon she made a copy of the diary, which was sent back to grandfather James Scott and passed down to other descendents until it was discovered in 1978 in Kansas. The original remained with her own family in Oregon. A few years later, at the age of twenty five, Abigail Scott Duniway used the diary as the basis for a long novel—the first commercially published novel in Oregon. (Another autobiographical novel, *Ruth Rover,* was published in 1854 by Margaret Jewett Bailey, who paid for her own private printing. The controversy surrounding its "scandalous" story of an abusive marriage and divorce undoubtedly sparked Duniway's interest and emulation.)

Abigail Duniway's *Captain Gray's Company, or Crossing the Plains and Living in Oregon* expressed the central themes of her lifelong women's rights campaign. It embodied in the editor-writer heroine who was clearly a projection of Abigail's own dream for the future. In 1905 she reworked the same themes again in *From the West to the West: Across the Plains to Oregon,* with a sanitized and romanticized story that conformed more closely to contemporary myths of the overland trail.

By the time the Scott family arrived in Oregon at the end of September 1852, they were impoverished and exhausted. While the rest of the children helped their father run a large boarding house, Abigail went off alone to earn a living teaching in a small schoolhouse near Salem. She had had less than a year of formal education, five months of it in "an apology for an academy" in Stout's Grove, Illinois. "I never did, could, or would study when at school," she later admitted. But she was a reader, with a thirst for knowledge, known as both the intellectual and the "burden-bearer" of the Scott family. Teachers were in great demand on the civilization-starved frontier; a distant relative was quick to recommend her for the job.

Only a few months later Abigail "met her fate," as she always put it, in the person of Benjamin Duniway—a handsome, horse-loving rancher, who had just returned from prospecting for gold on the Rogue River in southern Oregon. A tall, warmhearted, good-natured man with thick black hair and a resonant bass voice, he loved to sing and share whatever he had with his friends. Ben Duniway swept Abigail into marriage when she was eighteen and took her off to his isolated Clackamas County ranch thereafter.

For the rest of her life, Abigail Duniway talked about the drudgery of her life on that ranch—and the drudgery of farmers' wives in general. The rheumatoid arthritis that had begun when she was a child now recurred under the strain of childbirth, farm labor, and psychological frustration. She described the numerous "bachelor ranchers" who responded to Ben's hospitality, especially at mealtimes, "where it fell to my lot, whether the babies or I were well or ill, to feed the crowd to repletion, as is the habit of most wives and mothers of the frontier settlements unto this day." Twenty years later she told her readers sardonically:

We remember, when we used to follow the avocation of a supported and protected woman on the farm, that we were often so jaded and worn, and so tortured with pains and aches that we would involuntarily utter exclamations of pain, although we kept a-going about the usual occupations connected with our protected condition … .

These occupations included churning enough butter to sell and even to ship down to gold-rush California, raising sheep and chickens, plucking duck feathers and making quilts, slaughtering hogs, preserving enough food for winter, and hand washing heavy, dirty clothes. Doing the laundry was a task so onerous for all nineteenth-century women that it became a primary focus of rhetorical complaint in the women's rights movement. In addition to writing about it, Abigail soon encouraged Ben Duniway to invent mechanical agitators for barrel-based washing machines to sell throughout the Willamette Valley.

But even in the midst of complaints, she was already writing up her experiences "to read to my rustic neighbors … sufficiently diverting to attract crowds to our cabin home, often to remain over night, and always till after dinner." And she was getting her narratives published regularly in the local Oregon City *Argus,* a newspaper whose editor soon became one of the first backers of the newly founded Republican Party. Her columns about farmers' wives also began to appear regularly in the *Oregon Farmer.*

As the nation headed toward Civil War, even faraway Oregonians were well aware of the sectional controversies. Unionists and Copperheads squared off for verbal battle. Edward D. Baker from Illinois, one of Lincoln's closest political allies, who introduced Lincoln at his inauguration and was soon to be the first Union casualty of the war, became Oregon's Republican senator. Baker had been a principal agent of the Scott family's survival, when he gave bankrupt Tucker Scott in 1842 the exclusive rights to sell his portable saw mills in Illinois. Abraham Lincoln himself had once served as Tucker Scott's lawyer in the nearby Tremont, Illinois, courthouse. Abigail Duniway combined fervent allegiance to Republican politics with her commitment to women's rights—thus sparking Democratic party opposition throughout her career.

That opposition first surfaced clearly when her novel *Captain Gray's Company* was published in 1859. A controversy over women's rights was already sizzling in local newspaper columns. But Duniway's novel provoked scathing reviews of its "radicalism," "bad taste," and "slang." Duniway accused her critics of "prudery." But she was so devastated that she kept apologizing for her book the rest of her life. She even tried to buy up all the copies to prevent its distribution—one reason, perhaps, why there are only a few extant copies in various rare book libraries today.

Oregonians, including the Duniways, had many other problems to deal with in the years immediately after achieving statehood in 1859. The Duniways now lived on a beautiful farm, which they had bought in 1855 by selling the Clackamas County ranch. It was just outside of Lafayette, a thriving town with pretensions of becoming "the Athens of Oregon," and upriver from the sparsely settled village of Portland. But Abigail's hand-churned butter and her flock of hens' eggs (the main source of household cash) were selling at half the price of five years earlier, while cattle and fruit prices also fell. Ben planted several orchards, and he continued to buy adjacent land, ignoring Abigail's plea for household help. (Maids were in short supply on the frontier and could demand high pay, while farmhands were abundant and inexpensive.)

A terrible winter in 1859–1860 was followed by drought and heat that destroyed many crops. Then, during the fall of 1861, extraordinary snows and rain were followed by overwhelming floods. The previous summer had been a time of severe depression as Oregon products no longer commanded a monopoly of California markets. Many farmers had stored their entire wheat harvest, more than 80,000 bushels in Lafayette warehouses alone, in order to get better prices. Floods washed away all the warehouses.

The typically generous Ben Duniway, without asking his wife, had also co-signed a loan for a friend, using his farm as collateral. Although Abigail had been working just as hard as he had to keep the farm going and improve it, she had no ownership rights, and no control over its loss. She repeated the story for the rest of her life, in novels, editorials, and speeches, as one of the most basic issues in the women's rights struggle. Without the right to control their own property and income, without financial autonomy, women could never be truly equal or truly free. They were, in fact, slaves, she said—especially in the face of disaster.

And disaster did strike the Duniways. Not only had they sold their 1861 crop at depressed prices; in the spring of 1862, Ben Duniway once again tried the gold fields, this time in Idaho where another mini-gold rush was occurring. While Abigail opened a school (in addition to her farm duties and child rearing), they both hoped that Ben would "strike it rich." But he came back poorer than when he left. Meanwhile, the winter's floods had destroyed Ben's friend's livelihood, creditors were calling in all loans, and, as Abigail never failed to point out, the sheriff served papers—during Ben's absence—on *Mrs.* Duniway.

They had to sell the farm in order to pay. That fall, as Ben Duniway became a teamster to support his family, runaway horses ran over him with a heavy wagon and left him with a disabling back injury for the rest of his life.

Abigail Scott Duniway became the main economic support of her family from then on.

Although tragedy left feisty Mrs. Duniway with never-to-be-forgotten bitterness about her own marital circumstances, it also opened other doors for her. All through the Civil War years, she boarded students and taught at her Lafayette Union School. She gained both opportunity and reputation for intellectual expertise. In 1865, she sold the school "at a profit" and opened another one not far from her sister's home in Albany, Oregon—then the third most important town in the state with many entrepreneurial prospects.

Being a Unionist in communities where states' rights secessionists were politically powerful made Duniway often a target of controversy and complaint, which she did not fail to return in equal measure. She was proud in the face of criticism when her nine-and-a-half-year-old son declaimed the glories of the United States flag to the cheers of his class-mates. And she had no hesitation in returning the insults of "rebels" and "traitors." (Many of these same "traitors" remained implacable enemies of the woman suffrage movement for the next fifty years.)

Within a short time, Abigail Duniway also established a millinery shop in Albany, making fine hats and clothing for ladies and providing employment for numerous local women for whom sewing was one of the few ways to earn "pin money" of their own. Fashion was an important concern in post–Civil War America, and one of the most lucrative new sources of income for many ambitious women throughout the country. For Mrs. Duniway it was a gateway to all sorts of opportunities. She made business connections throughout the Willamette Valley. She discovered the legal inequities that afflicted many of the poor women who worked for her or sought her help, and even many of her wealthy customers who had no access to money of their own. And her buying trips to San Francisco, California, introduced her to influential women in the fledgling national women's rights movement.

Storekeeping was also an activity that a woman could pursue even during pregnancy. Teaching in the nineteenth century required "modesty"; a pregnant woman was not supposed to appear in a classroom. In 1866, when Abigail Duniway's "health failed," as she put it, converting her school into a store made good sense. She had the last two of her six children in 1866 and 1869.

By this time, throughout the United States, "strong-minded women" were beginning to organize to achieve equal suffrage. Western women were just as much in the forefront of the movement as easterners. From Connecticut to California, women established state suffrage associations, and from New Jersey to Washington Territory, a few intrepid women insisted on trying to vote, even as early as 1868. In 1872, Susan B. Anthony tried to vote in

Rochester, New York, hoping to carry her case to the U.S. Supreme Court. Meanwhile, in Portland, Oregon, voters in 1872 included the founders of the Pacific Northwest's first suffrage association: "Mrs. A. J. Duniway, a colored, and two white women."

Abigail Scott Duniway had made a new beginning for herself. During the winter of 1871, after attending a California Woman Suffrage Convention in December, she moved her whole family to Portland and bought an old printing press for her sons to learn the trade and produce a newspaper. Her brother, Harvey Scott, who was already the powerful editor of the Portland *Oregonian,* arranged for Ben Duniway to have a clerkship with a "few hundreds a year" salary at the Portland Customs House. (Harvey Scott's appointment by President Grant to be Portland's Customs Inspector gave him both political and economic clout.) It was a far cry from the country life that Ben loved; despite his disabling back injury, he had become well known throughout Oregon as a maker of washing machines and as an expert breeder of matching circus horses, but he acquiesced to her determination.

On May 5, 1871, Abigail Duniway launched the first issue of *The New Northwest,* a weekly newspaper devoted to all aspects of women's rights. It was also unabashedly western, committed to an outspoken assumption of manifest destiny that was shared by many of Americans of that time. The new editor told her readers that in her "chosen bailiwick"—which was to be the entire Pacific Northwest—the newspaper would represent "the onward march of improvement ... starting from the western shores of the Eastern World, ... which shall ... extend its career of conquest until it bursts upon the Old World."

In addition, Mrs. Duniway espoused unabashed utilitarianism, similar to that of Susan B. Anthony's *Revolution* and Victoria Woodhull's *Woodhull and Claflin's Weekly,* which she used as her models. Her paper would be "not just a Woman's Rights, but a Human Rights organ, devoted to whatever policy may be necessary to secure the greatest good to the greatest number ... fastened upon the rock of Eternal Liberty, Universal Emancipation and Untrammeled Progression." A few years later her masthead was rewritten to say that the paper was "Alive to all Live Issues and Thoroughly Radical in Opposing and Exposing the Wrongs of the Masses."

The New Northwest was a call to arms, especially for women, as well as an indispensable means of communication in the midst of frontier isolation. Farmers' wives were Duniway's most devoted readers—even if their husbands refused to allow subscriptions. They borrowed copies from friends, passed them on to neighbors, and read about the activities of women in the East and in Europe as well as in their local communities.

A few months after launching her newspaper, the intrepid Mrs. Duniway also launched her lecturing career. She persuaded Susan B. Anthony, who was already on tour in California trying to earn money enough to pay off her own newspaper's debts, to extend her trip northwards. Duniway planned a two-thousand-mile itinerary that traveled in the rainy season by stage-coach, steamboat, wagon, and canoe from September to November 1871. The tour even included seven days of camping in a tent with the entire Duniway family at the Oregon State Fair. For Anthony, most of the experience was "mortal agony." For Duniway, it was a tremendous publicity success and personally exhilarating.

Anthony was already widely known for her suffrage activities and widely vilified as an "old maid" activist. Thin, serious, and shy, Susan B. Anthony had become the prime heroine—and the prime scapegoat—of the national suffrage movement. She faced the same personal challenges on this frontier adventure, which made it even more difficult.

But Abigail Duniway thrived on controversy and on rough-and-tumble frontier politics. She garnered many new subscribers during the trip, and she discovered her talent for the lecture platform. Although Susan B. Anthony warned her to prepare all her speeches carefully, and memorize her words, Duniway loved to speak extemporaneously, playing the audience, being quick with repartee, and using an endless repertoir of metaphors and illustrative incidents drawn from experience.

For the next sixteen years, she spent more than half of every year traveling throughout her far-flung territory—all of Oregon, southern Idaho, eastern Washington, and the Puget Sound and coastline areas—at a time when most of the farms and settlements were still brand new, their roofs unfinished, their hopes unlimited. Under these circumstances, the illustrious Mrs. Duniway was almost as exciting an entertainment as the traveling circus. And for many a culture-starved, isolated frontier housewife, she also brought hope and encouragement and dreams of new possibilities for themselves and their children.

Frequently, Mrs. Duniway offered the use of her home to young women who wanted to come to the city to go to school or to work. Boarders could attend an academy or get training as typesetters—opportunities that existed only in the city. A woman like the soon-to-be-notable doctor, Bethenia Owens-Adair, could leave her adolescent son with the Duniways for a year while she went east to medical school. And editor Duniway was pleased to publish stories and poems by Pacific Northwest women in her pages. She also reprinted excerpts from numerous contemporary writers of distinction like John Ruskin, Bret Harte, Mark Twain, and eastern women novelists.

Duniway edited her newspaper on-the-go and wrote detailed descriptions of her travels and the people she met, which were published each week in the paper. (The postal service, even on the frontier, was then reliable enough so that her essays almost always reached Portland in time for each Thursday's issue, no matter where she happened to be.) And she wrote serialized novels, seventeen of them, which often incorporated some of these same people and events in fictionalized form. On all her travels she visited with a wide network of sisters, cousins, aunts, and assorted friends, paying her way by lecturing in any available town hall or village square. She would lecture in churches too—if the ministers did not forbid her presence, and even occasionally in the back rooms of taverns.

Mrs. Duniway traveled across the country four times during those two decades to attend National Woman's Suffrage Association conventions in the East. This was a formidable journey for a woman alone, since railroads did not reach across the Rockies to Oregon until 1883. Even then the Pullmans were too hot, the snows at times too deep, and the schedules too complicated—as she often described them in her narratives. It was the stagecoach drivers that Duniway most admired, sharing the outside buckboard seats with them whenever she could, especially in travelling some of the most difficult mountain terrain. On one occasion she wrote: "If there are degrees of exaltation in the great hereafter, where merit meets its just reward, faithful stage drivers will occupy some very high seats, despite their temptations and falls."

Mrs. Duniway took a steamship to San Francisco and then the railroad east in 1872, but in 1876 she started up the Columbia River and took whatever transportation was available the rest of the way. Visiting relatives in Illinois, she also spoke on that trip to the Illinois Legislature. With indomitable spirit and unstinted praise for western initiative, plus claims of widespread western support for woman suffrage, Duniway won admiration from eastern women activists of every sort.

In 1876, after she attended the Philadelphia Centennial Exposition, other suffragists encouraged Duniway by sponsoring an east coast lecture tour from Washington to New York and Hartford and Boston. She spoke to packed audiences who loved the raw vigor of her speech and manner. They saw her as the ideal representative of "western ways," of independent womanhood nourished by frontier freedom. She was away from Oregon and her family for more than ten months.

During this tour the prestigious publishing firm of S. R. Wells & Co., which had published many of the nineteenth-century's leading abolitionist and women's rights authors, also published Duniway's only book of poetry, *David and Anna Matson*. Dr. Clemence Lozier and other well-known New York suffragists hosted author receptions for her.

But the epic poem, on a theme borrowed from John Greenleaf Whittier about undying love and enslavement to Barbary pirates (used far more successfully by Alfred Lord Tennyson in "Enoch Arden"), was unquestionably bad. A typical review, this one from the *New York Graphic,* said, "It is a sad, sad story, and we congratulate Mrs. Duniway upon having got rid of it." Abigail Duniway told her *New Northwest* readers that the book was a great success, and she carried copies with her to sell on her lecture tours. But her self-taught literary talents were obviously best expended on the western landscape that she knew so well.

The fiction with which Duniway always hoped to "make her fortune" was incorrigibly didactic, romantic, and derivative—a worst-case exemplar of nineteenth-century sentimentality. Its interest today lies mostly with what she revealed in spite of herself about her own life and about the issues and conditions of frontier life.

For example, in 1874–1875, shortly before her own daughter's marriage, Duniway serialized *The Happy Home: or, The Husband's Triumph.* The plot concerned a woman who wanted to postpone marriage for the sake of her personal independence and to prove that her beloved could control his sexuality for the sake of true love. "Humanity," she wrote, "is ignorant of the moral and natural laws of constancy and self-control," echoing the advice of hydropaths and eminent scientists of the time. The story's hero explains to his mother that he will wait patiently and stifle his selfish passion, "believing that a husband's greatest triumph consists in conquering himself."

In 1874, as anti-Duniway political and temperance issues heated up in Oregon, Mrs. Duniway serialized *Amie and Henry Lee.* It was one of her many outspoken attacks on social snobbery, set in the town of "Portsmouth," with a virtuous dance-hall hostess as heroine and many opposition characters obviously modeled on leading citizens of Portland. In the novel the destitute heroine's editor-brother, who had refused to help her because of his social ambition, gives an anti-suffrage lecture at a Democratic victory banquet. He claims that women already control politics, especially the women of the saloon: "We who are leaders in politics, through them and the influence they wield with arts and embraces and whisky are enabled to carry elections just about as we choose." The narrative must have amused many readers—and infuriated many others!

Anti-Chinese riots and labor strikes were terrifying the cities and industrialists of the Pacific Northwest in 1886 when Duniway wrote *Judd and John Mundane.* Poverty-stricken John Mundane becomes a labor organizer advocating hard work and joint stock companies, to the horror of his affluent brother, Judge Judd Mundane. John's wife becomes a laundress for the judge's family because the labor movement has hounded the Chinese laundry out of business. But the judge is converted and agrees to surrender a mortgage without interest to the laborers' new company. The "Anti-Coolie League" changes its name to the "Workingmen's Cooperative Union," and Duniway's novel concludes triumphantly that "labor and capital gave up quarreling and joined hands in fostering mutual interests."

In 1893, Mrs. Duniway urged her son Clyde to persuade eastern magazine editors to publish her *Margaret Rudson* about an "Altrurian Ranch" in Idaho. She had probably borrowed the term from, and given a western locale to, William Dean Howells's *A Traveler from Altruria,* recently serialized in *Cosmopolitan.* She described a cooperative industrial-agrarian enterprise sponsored by a wealthy young woman who converts a handsome young man to the cause of women's equality. It will have a huge H-shaped hotel for one hundred women, two hundred men, and four hundred children, with a public kitchen and dining hall and a workers' directorate. Her egalitarian spouses will even call themselves Mr. and Mrs. Rudson-Horner.

Mrs. Duniway's ideas were widely current in that era; Edward Bellamy's famous *Looking Backward* (1888) and Charlotte Perkins Gilman's *Women and Economics* (1898) enjoyed publishing success, while various utopian and cooperative groups were springing up throughout the country. Thus she had some justification for thinking that eastern publishers favored eastern writers. In later years Abigail Duniway complained bitterly about the lack of respect, and acceptance, of her writing among those publishers, perceiving it as personal animosity, anti-suffragism, or cultural elitism. In this attitude she mirrored many westerners' suspicions about the changing power structures of American society after 1890.

And these changes were real. For example, when Abigail Scott Duniway began her public career, men still controlled the temperance movement. One of her first confrontations about women's rights occurred when she tried to speak at a temperance convention in Portland and was ruled out of order because she was a woman. Furthermore, many frontiersmen—farmers and small businessmen—initially favored woman suffrage. They saw women as their allies in achieving political control vis-à-vis land speculators, business monopolies, railroad conglomerates, and the laboring "rabble" or foreign immigrants who were pouring into western communities during the post–Civil War years. Thus Wyoming settlers granted women the right to vote in 1869 at the same time Wyoming became a territory. Utah similarly held on to Mormon hegemony. Washington Territory's legislature mustered a substantial minority to vote for woman suffrage in 1873, 1875, and 1881; the territory's constitutional convention in 1878 almost approved suffrage, defeating it only eight to seven. In 1883 Washington Territory granted votes to women, though the law was rescinded in 1887 and not included in the constitution when Washington became a state in 1889.

In Oregon's legislature in 1872 the vote was even closer—twenty-one in favor of suffrage, twenty-two opposed. But a "women's war on whiskey," which spread across the country in 1874, was the first stage of a massive social change in frontier society. Starting in a small town in Ohio, the popular ladies' "pray-ins" at local bars and taverns became a major campaign in the rough-and-ready seaport of Portland that winter. Women who had shown no interest in woman suffrage, or who had vehemently opposed both Mrs. Duniway and voting rights as unladylike, were now singing hymns in public bars and being jailed in large groups for their intrepid piety. The aim was to close the taverns and also the city's notorious houses of prostitution in order to protect men from damnation and their wives from the living hell of alcohol's influence.

Abigail Duniway heartily agreed with the goal, but she thought the ladies were hypocritical in their disdain for her and for the "power of the ballot." She had been railing against prostitution and political corruption in the *New Northwest* in almost every issue. She continued to favor personal temperance, but she was implacably opposed to the movement for legal prohibition of liquor that was led by the ever growing Women's Christian Temperance Union in the 1880s. At the same time, WCTU women began to take on the suffrage issue—as a means of achieving temperance. Duniway claimed they were "making suffrage the tail of the prohibition kite" and thus alienating the male support that the suffrage cause so badly needed. They claimed she had "sold out to whiskey."

WCTU members in general were more "refined" and eastern-educated than Duniway. They were mostly evangelical Christians, too. Although Duniway frequently quoted the Bible and saw herself as a religious woman, she espoused a freewheeling, pioneer resentment of organized religion. She had never forgotten the Methodist preacher who accused her of licentious writing in her first novel, nor the hell-fire-and-damnation preaching that terrified her throughout her childhood. In her typical "blasphemous" rhetoric, Duniway defended the alternative Open Temperance Society meetings that she organized. She told her readers:

> These hide-bound believers in a seven-by-nine heaven, who would vastly prefer to send all people to a Miltonic hell rather than have them gain everlasting paradise by a route not pointed out by themselves, are jealous of the audiences these meetings draw, the enthusiasm they excite and the good that they do, untrammeled by creed and cant.

In Oregon, as in the West generally, antagonism between the "civilizing influence" of evangelical religion versus the "unchurched" was a current that ran very deep. (Protestants saw Catholic "papists," of course, as equally dangerous to civilization, especially because western Catholics usually supported minority and women's rights and were in theological opposition to the evangelical missionaries who tried to replace them in the Pacific Northwest.)

Abigail Duniway also took her Republican political loyalties very seriously. Democrats had always been among her most implacable enemies. With new, burgeoning industries and growing immigration during the late nineteenth-century Gilded Age, the Democratic party seemed to be organizing the laborers and "rabble foreigners" who were most likely to be opposed to women suffrage, while western pioneers, like Duniway and her powerful brother Harvey Scott, were now among the business leaders from whom she expected support. As this profound cultural change was occurring throughout the West, woman suffrage became the lightning rod for every political discontent.

When Abigail Duniway began publishing *The New Northwest* in 1871, she thought, like most other American woman suffragists of the time, that votes for women would be quickly achieved. Not only had African American slavery been outlawed, all black Americans had also been declared citizens, and all male citizens had the right to vote. Women opposed the use of the word "male" in the Fourteenth Amendment—the first such limitation of citizens' rights in the Constitution, but they thought they could effectively argue their own rights from the clause that defined "all persons born or naturalized in the United States" as citizens. They were outraged that former slaves could become to-be voters while women were ignored.

But it was to be fifty years before the Nineteenth Amendment finally enfranchised all American women. That was in 1920, shortly after World War I; and after the Eighteenth Amendment established national prohibition. With that issue out of the way, it was safe at last for politicians to admit women to the polls.

But several western states enfranchised women much earlier, and Abigail Scott Duniway was one of the most important catalysts of that enfranchisement. Aside from Wyoming in 1869, there was Colorado in 1893, Utah and Idaho in 1896, Washington in 1910, California in 1911, and then Oregon in 1912. Arizona and Kansas followed also in 1912. Illinois (Duniway's home state) enacted presidential suffrage in 1913. Montana and Nevada passed state constitutional amendments in 1914. Thus there was a substantial block of legislators from suffrage states when the amendment finally passed in the national Congress in 1919.

For Abigail Scott Duniway, the issue was never as simple as voting rights alone. From her earliest writings and speeches and throughout her lifetime, Duniway argued for women's autonomy in economic and social matters as well. She argued for married women's property rights, which Oregon legislators finally granted in 1878. She promoted a Sole Trader Act that was passed in 1874, allowing women to manage their own business finances without regard to marital status.

And Duniway insisted on a married woman's right to protect her health and limit her pregnancies. Her advice, like that of most nineteenth-century reformers, was about the importance of spirituality in marital love and about the necessity of male restraint for the sake of a wife's well-being. Nevertheless, the doctrine of "voluntary motherhood" was considered sufficiently radical at that time to call forth anathemas both from religious leaders and from assorted editors and politicians defending their "masculine rights."

Many historians of the women's rights movement have portrayed its reform issues as the product of evangelical sensibilities, middle-class status, and more advanced educational and social opportunities in the eastern states. But Abigail Scott Duniway was promoting economic and sexual freedom, political autonomy, and career development for women just as early as any eastern suffragist. And she was finding like-minded women throughout the frontier towns and farms of the Pacific Northwest. Nineteenth-century feminism was far from a minority movement, and it was western women who were often most receptive to its ideas.

By the 1890s, however, a new generation of women's rights activists came along. The WCTU prohibition movement was an important part of their formation. Middle-class suspicion of immigrants, laborers, lower classes, and freed African Americans of the South also included disdain for the "crudeness" of western pioneers. The two National Suffrage Associations—American (led by Lucy Stone and based in Boston) and National (led by Susan B. Anthony and based in New York)—agreed to merge in 1889, with strong WCTU support and many of the same leaders. Although Abigail Duniway had maintained cordial relationships with both groups throughout her *New Northwest* years, and was a member of the merger committee, she sensed her displacement at that 1889 meeting. As she later noted in her autobiographical *Path Breaking*, Susan B. Anthony pointedly ignored Duniway and lavished attention upon the Reverend Anna Howard Shaw—who would soon become president of the national association and an implacable enemy of "the incorrigible Mrs. Duniway."

Serious troubles for Abigail Duniway started in the 1880s. In 1883 the Washington Territorial legislature approved woman suffrage, for which she had vigorously campaigned for years. There was bitter factionalism, including cries that Mrs. Duniway's presence would ensure defeat not victory, but despite the insults she claimed it as her victory. At the same time the Oregon legislature approved a suffrage referendum, to go before Oregon voters in June 1884. Mrs. Duniway was so confident of victory that she had even commissioned a victory engraving, showing the "Goddess of Liberty in the act of crowning kneeling womanhood."

But she reckoned without political trickery. Among the many harassments she endured was the short-lived establishment of a rival newspaper called the *Northwest News,* which was an outspoken, pro-whiskey publication apparently funded by her enemies. When she took them to court for misusing her paper's name, the case dragged on for months, until two weeks *after* the suffrage referendum. The judge had long been one of her political opponents; the court's bailiff was a man whom Duniway had publicly exposed for going to "houses of ill fame"; the man's father, who was influential doorkeeper of the state legislature, had claimed that he "*could* and *would* defeat the amendment" in order to get back at her.

Meanwhile, WCTU lecturers began campaigning for suffrage as a means of achieving prohibition. And newly enfranchised Washingtonians passed numerous "local option" laws. Duniway insisted that this would scare voters and thus antagonize many potential supporters. "Prohibition," she said, "is not temperance, but intolerance and quackery." And she suggested the following scenario to Washington women voters:

> If, instead of joining men in this conflict for prohibition, which … cannot be enforced, except by bullets, you will utilize your newly acquired power by forming a corporation to buy or lease that great building [Mrs. Stahl's Walla Walla brewery]—if you will convert it into a cannery, or creamery, or both, and give employment to that woman and her children, and to the wives and children of all the men in your midst, … the fame of your philanthropy … and the success of your business methods will inspire the voters.

Prohibitionists were appalled at such practical solutions.

The word of Duniway's iniquity spread across the country. A whole generation of eastern women first learned about Abigail Scott Duniway through WCTU anathemas. In Massachusetts that summer of 1886 the Woman's Christian Prohibitory League meeting in a Baptist Church in Boston decided that she had "brought disgrace on the Woman Suffrage cause." They censured her attempts at "conciliation" and said, "we voice the sentiment of every true woman in America when we say: God grant that the ballot may never be given to women if, in order to obtain it, we must conciliate men."

Duniway trusted her editor-brother and other businessmen who had always been on her side, but the *Oregonian* ran anti-suffrage editorials all that spring. Liquor dealers printed bogus ballots and financed vote-buying among newly unemployed railroad workers and immigrants in the city of Portland. (The Northern Pacific Railroad had just been completed down the Columbia River to Portland in December 1883. Breweries and hops-growing agriculture were now major industries in the Pacific Northwest.) Woman suffrage was defeated by the negative votes of Portland's Multnomah County, though all the other rural counties had positive pluralities.

In addition to the opposition she faced from corrupt politicians and from prohibitionists, Abigail Duniway also faced the grief of losing her only daughter. Clara Belle, the first of her children, had married a man whom Duniway thoroughly disapproved of, while her mother was away in the East in 1876. Duniway had great hopes for Clara Belle's musical talent; she often sang for suffrage meetings and parlor gatherings. But Clara Belle developed tuberculosis ("consumption") and came home with her small son to spend the last few months of her life at her mother's house before she died in January 1886. The end of 1886 also marked the end of the *New Northwest*.

At this time, the Duniway "boys" were getting increasingly restless about the newspaper. They wanted to strike out into their own businesses. Along with their father Ben Duniway, and encouraged by Harvey Scott, they wanted to try ranching in southern Idaho. The land-rush of the 1880s gave even Abigail Duniway great hopes for future profits. They were all glad to take advantage of the Preemption Act, the Homestead Act, and the Desert Reclamation Act to purchase the land.

Duniway, in fact, also saw the ranch as an opportunity to establish a joint-stock egalitarian cooperative community—of the kind she had been advocating for years in her newspaper. She envisioned irrigation systems and development potential, including new opportunities for women, which were a generation ahead of her time. A chance to sell her newspaper, with the promise that she could continue writing for it, seemed too good to refuse.

She did sell the newspaper, to one of Harvey Scott's friends, but he went out of business two months later. Perhaps the whole deal was a way of destroying her public voice for suffrage. The Duniways bought the Idaho ranch, and the economy soon changed for the worse. Ben and the boys insisted on simply raising horses and cattle and vetoed any utopian community ideas. The ranch was never successful, and Abigail Duniway hated it. She also felt she had been "robbed," since the sale of her paper had paid for the ranch, and she no longer had her own financial autonomy. Except for brief visits, she continued to live in her Portland home, to which Ben eventually returned for her to nurse him through his last years of illness before he died in 1896.

During the 1890s Abigail Duniway continued writing and lecturing on her own, including a stint as editor of the *Pacific Empire* and the short-lived *Coming Century,* but she never again had the clout that her newspaper had given her. She participated with other leading Oregonians in study-group discussions of the so-called "Australian" secret ballot, initiative and referendum, and direct election of senators legislation—all of which eventually became known as the "Oregon system."

Although Americans today take the secrecy of the voting booth for granted, there was seldom any such secrecy before the twentieth century. Voters voted by voice or by hand, or marked their ballots in public where politicians, ward bosses, and others could easily keep track of their choices. Referendum and initiative legislation enabled citizens to participate in the legislative process outside of strict party control by elected representatives. Its immediate effect was to enable statewide woman suffrage referendums to take place, in Oregon (after 1902) and elsewhere, without the law first passing both houses of the legislature in two successive sessions. Westerners led the way for the entire country's legal changes during the Progressive era.

Abigail Duniway was also an active participant in the burgeoning Woman's Club movement of that time. She was president of the Oregon State Women's Suffrage Association, becoming a mentor for numerous young women who would become major activists. As a member of the Portland Woman's Club, and then as president of the State Federation of Women's Clubs, Duniway continued to face antagonism as well as appreciation in regard to her leadership methods.

There were five more woman suffrage referendums in Oregon, more than in any other state. In 1900, Duniway's carefully planned, but quiet, campaign almost achieved victory. The vote was 28,402 No to 26,265 Yes—only two thousand short, and the negative plurality again was mostly due to Portland voters. Two weeks before the election, the Portland *Oregonian*'s antisuffrage editorials (while Harvey Scott was "out of town") helped scuttle the cause—to Abigail Duniway's disgust and rage. The family battle that ensued left such bitter enmity that Harvey Scott's children were still ashamed of their "crude" and "radical" aunt as late as the 1940s. In their book, she was no lady.

Meanwhile, national suffrage movement leaders in the East, like Carrie Chapman Catt and Anna Howard Shaw, had begun to believe the rhetoric about western freedom, which Duniway herself so often used. Catt had been very involved in the Idaho victory of 1896, repudiating Mrs. Duniway in the process. Believing that an Oregon victory in 1906 would be a marvelous opportunity to honor Susan B. Anthony, who had died soon after the 1905 Lewis and Clark Centennial Exposition in Portland, the NAWSA organization took over the 1906 referendum campaign. With the help of Duniway's prohibitionist Oregon opponents, they canvased the state wearing white WCTU ribbons, spending thousands of dollars that the Oregon Suffrage Association would later have to repay, and stirring up the well-enforced, fraud-filled opposition of the Brewer's and Wholesale Liquor Dealers' Association. Suffrage was roundly defeated. Abigail Duniway was blamed in all subsequent suffrage histories.

Not until 1912 did Oregon voters accept woman suffrage. By that time, Abigail Duniway was severely disabled by arthritis, and Harvey Scott had already died. Her age and illness, plus her long years of dedication to woman suffrage, made her seventy-eighth birthday banquet just before the election a wonderful publicity culmination of the campaign that younger women had organized. Governor West, who remembered her stump speeches from his childhood, asked Abigail Scott Duniway to sign the official Suffrage Proclamation after it became law. In 1914 she became the first woman in Oregon to cast her vote.

Abigail Scott Duniway (center) with her two friends at the Oregon polls in 1914, about to cast her first vote. (Courtesy of Oregon Historical Society)

Duniway's friend Emma Smith DeVoe founded a National Council of Women Voters in 1911 after Washington State women became voters. She named Duniway honorary president and always praised her work and her methods. DeVoe was as proud of the West as Duniway was, and she admonished "the non-voting suffragists of the East [to] cease publishing their bickerings and jealousies and concentrate their energies on the vital issue, woman suffrage, and show a disposition to give praise to the woman who has succeeded wherein they have failed."

But the League of Women Voters, for which Carrie Chapman Catt took credit, superceded and absorbed the National Council of Women Voters after 1920. By this time East-West antagonism was so strong that no one cared about including western leaders (like Idaho's founding member Margaret Roberts, for example) into the national superstructure. The post-World War I industrialized East now held the balance of American political and social power, eclipsing the hegemony of the pioneer West for more than a generation. Abigail Scott Duniway's lifetime achievements were relegated to short asides in the standard suffrage histories.

Eighty-one-year-old Abigail Duniway, tall and gaunt and feisty to the last, finally died of a foot infection in 1915. Without modern antibiotics, and after weeks of suffering, her aged body could no longer sustain her active mind and fighting spirit.

But Oregonians have remembered her. A large park in downtown Portland bears her name, as does an elementary school not far from Reed College. The University of Oregon named a dormitory after her, and an entire collection of Duniway Family Papers are housed in the university's library. Above all else, Oregon women, and all American women, continue to benefit from the many civil rights that she worked so hard to win for them.

Abigail Scott Duniway epitomized the independent spirit of America's pioneer women of every era—from colonial settlers to modern space travelers. Her resourcefulness, outspokenness, and self-confidence provided both encouragement and practical tools for other women, giving the lie to any notion of innate female inferiority or weakness.

Abigail Duniway was also one of the prime creators of the myth that westerners were more politically free and more open to women's rights and human rights. Like so many others, she believed that land development and business entrepreneurship would always lead to the greatest good for the greatest number. Yet she herself, like so many other women, was victimized by the political and social forces she sought to control. Through her experience one can see how attitudes toward women's rights reflected the political and social climate of time and place. The western frontier both destroyed and nurtured women's lives and freedom. The women's rights movement took place within a context of economic realities and theoretical constructions, which created both support and opposition.

As for Abigail Duniway's importance to western history, an 1888 episode is revealing. Her son Clyde told the story:

> Two ruffians "jumped" one of the family "hay claims" on Antelope Creek. Ralph brought the news to the Alder Creek cabin, some eighteen miles, where Mother and I were. That same evening Willis arrived by buckboard from Challis. There was a solemn family conclave on the crisis. Helped by the pioneer experiences and spirit of Mother it was decided that lawless force must be met by force—there being no peace officers within sixty miles, and the sentiment of the frontier requiring all but cowards to defend and vindicate their rights. Never shall I forget the Spartan courage and advice of Mother as she stood beside me while I was loading the magazine of my Winchester rifle. "Be awful careful, son. Don't shoot unless you have to. But if you must shoot, be sure you kill the wretch the first shot."

Later, when the constable tried to arrest her three boys, fifty-four-year-old Mother Duniway gave him a "tongue lashing" and insisted that Clyde should be allowed to leave as planned, immediately, to get his education in the East at Cornell University.

Abigail Duniway was always a spokesperson for the dignity and rights of westerners, and the "progressive development" of western civilization. In her publications and in her notorious "tongue lashings" she gave courage to the fearful and voice to the voiceless throughout her long life. And in her admiration for education and desire for recognition, not only for her children and herself, but also for all women, she helped keep the issue of woman suffrage in the forefront of western politics for fifty years. With suffrage achieved throughout much of the West when she died in 1915, there was a solid foundation for national recognition of the political equality of all American women in 1920. Westerners have good reason to be proud of Abigail Scott Duniway.

SOURCES AND FURTHER READING

All information and quotations in this essay are fully documented by Ruth Barnes Moynihan in *Rebel for Rights: Abigail Scott Duniway* (New Haven: Yale University Press, 1983), still the definitive biography. This book also contains an extensive bibliography. More detailed information and more extensive quotations from Duniway's own writing can be found in Moynihan's "Abigail Scott Duniway of Oregon: Woman and Suffragist of the American Frontier," 2 vols. (Ph.D. diss., Yale University, 1979).

For Abigail Duniway's own writing, see *Path Breaking: An Autobiographical History of the Equal Suffrage Movement in Pacific Coast States* (1914; New York: Schocken Books, 1971). This book begins as an autobiography, but the latter half becomes mostly a collection of her speeches. Microfilm editions of *The New Northwest*, 1871–1887, are available at the Oregon Historical Society and the Smith College Library. *Captain Gray's Company, or Crossing the Plains and Living in Oregon* (Portland, OR: S. J. McCormick, 1859) can be found in Yale University's Beinecke Rare Book Library, and in half a dozen other rare-book collections. *From the West to the West: Across the Plains to Oregon* (Chicago: A. C. McClurg, 1905) is somewhat less rare. Abigail Jane Scott's "Journal of a Trip to Oregon," edited by her grandson David Duniway, was published in 1986 by the Arthur H. Clark Co. of California; it is now available in a reprint edition from the University of Nebraska Press (1997).

The journal has an interesting history. The original copy is part of the Duniway Family Papers, now at the University of Oregon. But Abigail and her sister Margaret had copied the journal during the winter of 1853 in order to send it back to grandfather James Scott in Illinois. They made some revisions, leaving out a few things and adding details that were not in the original. Not until 1978 did anyone in Oregon know that the revised copy had survived. R. Edwin Browne of Independence, Missouri, another great-grandson of James Scott, used the diary, which had been handed down in his family, to make a trip west following its description of the route of the Oregon Trail. When he arrived at Portland's Oregon Historical Society he inquired about whether anyone there had ever heard of Abigail Jane Scott and her family. He was immediately introduced to David Duniway, who compared his own copy with Edwin Browne's and recognized a kinsman.

Unfortunately, knowledge of Mrs. Duniway and her work was eclipsed for much of the twentieth century by the prejudices of her political and social detractors. It was the latecomers to both Oregon and woman suffrage who wrote their version of Duniway's history for many years. In *The History of Woman Suffrage,* vol. 1, eds. Elizabeth Cady Stanton, Susan B. Anthony, and Matilda Joslyn Gage (1881), Mrs. Duniway told her own story. But in vol. 6, published by the National American Woman Suffrage Association in 1922, Clara Colby, a leader of the opposition faction against Duniway among Oregon women during the 1906 campaign, wrote the history of Oregon's suffrage movement. Her negative account of Duniway's methods influenced all later suffrage histories, including Eleanor Flexner's *Century of Struggle* (Cambridge, MA: Harvard University Press, 1959).

Abigail Duniway's own sons, however, remained convinced of her achievement. Clyde Duniway, who went on to become a history professor at Stanford University and then president of Carleton College in Minnesota, saved all her letters and personal papers. And his son David Duniway, who became State Archivist of Oregon from 1946 to 1972, gathered even more documentation and organized it all into useful form. This extensive collection, now housed at the University of Oregon Library, is an indispensable foundation for knowledge about Duniway's life and work.

Two University of Oregon M.A. theses, Martha Frances Montague's "Woman Suffrage Movement in Oregon" (1930) and Letitia Capell's "Biography of Abigail Scott

Duniway" (1934), provide valuable information. Leslie McKay Roberts's "Suffragist of the New West: Abigail Scott Duniway and the Development of the Oregon Woman Suffrage Movement," a B.A. thesis at Reed College (1969) is also excellent. Gayle R. Bandow's " 'In Pursuit of a Purpose': Abigail Scott Duniway and the *New Northwest*," a 1973 M.S. thesis at the University of Oregon is useful, but not comprehensive.

The first description of Duniway for the wider public was by Nancy W. Ross in *Westward the Women* (New York: Alfred A. Knopf, 1944). Elinor Richey carried on the legend in "The Unsinkable Abigail," *American Heritage* (February 26, 1975), whereas Dorothy Nafus Morrison wrote a children's book about her, *Ladies Were Not Expected: Abigail Scott Duniway and Women's Rights* (New York: Atheneum, 1977). Helen Krebs Smith put heroic effort into writing *The Presumptuous Dreamers, A Sociological History of the Life and Times of Abigail Scott Duniway*, vol. 1, 1834–1871 (Lake Oswego, OR: Smith, Smith and Smith Publishing Co., 1974), but she made up anachronistic conversations and motivations, which tend to obscure rather than illuminate her subject. The title of the book promises a great deal more than its author was able to produce.

❧ **10** ❧

Mother Katharine Drexel: Spiritual Visionary for the West

ANNE M. BUTLER

❧ ON MARCH 3, 1955, a ninety-six-year-old Roman Catholic sister, Mother Katharine Drexel, died peacefully in her convent at Cornwells Heights, Pennsylvania. Laid to rest far from mountain, prairie, or desert, this private woman of the cloister seemed an unlikely figure to have shaped an entire segment of Catholic education in the American West. Katharine Drexel, through her religious zeal, great wealth, business acumen, and organizational skill did exactly that and, in the process, transformed herself into one of the most unusual adopted daughters of the West. Her impact on the West began in the 1880s; it remains a powerful example of the ability, intelligence, and far-reaching influence women brought to the westering experience and underscores the historical complexity of Indian and Anglo relationships. Further, the religious community Katharine Drexel founded, the Sisters of the Blessed Sacrament for Indians and Colored People, demonstrates that single women, who eschewed traditional marriage and family roles, devised legitimate ways to participate in western settlement.

Little in Katharine Drexel's early life in Philadelphia, Pennsylvania, suggested her future as an influential figure in the women's West. Born November 26, 1858, to a wealthy banking family, Katharine grew up surrounded by family privilege. The Drexel parents, Francis and Emma, lived out the extravagant rituals of the nineteenth-century elegantly rich. In keeping with America's Gilded Age, they owned multiple residences, lived fashionably, traveled extensively, and presented their daughters to Philadelphia society.

Actually, Katharine's biological mother had died when the infant was only five weeks old, leaving a widowed husband to care for two young daughters.

Katharine's stepmother, Emma Bouvier, married Francis Drexel sixteen months after the mother's death. Emma Drexel, a forceful personality, closely monitored every aspect of the educational and social development of Francis Drexel's two daughters. The birth of a third Drexel child, Louise, in 1863, enlarged the family, where for many years the older girls remained unaware that Emma was their stepmother. The news, although stunning to Katharine and her sister Elizabeth, did not weaken the family influence of Emma Drexel, nor estrange the older girls from their younger half-sister, Louise; the siblings bonded into an unusually close threesome.

Both Francis and Emma Drexel exerted a powerful presence in the family, focusing their personal and professional routines on a vigorous and highly visible commitment to the Roman Catholic church. The three girls received their religious training from the French-speaking Madames of the Sacred Heart, the parents generously endowed numerous Catholic institutions, and the Drexel homes contained chapels for individual and group prayer. The family mixed with an aristocratic international set and commonly entertained high-ranking members of the Catholic clergy in their home or met in private audience with the pope when abroad. Emma Drexel molded her daughters with a philosophy, expressed in intensely religious terms, that emphasized the privilege and responsibility of the wealthy.

The premature demise of Emma B. Drexel in 1883 and Francis A. Drexel in 1885 left the three daughters both devastated and heirs to a highly publicized fortune. Katharine and her sisters shared an estate of fourteen million dollars, a separate million and a half bequeathed to Catholic institutions and religious orders in the Philadelphia area. No shortage of other Catholic organizations hoped the sisters, each estimated to receive an annual income in excess of $350,000, would continue the family tradition of beneficence.

Like Francis and Emma Drexel before them, all three Drexel daughters quickly established a record of Catholic philanthropy. After the mid 1880s, however, the three heiresses centered their charities on education, especially for people of color. Schools for African Americans in the South and Native Americans in the West increasingly appealed to these Philadelphia socialites as the theme for their benevolence.

With her family background thus shaping her, two distinct factors cemented Katharine Drexel's connection to the American West. The first involved the direct impact made on her by two western tours: one through the Dakotas, the other in Minnesota. The second element drawing Drexel to the West concerned her inner struggle to select a personal direction in life.

In the first instance, the regional power of the American West made its way into the mind of Katharine Drexel shortly after the loss of her parents.

Katharine Mary Drexel in 1888 at age twenty-nine, just prior to entering the convent. (Courtesy of the Sisters of the Blessed Sacrament, Bensalem, Pennsylvania)

In 1887, Katharine and her sisters, Elizabeth and Louise, now the sole heirs to one of the great banking fortunes in the East, stepped onto the grounds of the Rosebud Indian Reservation in South Dakota. Although they had once taken a sightseeing excursion across the West, this experience brought the Drexels to the everyday world of western people. Under the escort of two family friends, Father Joseph Stephan, director of the Bureau of Catholic Indian Missions, and Bishop James O'Connor of Omaha, Nebraska, these eastern women arrived to assess the circumstances of Native Americans.

After a short visit at the Rosebud, the little group continued across the Dakotas, stopping at one after another of the Catholic missions, where Indian hospitality had been arranged for them. Everywhere the travelers met Indians, dined with them, attended their dances. At each stop, as they joined in these events, the Drexels evaluated the Catholic services in place for Native Americans. Overall, as the small party moved deeper into the hinterlands, its members watched the poverty of the Indians and the handful of Catholic missionaries worsen. Although the Drexels may have overlooked the political subtleties in Indian/missionary relationships, they did see that the two groups lived together in a shared environment of economic deprivation.

Both suffered from bitter want. Missionaries clung to a stark existence. They built rough chapels, lived in rudimentary housing, and tried to stay alive on meager diets. Indians, constrained by crippling economic and political federal policies for Native Americans, lived in an even more restricting poverty. Unlike the missionaries, who ultimately could retreat from the ungenerous surroundings to their own cultural centers, Indian people remained bound to a circumscribed terrain and closed out of a mainstream economy. Well versed in the styles of white society, Indians brought their own culture, religion, and politics into the mission. What resulted from these poverty-driven interactions were highly complex relationships, in which the participants both clashed and accommodated, liked and disliked each other.

Katharine Drexel looked about the Dakotas and saw a somewhat different dynamic. In her view, the reservation called forth a simpler meaning: in a world invented by a neglectful government, disadvantaged Indians had been abandoned to poverty and ignorance. The reservations doomed Native people to prejudice, illiteracy, unemployment, and godlessness. This situation existed, Drexel believed, because most priests and nuns refused the extreme hardship of the Indian mission call. The few willing missionaries simply did not have the resources to maintain themselves or reverse conditions for Indians.

Drexel's vision took on its own hues, some of which would not have colored the perspective of the Indians, the government, or the missionaries of other denominations. Nonetheless, for Katharine Drexel, in whom personal privilege demanded social responsibility, the Dakota trip fixed her determination. She decided to use her fortune as an educational lever for those who had no money, no champion, no opportunity in white society.

In keeping with an American spirit, she believed in the power of education, especially when taught through a Catholic lens, to elevate humankind. Further, a widely publicized 1878 challenge of Catholic newspaper editor James A. McMaster to the American church to "atone for wrongs our people … have … done to the poor Indians," could not have escaped her. In the Dakotas, she bonded the two forces of her life, belief in the value of Catholic education and in the moral obligation to make institutions of learning available to Native Americans.

Katharine Drexel returned to the East and set into motion the first phase of her plan to enhance the educational experience of Native Americans. Unwilling to be distanced from the operation by simply donating to the Bureau for Catholic Indian Missions, she retained personal control of a massive organizing feat. Her strategy superimposed eastern business tactics and pedagogical thinking onto a western stage. Dipping into her considerable monies, Drexel purchased land along the perimeters of several different Indian reservations, hired architects to design school buildings, and paid construction costs, including salaries for local brickmakers, lumber workers, and carpenters.

In 1888, with this ambitious project underway, Drexel agreed to another trip into the West. Again she set forth with her sisters and a clerical escort, headed for the White Earth and Red Lake Reservations of Minnesota. For a second time, the three sisters moved through Indian communities, visited inside homes, attended chapel services, and watched dances.

The trek included travel across "corduroy roads," beds of "ticks filled with fresh hay," and morning ablutions from a "tin pudding dish." Hazardous terrain, unpolished accommodations, humble meals—these, nor any combination of them, elicited from the three the pinched comments of the idle rich. They appeared captivated by the West and its ways of life. Their letters and diary entries blended appreciation for the mountain landscape with vignettes of Native American life, droll anecdote with religious expression.

Katharine returned to Philadelphia and focused her attention on the school-building program. She named among her beneficiaries the recently visited Benedictine Sisters at White Earth, where for a decade a little group scratched out a slim life. Two White Earth Benedictine missionaries, Sisters Philomena and Lioba, managed day students, boarders, orphans, and an annex school eight miles distant, with slight emotional and monetary support.

The two teachers witnessed the remarkable help an infusion of $40,000 could make for their outpost station. A new three-story brick school that accommodated 150 children opened in 1890. At White Earth, Indian families proved willing to support the improved facility, where student enrollment rose from fewer than fifty to around one hundred. In the Benedictine motherhouse at Saint Joseph, Minnesota, administrators responded by assigning additional personnel to the school. In a short time, these changes strengthened the mission, internally and externally.

White Earth was only one of many missions to receive assistance under Drexel's plan. Between 1888 and 1893, as acreage was acquired and buildings rose at distant sites, Drexel deeded the finished products—lands and physical plants—in Wyoming, New Mexico, Idaho, Montana, California, Oklahoma, and Washington to the Bureau of Catholic Indian Missions. That agency, by negotiating federal government contracts for reservation schools and acquiring teachers from congregations of sisters, agreed to operate the new facilities. Within five years, Drexel organized and oversaw the completion of mission schools for several prominent tribes, including Cheyennes, Arapahos, Sioux, Nez Perce, Chippewas, Cherokees, Comanches, Osage, Crows, Blackfeet, and Pueblo Indians. Drexel's efforts made it possible for missionaries from numerous congregations—among them Franciscans, Dominicans, Benedictines, Daughters of Providence, Ursulines, Jesuits, Grey

Nuns, Daughters of Charity, and Mercy Sisters—to have sufficient economic support to live and educate in the West.

Thus, this child of the East channeled her business interests in ways that changed the economic and educational face of the American West. The construction of mission schools stimulated the local economy and planted small enterprises across reservation lands. Sisters and priests from many different groups found employment at the missions, as did Native Americans who worked as head farmers, cooks, housekeepers, drivers, carpenters, herders, and interpreters. The schools became magnets for Native Americans consigned to remote reservations with few Anglo institutions from which to extract jobs, schooling, or economic growth. Both Indian children and adults called on the missionaries for spiritual ritual and secular learning, and in the process taught nuns and priests about the patterns of Native American culture.

Katharine Drexel did not end her support for Indian schools with the construction of buildings. She also paid tuition and board fees for indigent children, monthly salaries to priests and nuns, insurance on mission buildings, grocery bills, and travel expenses. She funneled her money through the Bureau for Catholic Indian Missions and sent stipends directly to missions. Her charities eventually became so extensive and widespread that a complete recording of them proved impossible.

Secure in a plan for the appropriate disposition of her fortune, Katharine Drexel continued to wrestle with decisions about her personal goals. This second determining factor in her life grew from the Drexel family's highly spirited Catholicism. This element, like her wealth, tied Katharine Drexel permanently to the American West.

For several years, Katharine Drexel increasingly felt drawn to religious life in a convent. Following the death of Emma Drexel in 1883, Katharine spoke more openly about joining a community of Catholic sisters. Her interest lay with active mission sisters—those who renewed simple vows annually and developed a social ministry outside the cloister. Drexel decided against an order of nuns—those who took solemn perpetual vows, chanted the Divine Office daily, and followed the European enclosure rule, which meant sequester within a cloister.

Katharine knew this last constraint caused enormous adjustment problems for immigrant nuns. Some congregations worked for years to reach agreement on an enclosure definition that satisfied interior convent life and exterior mission demands. Ultimately most American convents abandoned or modified enclosure, but Drexel wanted to join a group with rules already in place for complementing America's social organization. To find the best choice among the hundreds of religious congregations available to American women, the twenty-five-year-old Katharine turned for advice to the Omaha bishop James O'Connor.

In general, the clergy gave hearty encouragement to young women of the nineteenth century who thought about convent life. Katharine Drexel received the exact opposite. For the next five years Bishop O'Connor, who before his appointment to the West had been pastor of a Pennsylvania church frequented by the Drexels, vehemently discouraged her decision to enter religion. He suggested the change from a home of opulence to the "cell of a nun" would be too drastic; he questioned the stability of her health; he insisted that her good works demanded she have complete freedom; he worried about what would happen to her contributions to the poor; he assured her that if God had other plans for her, He would inform the bishop. O'Connor's greatest concern, no doubt, centered on his own knowledge of the monetary policies of religious orders.

If Katharine Drexel entered a recognized religious convent, such as one she admired, the Sisters of St. Francis of Glen Riddle, Pennsylvania, her wealth at the time would have gone into the coffers of the community she joined. Thereafter, a Mother General and her advisory board would have decided on its uses, directing it exclusively to the projects of their sisterhood. These sisters would have acted on their own initiative or perhaps with the advice of their community's spiritual director\business advisor. Katharine Drexel, as a junior member of the order, would have surrendered her right to allocate the funds or be queried for her opinion in the matter. At risk, in this scenario, was the influence of the western American clerics over the Drexel disbursements that flowed so regularly from east to west and currently aided many different congregations.

The advice of Bishop O'Connor, who knew this one woman endowed the western missions more generously than the entire American Catholic community, also appeared to be tied to his knowledge of the will of Francis A. Drexel. According to that document, a spouse of any of the three daughters could not inherit the Drexel money; only future children of Elizabeth, Katharine, and Louise were eligible heirs to the trust. If a Drexel daughter died leaving no children, the surviving sisters divided that portion of the trust income. Should all the sisters die without offspring, the estate reverted to the Philadelphia-based Catholic institutions endowed at the time of Francis Drexel's death in 1885.

Any decision of the reluctant heiress to relinquish control of her money— either through matrimony or membership in a religious community—threatened the mission enterprise in the West. For Native Americans, the very linchpin of Catholic education, only recently secured by the bishops, would be lost. O'Connor, seeking to protect the financial interests of the missions and his own power among the American clergy, contrived a double-edged counsel for Katharine.

On the one hand, he wanted her to remain in the world, where she retained control of her money. On the other, if she continued to circulate in Philadelphia's elite society, the chances of her marriage to a person of means increased. Not only did O'Connor insist that Drexel belonged "in the world," but he tried to manipulate the conditions of that worldliness. He suggested Katharine take a vow, renewed each year, to follow a celibate life. This constraint, although not an absolute guarantee, would have inhibited marriage and motherhood, while eliminating the possible persuasions of a less charity-minded husband.

Perhaps never in her life did Katharine Drexel demonstrate more the strength of her own intellect than in her refusal to yield to Bishop O'Connor's arguments. Reared in a religious tradition that taught women to honor male clergy and defer to priestly authority, Katharine Drexel held her ground. On November 26, 1888, Katharine wrote to the bishop, "It appears to me, ... that I am not obliged to submit my judgment to yours, as I have been doing for two years ... ." Katharine Drexel had resolved to remove herself from the management of her money, leave it in the care of Elizabeth and Louise to benefit people of color, and join a religious order of women. A careful and informed thinker, she would not be dissuaded, even by a bishop.

Katharine Drexel entered the novitiate of the Sisters of Mercy at Pittsburgh in May 1889. In the face of Drexel's determination, O'Connor reversed his long opposition. He then lobbied Katharine to organize her own community of sisters, one dedicated to her mission interests among Native Americans in the West and African Americans in the South. Reluctantly, she yielded to O'Connor's insistence that the outcome of her religious training be the formation of a new congregation.

The introduction to the convent proved taxing for Katharine Drexel. Obeisance and obedience replaced self-sufficiency and personal decision-making. Although most young women entered the training program of a cloister between the formative ages of fifteen and twenty, Katharine approached her thirty-first birthday as she crossed the threshold of the Convent of Mercy. Already a mature woman who routinely made professional business decisions, Katharine faced the challenge of allowing others to mold her words and actions.

Although she responded to the convent prayer routines easily, she chafed at some of the work assignments, especially with school children. In addition, she took on this world of rule and ritual separated from her two sisters, who had shared everything in her life. No matter how much Katharine Drexel sought religious life, the novitiate required this privileged and independent woman to yield to new patterns and behaviors.

At no time, however, did Drexel's early training as a sister adhere strictly to all regulations for first-year candidates. She did not surrender her money. She continued her massive correspondence to mission convents in the West. She sifted through requests and made bequeaths. Not only did she maintain these business interests, but she even left the convent on occasion to conduct certain transactions. Along with various other disciplinary exemptions, she received intense schooling from the Sisters of Mercy in all aspects of convent administration, not among the usual lessons for young novices.

When Bishop O'Connor died in 1890, one year after Katharine joined the Sisters of Mercy, Philadelphia Archbishop P.J. Ryan, a Drexel family confidant, assumed the role of her spiritual and business advisor. Although not of the western dioceses, Archbishop Ryan was well acquainted with the Drexel heritage and the family personalities. The cleric also knew exactly how much his archdiocese had benefitted from Drexel generosity. He was well informed about the new religious community and hoped he could keep it centered in Philadelphia. Within two days of O'Connor's death, Archbishop Ryan reiterated the late bishop's theme about the necessity of Katharine Drexel's specialized work, deflecting any inclination she harbored to remain with the Sisters of Mercy.

Reverend Mother M. Katharine Drexel as superior general of the Sisters of the Blessed Sacrament. (Courtesy of the Sisters of the Blessed Sacrament, Bensalem, Pennsylvania)

Confronted with intense clerical lobbying and faced with a series of difficult decisions, Katharine Drexel was ill-prepared for the sudden death of her older sister at the age of thirty-five. Elizabeth, who had married in January of 1890, passed away during childbirth the following September. The premature infant died as well, thus leaving no offspring to inherit Elizabeth's portion of the estate. Elizabeth's share of the Drexel trust income was divided between Katharine Drexel and her younger sister, Louise Drexel Morrell. Each used a substantial part of it to memorialize Elizabeth by continuing for many years her philanthropy to the Pennsylvania Saint Francis Industrial School for orphan boys of all religious and ethnic backgrounds.

Following the death of Elizabeth, Katharine Drexel focused more purposefully on the formation of her own order of religious women. She may have finally accepted the argument of O'Connor and Ryan that no other congregation would devote itself exclusively to her mission interests. She, vowed to poverty, may have conceded the administrative and emotional difficulties of totally disengaging from a fortune just increased by half in both dollars and responsibility. She, vowed to chastity, may have chosen the personal stability of remaining with kinfolk, the much cherished younger sister Louise and brother-in-law, Colonel Edward Morrell. She, vowed to obedience, may have realized her own order was her only guarantee of regular visits to the beloved West. Or she may have recognized that her background better prepared her to be leader as mother superior, rather than follower as junior-professed teaching sister.

In February 1891 Katharine Drexel pronounced her religious vows as the first Sister of the Blessed Sacrament for Indians and Colored People. Now known as Mother Mary Katharine Drexel, she withdrew from the Mercy Convent. Accompanied by a Mercy nun, Sister Inez, on "loan" to further the training in religious decorum, Mother Katharine led a small band of thirteen women to the Drexel summer residence. There, under the direction of Sister Inez, the first Sisters of the Blessed Sacrament for Indians and Colored People immersed themselves in building a community identity.

For those young women who chose to cast their lot with Katharine Drexel, the new congregation offered exceptional opportunity in religious life. Catholic Sisters moved through a complex network of power that included the politics of their community along with the general authority of the masculine church. Professional advancement could be maddeningly slow or simply halted, depending on alliances in and out of the convent.

As the founding member in a new congregation, each young sister was almost assured a more rapid rise in the power structure of the community. By standing with Katharine Drexel, these new sisters bonded with perhaps the most powerful woman in the American Catholic church, she who had the respect of priests and pope. Drexel's position as a lay woman was secure, but as a religious she needed these women to execute her larger design.

In addition, by its very title, the Sisters of the Blessed Sacrament for Indians and Colored People, the new congregation captured the impulses of reform that swept through America in the early twentieth century. Although much of that reform resonated within secular groups, it intensified when reinforced by religious philosophy. The civic duty to eradicate national social ills took on moral obligation under a denominational rubric.

For Catholic women, Katharine Drexel with her firm personality, clear social message, established philanthropy, and sizeable fortune made an attractive leader. Demanding and exacting, she radiated a confidence in her position that complied with Catholic notions of authoritarianism. Drexel fit with traditional images of the mother superior, but she offered the excitement of new horizons.

Katharine Drexel avoided vague idealism and concentrated on practical plans, devising a Catholic agenda for women reformers. She not only talked about improving society but aggressively undertook the projects she thought would do so. Drexel reached out to the singular most western ingredient of the American West—Native people—and made it possible for eastern women to enter their world. With her many qualities and experiences, Katharine Drexel had no problem convincing her new sisters that she would lead them to the West.

Although seemingly pleased that the congregation was finally under way, the foundress refused to allow its business to divert her from her first interest, building and fortifying Native American missions. In June 1891, leaving those at the Drexel home under the supervision of Sister Inez, Mother Katharine journeyed to St. Stephen's Mission, deep in the Wind River Reservation of Wyoming. She intended to set the mission on a stable course.

An Arapaho/Shoshone mission with a troubled history, the small station had received Drexel money since 1885. Despite Katharine Drexel's many contributions for building construction and local salaries, improvements at St. Stephen's had not materialized. Business dishonesty, faulty workmanship, poor administration, continuous feuding, erratic mission personnel, missionary illness, extreme isolation—all resulted in chaos for St. Stephen's and misuse of Drexel money.

In 1888, the Sisters of Charity of Leavenworth had agreed to send missionaries, but they arrived to find the conditions less acceptable than the resident priest indicated. The convent proved to be nonexistent, and the sisters had to seek shelter in a dilapidated cabin, gathering nuts and berries to supplement their meager pantry. After a difficult two-year stay, the Sisters of Charity of Leavenworth, an extremely popular order in the mission West, left to answer other more promising calls for teachers. Dismayed that these sturdy missionaries decided to retreat, Mother Katharine set forth to investigate the conditions at St. Stephen's. She planned that, after an on-site inspection, she would resupply the mission and staff it with her own sisters.

Before Mother Katharine returned to Philadelphia, Archbishop Ryan blocked her plan to staff St. Stephen's. He greeted with coolness Katharine's letters that had described two newly minted sisters taking public meals at stage stops or walking down Beaver Canyon at four o'clock in the morning. Mother Katharine, accustomed to her unique standing among the clergy, misjudged her rank as a religious. She failed to perceive that church leaders looked on the Sisters of the Blessed Sacrament as unseasoned recruits, lacking maturity in their religious vocations.

In the archbishop's assessment, temporal and spiritual influences, exacerbated by great distances from Philadelphia, could lead to any number of disagreeable situations. Maintenance of convent behaviors, known as the Holy Rule, might falter among the ill-trained. More than one outpost mission band had set aside community conventions, fallen into bickering, or tried to separate itself from an eastern motherhouse. Just as dangerous, from the archbishop's perspective, were the western bishops who might declare jurisdiction over Blessed Sacrament Sisters, leading to a clerics' political struggle. Such disputes filled the annals of the nineteenth-century American church.

Mother Katharine recognized the discretion in conformity and suspended her intent to send her sisters to the West. With these early difficulties at St. Stephen's as a reminder, Mother Katharine focused on sending funds, requiring missions to justify requests and to demonstrate the money had been spent for its stated purpose. She reviewed construction designs and projected costs. When a new building appeared overly extravagant, she returned the plans for modifications to make the expenditures less burdensome. Ever courteous, even deferential in her business letters, Drexel did not hesitate to press for an overdue account. She acknowledged each installment on a debt, with long prayerful letters, always reminding the sender that other equally desperate missionaries awaited the money. She retained all correspondence and amassed a collection of nearly 20,000 business letters, which she used as a base for keeping abreast of her investments.

Mother Katharine developed explicit guidelines for her disbursements and maintained an inflexible policy in that regard. She permitted her funds to be expended only for the education of Native Americans, as she defined it. The argument that white students brought tuition money to a small mission meant nothing to her; she dropped her support accordingly.

St. Catherine's Convent and Boarding School, Santa Fe, New Mexico, in 1887. This was the first missionary location for Mother Katharine's community. (Courtesy of the Sisters of the Blessed Sacrament, Bensalem, Pennsylvania)

When one bishop encouraged a group of sisters to use a donation for furniture rather than for tuition and board for students, Drexel disallowed the purchase. She declared the new furnishings outside the benefit of Indian children, refused to replace the amount in the tuition fund, and withdrew her pledge for that school term. The bishop himself restored the $1,890 to the Pottawatomie school fund, thus dampening the rancor of the mission sisters for his bad advice and Mother Katharine for his presumptuous judgment.

Through this watchfulness and singleness of purpose, Drexel maintained sufficient funds to continue allocations. As her own community expanded, she reduced support to other congregations, but never entirely closed down her friendly assistance. Using careful business strategies, she gave approximately $70,000 a year to the mission schools of the West. By 1907, close to $1,500,000 in Drexel money had been directed to the education of Native Americans.

For her sisters, not until 1894 did Archbishop Ryan lift his restriction and allow Mother Katharine to send members of her community to the missions. With the arrival of these first sisters at St. Catherine's Mission in Santa Fe, another phase of the impact of Mother Katharine Drexel on the American West began. For the previous ten years, her endeavors on behalf of Native American missions sprang from her individual action. Her great wealth permitted her to give shape to her inner convictions in a tangible, monetary manner. Yet, the continued scarcity of mission personnel

restricted her efforts; schools opened and closed as missionaries in twos and threes came and went. Further, without a local representative to protect Drexel's interests, her control over the schools remained limited, as seen in the unfortunate events at St. Stephen's. Locating her own religious community in the West promised to broaden the scope of her influence and to steady its direction.

The Sisters of the Blessed Sacrament sent to the West brought with them the values and philosophy of Mother Katharine. They cared about protecting her definition of missionary labors and her monetary investment. With their frequent letters about mission life, the western sisters fueled the enthusiasm and resolve of those still assigned to the motherhouse to come to the West. This western presence allowed Mother Katharine to monitor the tone of mission management, as well as the conduct of sisters in the field. With these developments, Mother Katharine's western focus shifted to the sisters of her congregation, and in her position as their undisputed leader, she lengthened her shadow across western education.

In addition, these sisters learned how to be women of the West. Their experiences as travelers and workers in the West exposed them to the personal growth and change that marked the western newcomer. For them convent life did not mean the seclusion of a hermitage. Quite the opposite was true. Typical of women's congregations founded in America, the very essence of Katharine Drexel's community called for a sisterhood that worked among its constituency.

Once the first mission sisters arrived in Santa Fe, they quickly involved themselves in the community. Disappointed by the low enrollment at the school, they attended Indian festivals and began a hospitality program to make themselves known. Usually, ten to twelve Indians stopped for supper and slept on the grounds each night. Finally, Mother Katharine had placed her own sisters among Native American people. Pleased, she journeyed to St. Catherine's for a brief inspection.

Mother Katharine's expectations for the missions prodded single young women in her community to make a place for themselves in western society. Outside the typical structures of marriage and family relationships, sisters were required to develop meaningful community relationships and viable economic support for the mission. The sisters lost no time in carving such a place for themselves in Santa Fe. In doing so, they helped to push back western gender limitations and enlarge the definition of the woman's West.

By the following year, the sisters were traveling to the pueblos for community celebrations. There, over one two-day period, pueblo residents performed an elaborate set of Catholic rituals, more ornate than the sisters had ever witnessed. At the Indians' insistence, the sisters led the choir, attended a torchlight procession, a wedding, and a community feast. Although the exact ceremonial display differed from the sisters' experience, its spirit and theology provided a unifying sense of Catholicism. These kinds of social events fell beyond the usual allowed to professed sisters. They reflected the changing demands the West imposed on the traditional sister's role and the adaptations that mission sisters made to regional circumstances.

The sisters' interaction with the Native Americans, however, turned on more than one element. The New Mexico tribes, unlike Native Americans in many other areas of the West, came from a long tradition of Catholicism. They knew Catholic missionaries and understood how to define relationships with them.

The Indians also knew how to bring more than a dash of cultural selectivity to their Anglo associations. During her second visit to St. Catherine's, Mother Katharine, ignoring the advice of government officials, charged out to the San Domingo Pueblo during an epidemic. Fired with zeal for some direct missionary experience, she misread the temper at the pueblo.

When the Indians flatly refused her admittance, she explained away the rejection as an example of Native concern for her personal health and well being. It more likely reflected the political sentiment and religious feeling inside that pueblo, as well as her status as a stranger to the Indians. Six years later, at another pueblo, Indian residents sent for two nearby Blessed Sacrament Sisters to minister in their homes during a malaria epidemic. At the request of Indian families, these two sisters lived at the pueblo for several weeks cleaning homes, preparing food, and tending the sick and the dying.

By 1900, with St. Catherine's on firm footing, Mother Katharine wanted to increase her mission houses among Native Americans. She expanded an existing arrangement she had with Franciscan Fathers in Arizona among the Navajo and drew up plans for a convent and school called St. Michael's. Again she absorbed construction costs, bought furniture, paid salaries. On this occasion, she moved to the mission location, spending several weeks reviewing and approving all aspects of the work.

Unlike St. Stephen's, where her absence hurt her investments, St. Michael's felt Drexel's presence, whereby she badgered the work to completion. By the fall of 1902, she had the school ready for occupancy. The reception, however, of her missionary sisters among the Arizona Navajo proved different from the New Mexico experience.

In 1900 the Franciscan Fathers and Mother Katharine had met with Navajo leaders to convince them to send children to the St. Catherine's school in New Mexico and to support the new St. Michael's when it opened. The Arizona Indians vehemently rejected these suggestions. They protested the

Mother M. Katharine Drexel with Navajo man and Franciscan priest at Lukachukai, Arizona. (Courtesy of the Sisters of the Blessed Sacrament, Bensalem, Pennsylvania)

separation from their children, they questioned the benefits of Anglo education, and they doubted the healthfulness of living among the sisters. Although the Franciscans spoke the Navajo language, the sisters had no such skill, adding another layer to the distance between themselves and the students. Only five children went to St. Catherine's, and enrollment lagged at St. Michael's.

Eventually St. Michael's flourished, and in 1925 a Navajo tribal committee requested it be enlarged or a second school constructed in the area. Yet, at the outset of this mission, Mother Katharine misread important cultural indicators of Native feeling. She, who instructed her sisters to be sensitive to Indian parents, who wrote about the loving bonds between Native American fathers and their children, allowed her goals to blind her to the repugnance of family separation for the Navajo. She failed to see that absorption into the conventions of Anglo Christianity had limited appeal for Native people determined to retain their own cultural world. Given the overall attitudes she brought to her mission work, Drexel may have lapsed because she blurred the distinctions between her two ministries, one for blacks and one for Indians.

Eastern and southern African American families did not share with western Indians the same cultural response to the presence of Anglo schools in their communities. The group benefits perceived to exist in those schools differed for African Americans and Native Americans. Whereas the former used them in the struggle for entrance to mainstream white society, the latter preferred withdrawal from that environment. With the Sisters of the Blessed Sacrament administrative center in the East and closer to the philosophical underpinnings of its African American constituency, Drexel, despite her love for the West, lacked a regional compass to keep her grounded in western local culture.

Mother Katharine's own western experiences, limited to tours of mission houses, cast her in the role of visitor to the West. Although Drexel knew many Indians, she seldom had the opportunity to cultivate the long-term relationships that marked those who lived at the missions. For Mother Katharine, the West retained some of the initial romanticism that colored her first trips to the Indian missions. Distance and romantic feeling undercut her understanding of the West, particularly as the region altered across time. In 1902 Drexel, with a trip into Indian Territory, came to perceive some of these changes that had overtaken the West.

After years of relying on missionary letters for information, Mother Katharine wanted to see for herself the results of her donations to other congregations. At mission after mission, she barely concealed her shock at the appearance of the student populations. In all places, she saw the children as Caucasian, rather than Indian. She found it hard to believe the many youngsters with light hair and blue eyes could truly be Native Americans.

In fact, she did not consider a single Indian grandparent a sufficient bloodline for enrollment in her schools. Her distress mounted in those classrooms where she could not identify a single Indian child, even of mixed blood. She described herself as "dazed" by the prevalence of whites living on Indian land.

The Indian Territory trip renewed Mother Katharine's fervor to save the full-blood Indians, so "that they may not be cheated out of their land by the teaming [sic] population of whites." If no one would make this effort, she felt the full bloods destined to become "paupers and die out." Drexel reiterated her belief that, through education, Indians could be made ready to marry among white people, leading to the dissolution of racial division. She repeated these exhortations many times over the years, calling for a society in which Native Americans, African Americans, and Caucasians melded into one race. Although hers was a demographic picture that led all people into whiteness, it emphasized societal unity through marriage and procreation across races—a sexual notion abhorrent to most white Americans of the early twentieth century.

Above all, the trip through Indian Territory convinced her that over the years the intent of her donations had been diluted. It galled her that, even under the guidance of religious congregations, whites usurped the Indian right to education. She felt those bonded to the white community, mixed bloods among them, forced Indian boys and girls out of their own institutions and off their own land. As a result, full-blood Indian families retreated deeper into the reservation backcountry, having even less chance to secure an education for their children. Ultimately that meant a speedy death knell for Native Americans as their access to all mainstream economic opportunity collapsed.

Disturbed by what she had witnessed in the Indian Territory, Mother Katharine returned to the East, where the administrative concerns of securing formal papal recognition for her order required attention for the next several years. This demand necessitated that she spend an extended period in Rome. In 1908, with preliminary Vatican approval in hand, Mother Katharine was elected the first superior general of the community.

Free to refocus on the mission work, Drexel returned to the enjoyment of her annual inspections in the West. In 1911 the death of Archbishop Ryan sank her into a paroxysm of grief. The following year while in Santa Fe she fell dangerously ill with a lung infection, compounded by a heart problem. Both her physical and mental state teetered at the edge of collapse.

Now fifty-five and exhausted from years of travel and administration, Mother Katharine recovered slowly over the next year. Her community, never destined to attract huge numbers, had grown somewhat, and she yielded some management to the more experienced sisters. Finally restored, Drexel made a trip abroad, during which she sought European volunteers for her order.

Upon her return to the United States, much of her energy went into organizing new mission work among African Americans. In 1916 she visited the Sisters Servants of the Holy Ghost and Mary Immaculate, a small Texas congregation dedicated exclusively to the education of African Americans, Mexicans, and Mexican Americans. She left San Antonio and traveled to New Orleans. There her interest centered on the transformation of an old school into what became Xavier University, the first and only such Catholic institution of higher education for African Americans in the United States.

From its genesis, Mother Katharine's work, with African Americans and Native Americans, met with mixed social response in U.S. society. In the West, Anglos had not shown themselves sympathetic to Indian land claims and needs. In all areas, the African American missions had been greeted with suspicion, hostility, and violence.

East or West, not everyone looked on the Sisters of the Blessed Sacrament for Indians and Colored People as noble humanitarians. Many saw them as radicals—misguided at best, dangerous at worst. The institutional church showed little inclination to endow the parishes and schools of African Americans and Native Americans. Among themselves bishops acknowledged their relief that the missions of the "Indian and the Colored" could be left to Katharine Drexel.

Into her seventies, despite the dislike of some, the indifference of others, Mother Katharine continued funding schools for Native Americans and African Americans. Always somewhat secretive about exact donations, Drexel left no complete tally of all the money sent to Indian missions; over a period of fifty years, she invested approximately eleven million dollars in schools for African Americans. As an elderly woman she found satisfaction in managing these diverse charities and traveling to the mission houses.

Then at age seventy-seven, she was again taken ill while at St. Catherine's in New Mexico. She pushed on to South Dakota, where she wanted to explore the idea of a novitiate for Native American women who wished to enter the convent. Religious vocations among Native Americans always had been scarce. An occasional Franciscan here or a Benedictine there totaled the number of Native American sisters. Then in 1935, a priest at Marty, South Dakota, wrote to Mother Katharine about seven Sioux women anxious to form a congregation for mission work among their own tribe. Katharine Drexel agreed to assist this project with money and training staff.

She departed from South Dakota exhausted and unwell. In Chicago, Mother Katharine was stricken with a serious heart attack. Late in 1935, she returned to the motherhouse, never again to visit her beloved missions in the West. Drexel lived out her long life on the infirmary floor at St. Elizabeth's in Pennsylvania.

Mother M. Katharine Drexel (right) with Mother M. Francis Xavier and Navajos at Lukachukai, Arizona, in 1920. The baby was named Abe Lincoln. (Courtesy of the Sisters of the Blessed Sacrament, Bensalem, Pennsylvania)

The sudden death of Louise in 1943, fifteen years after that of her husband Edward, brought a wave of nearly unbearable sorrow. The prospect of life without Louise seemed unthinkable to the eighty-five-year-old Mother Katharine, who smothered her agony in terms of religious acceptance. Now the sole Drexel heir, she refused to dispute her father's will, whereby at her death the entire fortune would revert to Francis Drexel's original Philadelphia charities. Indeed, when Katharine Drexel died in 1955, her stubborn position about the will cut her community off from its financial base, a circumstance remedied by the intervention of the Philadelphia archbishop and the cooperation of the other beneficiaries.

Her fortune aside, the importance of relationships, which began with the Drexel family, in part explained her passion for bridging to others. Raised to be an independent woman capable of executive decision, she disliked opposition and rarely yielded to it. She considered her wealth cumbersome and determined to divest herself of its material trappings. Although she oversaw a vast fortune, she built a personal world ordered by a humble ambiance. At the same time, Drexel would not surrender her sense of the social responsibility that money and privilege imposed.

Her intense capacity for family bonding originated with her parents and siblings, Elizabeth and Louise. Later she shifted this allegiance to her associates in religion. An unmarried woman, she developed a maternal identity with the Sisters of the Blessed Sacrament and crafted in that organization an outlet for her business acumen, organizational skill, and leadership compatible with her religious beliefs.

Drexel greatly valued these personal relationships, whether with kin or friend. Separations by death caused exceptional pain for her, each one renewing the grief of earlier losses. Her respect for enduring human closeness perhaps even illuminates her refusal to tamper with her father's arranagements. She held to a code she deemed appropriate and was loathe to violate it.

Her code ignored racial boundaries and prompted her to think about divisive elements in American society. During years when white America, by custom and law, vehemently opposed integration, she introduced a measure of it, gave it a springboard from which to take form. By backing the missions across the West, Mother Katharine sponsored interaction between hundreds of western "culture brokers"—those from each side of the cultural fence willing to meet and to exchange ideas, experiences, custom, feeling. Their efforts to interact with one another rested on an avalanche of cultural imperatives and economic factors that necessarily included both the positive and negative for the participants. Nonetheless, Native Americans and Sisters of the

Blessed Sacrament reached for an ideal of cultural understanding and human decency that might guide America.

Above all, Mother Katharine's work focused on improving the lives of others, and she did so in the spirit of social justice. The entrenched social and economic conditions that stymied Drexel's vision for people of color drove her to articulate a moral philosophy about U.S. race relations that influenced American church-thinking. The American clergy could not indefinitely ignore her voice, her constituency, her money. Her early insistence on justice prepared both her students and her sisters to respond to its changing meaning and practice through the twentieth century.

As ethnic Americans redefined their place on the national stage and voiced their cultural expectations, the Sisters of the Blessed Sacrament responded with a Drexel-like spirit of action grounded in justice. In the 1960s, the sisters re-examined their purpose and goals. In an era when many religious congregations lost members, some African American and Native American women saw personal opportunity with the Sisters of the Blessed Sacrament and joined their ranks. By the 1980s Sister Juliana Haynes, an African American sister, had been elected president of the congregation.

In November 1988, members of the Blessed Sacrament Sisters and their friends gathered in St. Peter's Basilica in Rome for a beatification ceremony for Katharine Drexel. This procedure, a step leading to a pontifical declaration of sainthood, gave formal recognition to the major impact of this single woman on the Catholic church in the United States. The Sisters of the Blessed Sacrament, led by Sister Juliana Haynes, played a prominent role, but those served by Mother Katharine dominated.

Eagle Dancers from the Laguna pueblo in New Mexico swirled about the altar, Victor Bull Bear from South Dakota offered the Prayer of the Four Directions, Marie Tso Allen spoke the first Navajo ever used in a Vatican liturgy—Native American culture mingled with church ritual in unprecedented ways at the very center of Catholicity. Far from little mission schools in Wyoming, Montana, Oklahoma, and New Mexico, Native Americans gave witness to the enduring strength of their own heritage and the legacy of Katharine Drexel.

On that festive day, many would have agreed with a former student from St. Catherine's, who, in 1941, said of Mother Katharine Drexel, "Hers was a flaming desire to dream lofty dreams ... a vision that promised what you and I should be ... ." His remark captured the vision of this spiritual daughter of the West, Katharine Drexel, who brought together people of variant cultures and insisted they consider their common humanity.

Sources and Further Reading

Despite the unending fascination of Americans and scholars for the nineteenth-century West, certain groups of westerners remain underrepresented in the historical literature. Roman Catholic sisters, known in the vulgate as nuns, constitute one of the less studied of western residents. Current attention to women's history promises to remedy this situation, but for the present, scholarly work about western sisters remains limited.

No biography of Mother Katharine Drexel exists, other than those published by her congregation. This essay relied heavily on Sister Consuela Marie Duffy, SBS, *Katharine Drexel: A Biography* (Bensalem, PA: Mother Katharine Drexel Guild, 1987). Duffy, who knew Mother Katharine, offers a personal and partially documented account of Drexel's life. The volume, however, contains a largely pious description of all the characters. As a result, the account, rich in detail, is historically uncritical. The Sisters of the Blessed Sacrament at Bensalem, Pennsylvania, also have published several pamphlets about the life of Mother Katharine. These include "A Philadelphia Story" (reprint from the 1984 *Anthonian*), "Blessed Katharine Drexel," *Mission* (winter 1988), and the *Josephite Harvest* (winter 1988–1989).

Other secondary materials about Katharine Drexel can be gleaned from the histories of other congregations. For examples, see Sister Mary Buckner, *History of the Sisters of Charity of Leavenworth, Kansas* (Kansas City, MO: Hudson-Kimberly Publishing, 1898); Sister M. Grace McDonald, OSB, *With Lamps Burning* (St. Joseph, MN: St. Benedict's Priory Press, 1957); Sister Genevieve McBride, OSU, *The Bird Tail* (New York: Vantage Press, 1974); and Sister Dolorita Marie Dougherty, CSJ, et al., *The Sisters of St. Joseph of Carondelet* (St. Louis, MO: B. Herder, 1966). Although these works contain limited detail about Drexel, each is informative about the missions she supported for these congregations. Again, each is a pious history of the community's members.

The finest primary materials available about Katharine Drexel are to be found at the motherhouse archives of the Sisters of the Blessed Sacrament in Bensalem, Pennsylvania. The collections there include the diverse correspondence she received over her long life, matters relating to the establishment and maintenance of her community, the lengthy reports sent by the sisters at both the Indian and African American missions, and Mother Katharine's replies to her many supplicants.

The archives of other congregations also contain correspondence from Katharine Drexel or comments about her in the proceedings of the general council meetings. These materials are scattered at best and not always easy to retrieve. The motherhouse archives of the Sisters of St. Francis of Glenn Riddle, Pennsylvania, those of the Sisters of the Holy Spirit in San Antonio, Texas, and those of the Ursuline Sisters of Toledo, Ohio, are among the communities with limited records of Katharine Drexel. For reference to her work with African American missions, consult the archives of the Josephite Fathers in Baltimore, Maryland. A very small collection of material about Katharine Drexel is also held at the archives of Notre Dame Univeristy at South Bend, Indiana. The vast religious collection there, however, is illuminating about the western history of many different religious congregations.

For a general understanding of the complex religious history of the West, see Ferenc M. Szasz and Margaret Connell Szasz, "Religion and Spirituality," in *The Oxford History of the American West,* Clyde A. Milner II, Carol A. O'Connor, and Martha A. Sandweiss, eds. (New York: Oxford University Press, 1994), 359–91. For a vivid account of nineteenth-century missionary experiences and some of the personalities involved, see L. B. Palladino, SJ, *Indian and White in the Northwest: Or a History of Catholicity in Montana* (Baltimore, MD: John Murphy, 1894). For an appreciation for the politics of western church building, see Marvin R. O'Connell, *John Ireland and the American Catholic Church* (St. Paul: Minnesota Historical Society Press, 1988).

✃ Contributors ✄

ANNE M. BUTLER is the coeditor of the *Western Historical Quarterly* and Professor of History at Utah State University. Her research concerns the social history of the American West, with an emphasis on the experiences of women. Her major publications include *Gendered Justice in the American West: Women Prisoners in Men's Penitentiaries; Daughters of Joy, Sisters of Misery: Prostitutes in the American West, 1865–1890; Uncommon Common Women: Ordinary Lives of the West* (coauthor with Ona Siporin); *Major Problems in the American West* (coeditor, 2nd ed. with Clyde A. Milner II and David R. Lewis); and *U.S. Senate: Election, Expulsion, and Censure Cases, 1789–1986* (coauthor with Wendy Wolfe). She is currently preparing a monograph about Roman Catholic sisters in the nineteenth-century West.

RICHARD W. ETULAIN is Professor of History and Director of the Center for the American West at the University of New Mexico. A specialist in cultural history and historiography, he has authored, coauthored, and edited more than thirty books, including *The American West: A Twentieth-Century History* (coauthor); *Conversations with Wallace Stegner on Western History and Literature,* rev ed.; *Writing Western History;* and *The American West in the Twentieth Century: A Bibliography* (coeditor). His most recent volumes are *Re-imagining the Modern American West: A Century of Fiction, History, and Art; Researching Western History* (coeditor); and *Religion in Modern New Mexico* (coeditor). He has forthcoming *Basques in the American West* (coeditor).

JANET R. FIREMAN is Curator and Chief of History at the Natural History Museum of Los Angeles County. She has a B.A. in history and Spanish from the University of Arizona and an MA and Ph.D. in history from the University of New Mexico. Her research interests began with discovery and exploration in the Spanish Borderlands, and have broadened to include nineteenth- and twentieth-century popular culture in the West. Fireman is the author of *Spain's Royal Corps of Engineers in the Western Borderlands: Instrument of Bourbon Reform, 1764–1815* and a number of essays, reviews and addresses. Along with many activities in the field, Fireman is the president-elect of the Western History Association.

SUSANNE K. GEORGE is Professor of English at the University of Nebraska at Kearney. Specializing in nineteenth-century American literature, especially the literature of the American West, she has published two literary biographies, *The Adventures of The Woman Homesteader: The Life and Letters of Elinore Pruitt Stewart* and *Kate M. Cleary: A Literary Life with Selected Works.* She has also edited two collections, *Wellsprings: Poems from Six Nebraska Poets* and *The Platte River: An Atlas of the Big Bend Region* (coeditor). Past president of the Western Literature Association and on the governing board of the Willa Cather Pioneer Memorial Foundation, she is currently working on a literary analysis and collection of western works by Elia Peattie, turn-of-the-century Nebraska writer and journalist.

JANET LECOMPTE is an independent historian and author who has published two books, *Pueblo, Hardscrabble Greenhorn: The Upper Arkansas, 1832–1856,* and *Rebellion in Rio Arriba, 1837.* She is also the editor of several collections and sixty-plus articles relating to the fur trade of the American West and New Mexico during the Republican period (1821–1846). She lives in Moscow, Idaho.

VALERIE SHERER MATHES teaches history at City College of San Francisco. She specializes in American Indian history and western history. She has written *Helen Hunt Jackson and Her Indian Reform Legacy* as well as numerous scholarly articles. She is currently editing a selection of Jackson's Indian letters. She has received two Spur Awards from Western Writers of America for her book and an article on Jackson.

RUTH BARNES MOYNIHAN is a historian and writer specializing in the history of American women. She is the author of the definitive biography, *Rebel for Rights: Abigail Scott Duniway.* Her other works include, *So Much to Be Done: Women Settlers on the Mining and Ranching Frontier* (coeditor); *Second to None: A Documentary History of American Women, 1540 to 1993* (coeditor); and *Coming of Age: Four Centuries of Connecticut Women,* as well as numerous essays. She is currently working on several biographical projects.

GLENDA RILEY is the Alexander M. Bracken Professor of History at Ball State University in Muncie, Indiana. She specializes in women's history, especially women in the American West. Her books include *Frontierswomen: The Iowa Experience; Women and Indians on the Frontier; The Female Frontier; A Place to Grow: Women in the American West; The Life and Legacy of Annie Oakley;* and *Building and Breaking Families in the American West.* She is currently working on women in the American conservation movement. She has received many awards, including a Distinguished Fulbright and membership in the Iowa Women's Hall of Fame. She is President of the Western History Association.

MARY LEE SPENCE, Professor Emerita, supervised the undergraduate program in history at the University of Illinois, Urbana-Champaign campus, for some seventeen years and taught courses in the history of American women and the history of American Indian–white relations. With Donald Jackson, she edited *The Expeditions of John Charles Frémont* (3 vols., supplement, and map portfolio); with Pamela Herr, *The Letters of Jessie Benton Frémont;* and with Clark C. Spence, *Ten Years in Nevada* (by Mary M. Mathews); and *Narrative of My Captivity Among the Sioux* (by Fanny Kelly). *The Arizona Diary of Lily Frémont,* which she edited, has recently been published. She is a past president of the Western History Association.

QUINTARD TAYLOR is Professor of History at the University of Oregon where his primary teaching area is African American history in the U.S. West. Taylor is the author of *The Forging of a Black Community: A History of Seattle's Central District from 1870 Through the Civil Rights Era* and more than thirty articles on the black West that have appeared in several journals. He is presently writing *In Search of the Racial Frontier: African Americans in the American West, 1529–1990,* which W.W. Norton will publish in 1998. He is coediting with Lawrence B. De Graaf, *California and the Black West: Essays on African Americans in the Golden State* and with Shirley Moore, *African American Women in the American West, 1600–1990.*

✸ Index ✸

Note: **Boldface numerals** indicate an extended treatment of the subject.